GOD'S LOVE MYSTERY
THE PURPOSE FOR EVERYTHING

To Betty Smith ~~White~~

Blessings

David Carley

DAVID CARLEY

DEDICATION

To my loving mother, two beautiful daughters, and the memory of my lovely wife Cindy. I believe she was as close as humanly possible to being an angel on earth. Cindy shared God's love through her beautiful eyes, smile, and kind words. All who met her loved and adored her. Finally, to my wonderful grandchildren, I pray you find and utilize the knowledge and wisdom in this book that I wish I had known sixty years ago.

CONTENTS

Acknowledgments

I am grateful to God for allowing me to be used in His service since I was twenty-one years old. Although I have been a Christian since I was twelve years old, it was not until I was twenty-one that I dedicated my life to the service of God. I am grateful to Herbert W. Armstrong and his son Garner Ted for focusing my mind on God's Word and the importance of striving to live daily in God's truth. Striving to do that has been my journey since. For thirty-five years of my life I was a member of the Armstrong's Worldwide Church of God (WCG). I spent twenty-five of those years in the ministry of the WCG. At the end of that time span I was awakened to the true meaning of grace, and I decided to resign from the ministry and the Worldwide Church of God at the age of fifty-six. During that time I became deeply disillusioned after realizing that the WCG was not the only true Church of God on earth and that anyone in any Church who had repented of their sins and accepted Jesus Christ became a member of the Body of Christ.

In the ensuing ten years I stumbled warily down life's road, trying to put my shattered world back together and make sense of my present and past relationship with God. I did not understand why God would lead me down a torturous and legalistic religious pathway with the autocratic religious cult that had consumed my youth. It was not until the death of my lovely, precious wife Cindy that I came to my senses and got back on track with God. I returned to my faith with an intense spiritual hunger to find a church to attend and rededicate the remainder of my life to serving God's will. I visited many different churches, trying to find the one where I would feel spiritually at home. It took about two years of intense searching, but eventually I joined a recently started church called Generations Church. Its husband and wife co-pastors, James and Lori Roach, blessed and showered this little church with love and grace-filled sermons week after week during the three years I attended there. They were invaluable in reviving and nourishing me spiritually with the love and grace of God. Thank you, James and Lori. This book was eventually born out of a sermon you so graciously allowed me to give one Sunday. I want to thank the both of you for your inspiration and love during those years.

In the writing of this book I have been greatly influenced by the television ministry of Joseph Prince. Other ministries that have been helpful concerning the wonderful realities of the Grace of Christ besides that of James and Lori Roach, are those of Butch Bruton, Paul Ellis, and Creflo Dollar. Also Irwin Baxter's profound understanding of end time prophecies have been invaluable to help me understand what many of us will live through to the coming of God's Kingdom. All of you have been a great blessing. Thank you!

I am awed by how modern technology has made the research and writing of this book so much easier than when I was a young man of twenty-one. Back then, all I would have had available to help me in a project like this would have been a library, an electric typewriter, a lot of typing paper, and tons of liquid "white out" to make corrections. I am deeply grateful to the "Bible Hub" website for use of their various Bible translations as well as commentaries at: http://biblemenus.com/bh/topmenubh.htm. Also helpful was Bible Gateway at: https://www.biblegateway.com/, and several other online aids such as use of online dictionaries and a thesaurus. All have been invaluable to me. Online technology is truly amazing.

I want to thank God for the road He gave me to travel over the last seventy-four years of my life. It has been an exciting, wonderful, and at times heartbreaking journey. However, it has produced this book which I hope will have a profound and positive effect on your life and happiness. I can think of no greater blessing then if my life's spiritual journey with God would bring lost souls to Christ and help loosen the unnecessary legalistic burdens so many Christians are struggling with today.

It is possible you are one of those Christians who think that it is necessary to keep laws in order to maintain your righteousness standing with God and thus enter heaven. It is also possible you are not a Christian and have no interest in becoming one. You may believe "freedom" is doing your own thing, which requires the absence of Jesus in your life. Both of these beliefs are lies! The simple truth is that, "…where the Spirit of the Lord is, there is liberty." (2 Cor. 3:17b WEB). Any other "freedom" experienced is a delusion appealing only to fleshly desires and incapable of producing lasting love, liberty, peace, and satisfaction. Even a Christian's freedom can be diminished in the chains of legalism. This book will expose that reality to you and help set you truly free to enjoy the liberty that you hunger for which can come only from learning what true grace is and how to live in it. My goal in writing this book is to enrich your life and help guide you into the joy of the Lord eternally! If this book aids you in achieving that eternal joy, then this book's purpose will have been served.

PREFACE

The purpose of this book is to look at the most wonderful gift that God could possibly give us. The Bible refers to it many times as a "mystery." Within the mystery are contained many more secrets supporting God's ultimate purpose. However, Paul called it "…the mystery which has been hidden for ages and generations." (Col. 1:26a, WEB). This mystery reveals God's plans, which explains the reason and purpose for His creation of all things. I call it God's love mystery. In it is revealed God's astonishing love for the apex of all His creations, mankind. God's love for each of us is awe inspiring, and far beyond what any of us can truly grasp. It's because of God's love for mankind that He created the angels, time, space, and all the physical universe. How great is such a love? What a wonderful purpose He must have in mind for mankind, which is the very focal point and reason for everything. God's purpose was so great that God was willing to die to bring it to pass.

The understanding of God's supreme mystery and purpose for everything was revealed only in bits and pieces to a privileged few from Adam until the time of the apostle Paul two thousand years ago. Although this marvelous mystery was revealed to the first-century Christian Church, a brief three hundred years later, its understanding had been greatly distorted for Christians and has since been hidden entirely from the vast majority of mankind. Most of God's plans have remained hidden for His wonderful and grand purpose. These secrets will be revealed to every living soul to whom God has granted life on a day, at a time, and in a manner that God has predetermined. To each soul given life, God will offer this most precious mysterious gift. This gift can be received and opened by all who accept it when it is finally offered. Because it is freely offered, it must be freely accepted. It demands no price except that we embrace it with faith. This gift requires that each person must have "free will" to choose or reject it. So, because of man's free moral agency, our loving God will make sure that it is offered at the time and place in each individual's life when he or she will be most likely to say, "yes" and joyfully embrace it. The cards, so to speak, are stacked by God in each individual's favor.

This book examines the history and gift of God's great love mystery. It also tells the sad story of how the truth of God's love mystery has been abused. The apostle Paul was the first to unveil a proper understanding of God's love mystery, which brought peace and happiness to the lives of first-century Christians even though they suffered great trials and persecutions. This correct understanding drained away over the next three hundred years to give rise to a Christian Church bogged down in rituals and legalism. Satan was the driving force to shroud a proper understanding of God's love mystery among Christians. We will examine how it has been camouflaged and abused during the last two thousand years, causing incalculable unnecessary pain and suffering in the lives of Christians.

The preparation for the completion of the mystery of God required complex, detailed plans that have been in the process of being implemented in successive stages through several billion years. In the Scriptures, I have observed seven main sequential events which are the major building platforms which provide the launching pad for God's glorious plan for mankind and the universe for all eternity. The soon coming launch of God's love mystery, for all who are on board, will mark the extermination of all sin and misery and the beginning of the way God intends all to live, which is in real love, freedom, peace, and happiness. In this book we will discuss each of the seven stage platforms leading to this coming new universe for those blessed to live in it.

If you believe that earth was created only six thousand years ago, please do not close this book just yet. I, too, believe that is possible; however, as a creationist, I also believe God could have created the universe billions of years ago and still have been in perfect harmony with the His scriptures. I make a case, in the second paragraph below, for those of you who may disagree on this issue; so please keep reading.

We will travel to the place prior to the beginning of time when God's love mystery was formulated. We will take a look at God's creation of time and space and then consider the state of Lucifer and all the angels prior to and after the time of Lucifer's rebellion against God. We will discuss the purpose of the creation of our prehistoric world with dinosaurs. We shall then move into the Garden of Eden and from there journey through time to the present. We will explore why it was necessary that God allow free will and the possibility of sin entering the universe. We will explain why God has allowed mankind to march a bloody pathway through history in order to have access to God's plan and purpose contained in His love mystery.

I'm sure you will not believe, at first glance, some of the theological ideas that I will present to you. Some of them may be provocative to you. All Christians are not in perfect agreement on theological doctrine. Please be patient if I make a statement that does not exactly fit a doctrinal point of view that you have. In spite of the points where you may disagree with me, I assure you there is great redeeming value in where you might agree. Let me present my case to you, and if you don't agree, that will be fine. As the great writer and philosopher Elbert Hubbard wrote:

> Emerson loved the good more than he abhorred evil. Carlyle abhorred evil more than he loved the good. If you should by chance find anything in this book you do not especially like, it is not at all wise to focus your memory on that, to the exclusion of all else—bless my soul! ~ The Note Book of Elbert Hubbard

We can be Christian brothers and sisters and yet disagree on certain doctrinal points and still learn from one another. If we focused only on those writings with which we totally agreed, our religious library would be small indeed. Our ability to expand on spiritual truth and knowledge would be greatly hindered. We must not allow our wishes to dictate doctrinal beliefs. It is only human to try to understand God according to a favorite pastor or our own desires, rather than God's. Many Christians carry God in their hip pockets, using Him to justify what they want to believe and do, while ignoring any word from God revealing His true will for them. Some of our doctrinal beliefs may be driven by traditions. Some churches do some of the things they do just because that's the way they have always done it. After a certain amount of time, when things are done in one way long enough, this method of doing things becomes tantamount to a doctrine, not to be questioned. However, rather than allow traditions or personal desires to drive our doctrines, we must let the words and Spirit of God do the driving, no matter how disturbing the results might be.

We can all be Christians and still believe differently concerning certain doctrines and theological ideas. And quite frankly, few Christians, even within their own denomination, believe exactly the same thing on every theological point. The world is filled with thousands of differing Christian congregations. Many, if not most, disagree on details of how God wants us to worship Him. As I'm sure you well know, there are many different views concerning the meaning of the Scriptures. Many churches interpret Scriptures differently than others. It is astounding how many churches differ concerning what they read out of the same Bible.

What is it, then, that makes people true Christians? Is it any one particular doctrine? The answer to this is yes. There is one, and only one, doctrine that we all must agree upon if we are to be considered Christians, and it has nothing to do with which church is most correct in its theological beliefs.

The only doctrine an individual needs to know, accept, and believe in to be a Christian is that we must accept the sacrifice of Jesus Christ for the remission our sins in order to be saved. When we do this, we are born again by receiving the Spirit of God. This doctrinal understanding alone is what joined the thief on the cross with Jesus Christ in paradise that day after their deaths. It is the same for every Christian who accepts the gospel. God gives each one of us eternal salvation in

Christ, never to be lost. All doctrine in Scripture is important, but it is only that of salvation in Jesus Christ that will give you a new eternal body in the God's Kingdom.

In this book I will discuss several theological doctrinal concepts. Some you will agree with. Some you may not. Some of the concepts I will present as only speculation on my part. Yes, they are based on Scripture, but nonetheless I draw conclusions from them that may or may not be correct. I believe they are correct, but I allow that I may be wrong. I stake my salvation on none of them. As a matter of fact, I could be wrong on all of them and yet I am assured of eternal life with Christ in His Kingdom. You are free to pick and choose from them as you like. Some of my ideas will be new to you and I present them simply for your consideration. Brothers and sisters in Christ can differ on theological matters and still respect each other as fellow saints. Please do not let your differing views keep you from reading on to draw upon the various concepts that will be a blessing to you. Some of these ideas you may want consider.

My favorite televangelist, who has had a profound effect on my spiritual growth, differs with me on when the Rapture will occur. He believes in a pre-tribulation Rapture. I believe in a post-tribulation Rapture. I will, however, not let that keep me from listening to and learning from him in the future. He is a recognized world leader in preaching the grace of Christ. He has profound, spiritually strong, and positive sermons that help millions around the world weekly. Even though I disagree with him on a few doctrinal points, it would be to my loss not to learn from the many profound spiritual, life-changing insights that he has given me. We both agree on the question of what it takes to make an individual a true Christian. The answer to that question is what really matters!

In the last chapters of this book we will look at approximately the last ten years of prophetic events just prior to the return of Jesus Christ. We will find that the knowledge about God's love mystery will experience a renaissance, a new Great Awakening, which will propel the good news of the gospel around the world. The genesis of this Great Awakening is gaining steam now worldwide. However, this good news is facing a counter balancing false ideology which also now is being widely accepted around the world politically and religiously. Politically and religiously this belief in short is that a Utopian world can only be achieved through a union of all the religions of the world, which then will allow the nations of the world to remain sovereign yet politically unite. It's believed that a new religious and political world order can then emerge to give mankind the liberty, peace, and happiness that's been vainly sought throughout history.

To achieve this joyous universal union there must be political and religious compromises in order for this to occur. It's believed that only through religious and political correctness; fairness, equality, and world peace will come. "Political correctness" is the secular side of this striving to unify all peoples and nations. Political correctness, in effect, has the same aim as that of "Christian" inclusion beliefs. They both attempt to unify all people of the world to bring about a Utopian dream. The religious doctrine of Inclusion supports this world view of what must be done to achieve universal peace. Religious inclusionism acknowledges Christ, but in actual fact stands against a requirement of having to accept Christ in order to receive eternal salvation. How else could "Christianity" unite with non-Christian religions? All religious must be regarded as equal and acceptable. This inclusionism position, however, is actually being against Christ or "Antichrist." These false religious and political beliefs are being promulgated worldwide now. These beliefs will eventually be embraced resulting in a uniting of religions and nations worldwide. This union will have been achieved during the last three and a half years prior to the return of Christ. Satan, who is the real driving force behind this political and religious union, will use this united religious and political force to try and stop the manifestation of God's love mystery which ushers in God's Kingdom on the earth eternally. We will look closely at all these end time events in the closing chapters of this book.

Gaining a proper understanding of God's love mystery will greatly aid you in being able to enjoy your life as God intends. In this generation God has restored Saint Paul's understanding of God's love mystery to us. We will delve deeply into our present understanding of God's love mystery as it has now been revealed. Paul eluded to it and its purpose for us as "…a mystery, the wisdom that has been hidden, which God foreordained before the worlds for our glory…" (1 Cor. 2:7b, WEB).

Let's now begin to unwrap God's most precious gift to us. It must be something special indeed, for after all it is the purpose for everything. Our journey will be beautiful, exhilarating, and awe inspiring as we look into God's love mystery.

1

GOD'S LOVE MYSTERY

In the beginning, God created the heavens and the earth.
~ Gen. 1:1, WEB

The very first sentence in the Bible evokes the question, "Why did God do that?" God gave a very brief answer to that question in Isaiah: "For thus saith the LORD that created the heavens; God himself that formed the earth and made it; he hath established it, he created it not in vain, he formed it to be inhabited: I *am* the LORD; and *there is* none else." (Isa. 45:18, KJV). However, even this answer leads us to ask, "Why did God create the earth to be inhabited?" Solomon observed the difficulty of answering this question:

> When I determined to load up on wisdom and examine everything taking place on earth, I realized that if you keep your eyes open day and night without even blinking, you'll still never figure out the meaning of what God is doing on this earth. Search as hard as you like, you're not going to make sense of it. No matter how smart you are, you won't get to the bottom of it. ~ Ecclesiastes 8:16-17, *The Message*

Modern science and the world's greatest educational institutions all attest to this truth stated in Ecclesiastes. Apart from God, it is impossible for anyone to know or understand God's plan here on earth. It is indeed a mystery! Though God wrote of His mystery in the Scriptures, few have understood it and certainly no one has fully fathomed it. God's great knowledge and plans cannot be known until He reveals them to us.

Within God resides a great mystery that explains why He created the heavens and the earth. The reason has been kept secret since before the beginning of time from all but a few. This mystery contains the greatest gift that the omnipotent God could possibly give. Not only that, this gift—once accepted by the recipient—ensures an eternity of more surprising wonderful loving gifts. In essence, this great mystery of God is packed with even more mysteries, which will be endless revelations of gifts expressing the love of God for His creations. Winston Churchill said "Russia is a riddle wrapped in a mystery inside an enigma."[1]

This famous quote can be applied in an analogous fashion in helping us grasp the complexity of God's love mystery. It is a riddle wrapped in endless mysteries inside an enigma. Among the numerous secrets of God, there are many statements about a specific "mystery of God" in the New Testament. This particular mystery is God's enigma or master plan for all of His creative work. This enigma gives purpose to and is the driving force for all of God's actions. Furthermore, the Scriptures speak of other related secrets supporting God's all-encompassing majestic plan. One-third of the Bible contains prophecies having to do with God's great plan; some have already been fulfilled and many have yet to unfold.

The mysteries contained in the prophecies, along with the many other secrets of God, are not the primary secret, though they are intertwined with and support it. Yet all are vital stepping-stones in God's plans; you can't have one without the other. They all are pieces of God's puzzle designed to lay the foundation and structure that crescendo to the grand climax that ushers us into eternity in the Kingdom of God. The New Testament primarily refers to these building materials as mysteries, while the Old Testament calls them the "secrets" of God. An Old Testament prophet spoke of these mysteries, saying, "I will open my mouth in parables; I will utter things hidden from the foundation of the world" (Matt. 13:35, WEB). Prophecies spoke of these *"things"* which are secrets wrapped in God's master plan. The ultimate purpose of God's master plan is what I call God's love mystery. The ultimate manifestation of God's love mystery has been the driving force and purpose for the creation of all things.

Although God gave the Old Testament patriarchs some insight into the love mystery of God, He gave the apostle Paul the honor of unveiling to the world the main purpose of His great mystery. Paul said, "But we speak God's wisdom in a mystery, the wisdom that has been hidden, which God foreordained before the worlds for our glory..." (1 Cor. 2:7, WEB)—what in the world is Paul talking about here? Paul clearly states that this is a special mystery that is intended to accomplish a specific purpose. He further says that this wisdom of God, which he calls a mystery, was planned by God prior to the creation of time and space and kept secret to all but a few of mankind. Finally, this mystery was specifically formulated for the special purpose of ultimately producing "glory" in mankind.

When we understand the purpose of God's plan for "our glory," then we will begin to understand why God created angels and eventually the physical universe, setting into motion all that we call history. We will also see how God's mystery, His road map to our glory, has forged events in the past and will direct future events for all eternity to come.

The Main Mystery

Like God, the mysteries of God are limitless and therefore will never cease, their depths never to be fathomed. Anything in God's extensive and endless plans that has not been revealed to us is still a mystery. When God does choose to reveal some of His mysteries, with only a few exceptions these revelations are given only to the people of God. As the prophet Amos said, "Surely the Lord GOD will do nothing, but he revealeth his secret unto his servants the prophets" (Amos 3:7, KJV). God's Word reveals an outline of His secret plans and offers a clue to understanding the primary purpose of His plan.

In Colossians Paul repeated and amplified his 1 Corinthians 2:7 statement, declaring what his commission from God was "...I was made a servant, according to the stewardship of God which was given me toward you, to fulfill the word of God, the mystery which has been hidden for ages and generations. But now it has been revealed to his saints, to whom

God was pleased to make known what are the riches of the glory of this mystery among the Gentiles, which is Christ in you, the hope of glory.… " (Col. 1:25-27, WEB). He disclosed that the "glory" God was giving to mankind was in and through Jesus Christ and that the salvation that He offered was not just for the Jews but for all of mankind worldwide. Paul said the mystery's purpose was for the "glory" of mankind. Wow! I believe it will become obvious that the creation of the heavens and earth was for the glory of mankind? What an awesome empowering truth this should be for us! This book will help explain why and how God plans to glorify those who accept His offer of glory.

The apostle Paul also said that he and fellow minister Apollos were "…Christ's servants, and stewards of God's mysteries." (1 Cor. 4:1, WEB). Paul then added concerning Christians, "…that their hearts may be comforted, they being knit together in love, and gaining all riches of the full assurance of understanding, that they may know the mystery of God, both of the Father and of Christ…" (Col. 2:2, WEB). The mystery came from the Father in and through Christ who was and is the focal point of God's mystery.

Christians of Paul's day did not understand what all of that meant. There were many secrets in Christ yet to be revealed and understood. It is interesting to note that this pronouncement from Paul occurred several years after the Messiah had ascended back to His Father in heaven. Prior to His ascension to heaven, Jesus had taught His apostles the basics concerning salvation and His coming kingdom, yet He did not deliver to them many of the most important understandings concerning God's mysteries surrounding Jesus. He reserved the full unveiling of them for the apostle Paul.

Paul requested that the saints be "…praying together for us also, that God may open to us a door for the word, to speak the mystery of Christ…" (Col. 4:3a, WEB). Without Jesus, it would be impossible for the rest of the secrets of God to exist. He is at the heart of God's mystery, and in Him are contained all secrets to come. Paul did not say that all the secrets of God would be revealed in his time, just that what was given up until that point needed to be properly understood. Christ is the primary mystery, and in and through him will soon come the mysterious glory promised to mankind.

So, to sum up, we have several secrets or mysteries wrapped inside of the grand enigma, which is Christ. The revelation of some of these mysteries to mankind has been sprinkled throughout the Bible, with increasing understanding given to the servants of God from Genesis to Revelation.

God's mystery required detailed plans, all of which revolved around Christ. Hints of some of these mysteries are referred to throughout the Bible. As Jesus said, "… I tell you that many prophets and righteous men desired to see the things which you see, and didn't see them; and to hear the things which you hear, and didn't hear them." (Matt. 13:17, WEB). Blessed we are, indeed, if we but open our eyes to the wonders of the mysteries of God. There is only one way that man can know the ways and plans of God. The Scriptures clearly tell us that, "The secret *things belong* unto the LORD our God: but those *things which* are revealed *belong* unto us and to our children for ever…" (Deut. 29:29, KJV). Unless God reveals His plans to mankind, no one can know the mystery of God, though that mystery has been playing out from before the beginning of time to the present and will continue throughout eternity.

God's Diamond

All the descriptions of the mysteries in the Scriptures point toward Jesus Christ. Paul summarized the point of his preaching when he said, "Now to him that is of power to establish you according to my gospel, and the preaching of Jesus Christ, according to the revelation of the mystery, which was kept secret since the world began" (Rom. 16:25, KJV).

The time came for the birth of Jesus. Jesus epitomized and contained all the mysteries of God which is the gospel, meaning "good news." Jesus came as God's gift to a fallen world and mankind. Through Jesus the redemption from sin of both would occur. This indeed was and is the most glorious good news that could be delivered. Satan hated the gospel, which proclaimed this good news would be accomplished through the Messiah. After the birth of the Messiah, Satan strove to kill Jesus and thus terminate any possibility of the good news shinning forth to a dark world. Satan inspired the Jewish King Herod to destroy all male children aged two and under in an attempt to kill Jesus (see Matthew 2:16). As the Scripture says:

> Even if our Good News is veiled, it is veiled in those who perish; in whom the god [Satan] of this world has blinded the minds of the unbelieving, that the light of the Good News of the glory of Christ, who is the image of God, should not dawn on them. …seeing it is God who said, "Light will shine out of darkness," who has shone in our hearts, to give the light of the knowledge of the glory of God in the face of Jesus Christ." ~ 2 Corinthians 4:3-4,6b WEB

The gospel, which is epitomized in Jesus Christ, can be likened to the most valuable, beautiful, perfect diamond ever created. He is like a perfectly formed diamond reflecting His Father's dazzling light. As Paul put it, "The Son is the radiance of God's glory and the exact representation of His nature…" (Heb. 1:3a, BSB). His brilliance is beyond that of any sun in the universe, shining into a dark world. His various facets reflect the brilliance and likeness of God, His Father. They reveal and shine forth the good news of the New Covenant, which God offers to all who accept and believe in His sacrificial Lamb. Jesus was the Lamb of His Father to be sacrificed for all the sins of mankind, past, present, and future. It is Jesus Christ who makes possible all the rest of God's secret blessings coming to mankind. Without Jesus, there is no gospel for us, nor are there any of its blessings of faith, grace, peace, joy, mercy, happiness, salvation, the New Covenant, God's kingdom, eternity, or heaven.

Once we desire and agree to the New Covenant with God, all the facets of the gospel diamond reflect the blessings of Christ, which are ours to gaze upon, enjoy, and explore without ever being able to plumb the depths of His beauty. One of His sparkling facets shows our entry into the kingdom of God. Another facet reveals how we are born again into a new creation, becoming children of God. Another assures that we will be given an eternal new body and will reign with Christ when His kingdom engulfs the earth at His return. God's great love for us is another facet we see in this diamond. Shining brilliantly is the facet of God's glorious mercy and grace. The glowing beauty of God's diamond given to mankind produces in us God's love, thoughts, peace, joy, faith, charity, and hope.

Eyes That Can See

Jesus was the embodiment of God's love mystery, a fact that the world has not understood. As Paul said:

> But we speak God's wisdom in a mystery, the wisdom that has been hidden, which God foreordained before the worlds for our glory, which none of the rulers of this world has known. For had they known it, they wouldn't have crucified the Lord of glory.
>
> But as it is written, "Things which an eye didn't see, and an ear didn't hear, which didn't enter into the heart of man, these God has prepared for those who love him."
>
> But to us, God revealed them through the Spirit.
> ~ 1 Corinthians 2:7-10 WEB

Paul continued:

> But we received, not the spirit of the world, but the Spirit which is from God, that we might know the things that were freely given to us by God. Which things also we speak, not in words which man's wisdom teaches, but which the Holy Spirit teaches, comparing spiritual things with spiritual things. Now the natural man doesn't receive the things of God's Spirit, for they are foolishness to him, and he can't know them, because they are spiritually discerned. ~ 1 Corinthians 2:13-14, WEB

These Scriptures clearly show that only Christians can truly understand the secrets of God. What a blessing it is that God has given Christians insight into His secrets. And to think, God knew before time began who would be given this knowledge. As Paul said:

> …even as he chose us in him before the foundation of the world, that we would be holy and without blemish before him in love; having predestined us for adoption as children through Jesus Christ to himself, according to the good pleasure of his desire, to the praise of the glory of his grace, by which he freely bestowed favor on us in the Beloved…" ~ Ephesians 1:4-6, WEB

What a staggering statement this is! Here, laid out in beautiful, simplistic terms, is more information about God's wonderful plan and purpose for mankind. The "glory" to be revealed in us, hidden in God since before time began, is that God predestined us for adoption to become His sons and daughters because of His great love for us. Astounding, but true—God knew each of us before we were born and He knew who would choose to believe, embrace, and follow Him, becoming His adopted children and eventually being clothed with His eternal glory.

The sum of this chapter is this. There are only two realities in existence. One is spiritual and the other is the material universe. Material mankind is locked into only his physical reality, unless the unseen spiritual world reveals itself to him. There are only two spiritual forces in existence that affect mankind. Only one of them, which is God, has eternally existed. The rest of the spiritual world God created giving each being (e.g. angels) eternal life. God then created the physical universe and all life contained therein. Both creations, spiritual and physical, were created for the specific purpose of producing children for God. For reasons we will explore in later chapters, God kept the vast majority of mankind in ignorance of His grand overall ridding plan and purpose for mankind. This plan is God's love mystery. In it is contained all of God's secrets planned for mankind. Jesus Christ was the embodiment of God's love mystery and was essential in making possible the mysteries' purpose which is the birth of all new sons and daughters of God to populate

His eternal Kingdom. All of mankind will be offered an opportunity to become the eternal children of God. Those who embraced this opportunity will eventually be clothed with a new eternal spiritual body. For reasons we will explore later, the spiritual realities and the ultimate purpose for mankind were hidden to all except for only a few throughout the last six thousand years. Now, let's look more deeply into God's great desire for eternal children and how His great love mystery came into existence.

2

GENESIS OF THE MYSTERY

All I am about to tell you became intricately woven into the fabric of God's love mystery. Its eventual revelation to mankind became known as the gospel or good news. Before the beginning of time, there was only one kingdom in existence: the kingdom of God. It consisted of a Trinity that was God, the Word, and the Holy Spirit. The Trinity created and agreed upon a grand master plan that would produce children.

Prior to creating anything in eternity, the Trinity knew the end result of that creation. God knows the end from the beginning. Nothing catches God by surprise. He is the One who plans, leads, and acts. He is always in control and never has to be on the defensive concerning anything.

The gospel, the good news of the Bible, is the revealing of God's mystery to man. Paul speaks of the gospel's origin: "Therefore don't be ashamed of the testimony of our Lord, nor of me his prisoner; but endure hardship for the Good News according to the power of God, who saved us and called us with a holy calling, not according to our works, but according to his own purpose and grace, which was given to us in Christ Jesus before times eternal, " (2 Tim. 1:8-9, WEB). It is the mysterious love story of God. To better understand it, we must go back to before the beginning of time to follow its story.

Our Destiny

God tells us that, "In the beginning was the Word [Christ], and the Word

29

was with God, and the Word was God. The same was in the beginning with God. All things were made through him. Without him was not anything made that has been made." (John 1:1-3, WEB). From the spiritual world, God sent the Word, Jesus Christ, to become incarnated into a human being. Jesus Christ was to be the first citizen of a new race of mankind to come. Jesus Christ was called the last Adam. Just as the first man, Adam, caused all of mankind to fall under sin and death, through Jesus would come righteousness and eternal life for all who believe and embrace him (see Romans 5:15-19). This is the sum purpose, and totality of the mystery of God, kept secret from the beginning of time.

The Word stepped out of eternity into time and space to become a mortal man. Yet he was not just any man; He was also divine. He was the advance emissary and embodiment of what God's mystery would eventually produce in His new brothers and sisters who comprise His new kingdom. He was the ambassador to this world, representing and proclaiming the new kingdom to come, which will be populated by the children of God. This heavenly new kingdom will eventually conquer and save this world from destruction and usher in a new, Utopian world.

Let me make it plain: the main mystery and the purpose of Christ, mankind, time, and space is the birth of children for God who will make up a new kingdom ruled by Jesus Christ on this earth for one thousand years. After that time period, Jesus will hand over this kingdom to God, his Father.

Jesus Christ was the first one born into that coming kingdom, with many brothers and sisters to follow. As Paul put it, "For as in Adam all die, so also in Christ all will be made alive. But each in his own order: Christ the first fruits, then those who are Christ's, at his coming. Then the end comes, when he will deliver up the Kingdom to God, even the Father; when he will have abolished all rule and all authority and power." (1 Cor. 15:22-24, WEB). This is the simplest and purest explanation of God's mysterious plan. The new kingdom will consist of a new, superhuman race of people such as the universe has never seen. All other mysteries, be they hidden in prophecies or other secrets throughout the Bible, revolve around and support this main mystery: the creation of a new kingdom filled with a superhuman race of mankind, all of whom will live eternally. God's plan to produce this new kingdom was the gospel or good news that was announced to mankind.

Jesus was the embodiment of what the children of God would eventually be and look like. In Him was eternal light and life that would be given to His new brothers and sisters. As Adam stood for the fallen man, who would be mortal, decaying, and subject to death, Jesus Christ represented the new man, who would be, through His blood, sinless and eternal. The Scriptures tell us:

> So also it is written, "The first man, Adam, became a living soul." The last Adam became a life-giving spirit. However that which is spiritual isn't first, but that which is natural, then that which is spiritual. The first man is of the earth, made of dust. The second man is the Lord from heaven. As is the one made of dust, such are those who are also made of dust; and as is the heavenly, such are they also that are heavenly. As we have borne the image of those made of dust, let's also bear the image of the heavenly. ~ 1 Corinthians 15:45-49, WEB

You can't get much plainer than that. Our destiny as children of God is to be given a glorious, eternal, physical body just like Christ now has.

Jesus Christ was the bridge to heaven for mankind. He personified what the children of God would become. He epitomized what the main mystery, planned before time began, would eventually produce in mankind. He also was the key factor in making it all possible through His life, death, and resurrection. Therefore, He represents what the mystery is and what we can become if we accept His invitation to join Him in His kingdom.

The Marriage of God

So, the mystery of God revealed is the creation of a new kingdom filled with a family for God through Jesus Christ. It is a love mystery because it required the greatest loving act that ever has or ever will exist.

We can better understand God's mystery if we use the Bible's terminology, which uses the analogy of a love story between a man and a woman. Only this love story is about the love of God. It is about how Jesus fell in love with a woman (the Church) and wanted to marry her. This marriage could be made possible only by the eternal love of God. God uses this allegory to reveal His great mystery for the glory of mankind. Here is God's love story as He describes it: "I will betroth you [Church] to me forever. Yes, I will betroth you to me in righteousness, in justice, in loving kindness, and in compassion." (Hosea 2:19, WEB). Paul expounds on this: "I [Paul] married you to one husband [Christ], that I might present you as a pure virgin to Christ." (2 Cor. 11:2, WEB).

The wedding of Christ and His Bride will be celebrated with a marriage supper in heaven and is spoken of by the apostle John this way:

> "Let us rejoice and be exceedingly glad, and let us give the glory to him. For the marriage of the Lamb has come, and his wife has made herself ready." It was given to her that she would array herself in bright, pure, fine linen: for the fine linen is the righteous acts of the saints. He said to me, "Write, 'Blessed are those who are invited to the marriage supper of the Lamb.'" He said to me, "These are true words of God." ~ Revelation 19:7-9, WEB

We are also told that at that day, "…as the bridegroom rejoices over the bride, so your God will rejoice over you. " (Isa. 62:5b, WEB).

Let's continue with this allegory to follow the purpose of God's plan. God, the Word, and the Holy Spirit discussed and agreed upon wanting a family. The driving force behind God's plan, as God's allegory shows, was simply that the Word, who became Jesus Christ, would take a bride (the Christian Church) and produce many children (Church members) for Him. Christ wanted a family with whom He could share the love of God. However, there was a problem: the woman he wanted to marry would be under a death penalty because of the sin of her physical father, Adam.

Although Adam had free will, God is omniscient and knew that Adam would sin, introducing sin and thus the death penalty to all of his children who followed. Due to the many egregious sins of all mankind, there was only one way in which the bride could be purified of her sins so that a marriage to Christ could be made possible. God had to be willing to become a man and die in place of His bride. What kind of love does God have for His bride and for each of us? So great a love that He was willing to step out of eternity into time and space and die in order to give life to His bride and the many children she would produce for Him. There never has been, nor can there ever be a greater love than that! This thought is mind-boggling and far beyond our comprehension. "Behold what manner of love the Father has given to us, that we should be called children of God. And that is what we are" (1 John 3:1, BSB)!

Marriage was first designed by God and for God. It was only later that this pattern was used to create the relationship between a man and a woman. The kind of love necessary for God's marriage is exactly the same kind needed for a successful human marriage. Paul specifically addressed God's marriage relationship saying, "This mystery is profound, but I am speaking about Christ and the church" (Eph. 5:32 BSB). It is interesting that Paul goes beyond just calling the marriage relationship as a mystery. He says it is also profound. Please afford me the liberty to paraphrase Paul's comparison with added commentary, looking at these verses from the spiritual perspective of the relationship between Christ and his bride.

Paul tells us that the Church is to submit to Christ (see Ephesians 5:22). Why? It is because Christ is God, who is the bride's eternal Creator, and in Him alone resides all that she was created to need: love, truth, and eternal life; which only He can give her (see Ephesians 5:23). The bride was found with sins and was under a death sentence that had to be removed in order for God's love and righteousness to be instilled in her. Only Christ dying in her place could accomplish this. Because of Christ's great love for His bride, she is to look to Him and submit to His lead in her life (see Ephesians 5:25-26). Christ demonstrated His love by dying on the cross to make it possible for His bride to join him in a loving marriage relationship for all eternity (see Ephesians 5:27).

Love's Sacrifice

Jesus, the sinless, righteous Son of God, had to be willing to die in place of His bride! This would have to occur even while she hated Him. Jesus exercised a supremely loving, selfless act and exchanged places with her, becoming her sin and dying in her place on the cross, setting her free from death: "In this is love, not that we loved God, but that he loved us, and sent his Son as the atoning sacrifice for our sins" (1 John 4:10, WEB). Because of this atoning sacrifice, Christ's bride was offered the opportunity to symbolically die on the cross with Christ and in reality be transformed into His righteousness. Unbelievably, Jesus became her sin and she was able to miraculously become the very righteousness of Christ and be regarded in the Father's eyes as virginal and sinless. This was possible only by Jesus dying on the cross in her stead. The bride was then set free and transformed into the eternal righteousness of Christ, thus acceptable to the Father.

Something wonderful happened then that John simply but profoundly describes: "We love him, because he first loved us" (1 John 4:19, WEB). We literally had no real love to give until God the Father gave us His love through His Son. Now we have the love of God, which He has given us. We can now share His love with Him and with others. This was the reason why God was willing to give His creations free will, the freedom to choose to accept His love or not. He knew it would be worth it in spite of the sad fact that some would not choose to accept His love. Those who do accept His love will have chosen to receive it. God will not force His love on anyone.

The Father, Jesus, and the Holy Spirit so loved the world that they were willing to sacrifice the Creator of all things to purify the woman to make marriage possible with her. As the most famous Scripture in the Bible reads, "For God so loved the world, that he gave his one and only Son, that whoever believes in him should not perish, but have eternal life" (John 3:16, WEB). Eternal life, once given through the conditions of the New Covenant (which is another vital, glorious facet of the mystery of God), cannot be reversed. This great sacrifice of God laying down his own Son's life for the woman would cleanse her of all sins past, present, and future. Only a perfect and sinless sacrifice would be enough to satisfy sin's great demand for death.

After that perfect sacrifice was met in Christ, then He would make a proposal of marriage to the woman, which, if she accepted, would consummate their marriage. Christ's selfless, loving sacrificial act would make possible the impregnation in the heart of the woman God's loving Spirit, creating within her a desire to live with Him forever. Christ will return to earth at the end of this age to claim His bride. When Jesus asks you to become His bride, to accept His death to purify you, to make you ready for marriage with Him, He makes an agreement, or covenant, with you that spells out precisely what He and you agree to do for each other in the relationship. In the agreement, Jesus' part in this covenant is laid out, detailing how he will now and forever treat and take care of His wife. The agreement also reveals what the wife is to do for Christ. This covenant makes possible a totally loving relationship, which spirals upward in eternal bliss, between Jesus and His bride.

In conclusion, the good news that God reveals to mankind through Jesus Christ contains the secret mysteries of God's love that if accepted gives you access to that which will fulfill all your desires and give you entry into God's eternal Kingdom now. As citizens of God's Kingdom, you will be given at the return of Jesus a new eternal body like His. Those so blessed will have completed God's ordained predestined journey required for the creation of a new superhuman race of people far beyond the grandeur of what even fiction writers have ever dreamed of. This superhuman race will reign with Christ after His return over the remaining physical people and nations of the earth for the next thousand years.

The relationship God the Father, Christ, and this new superhuman race is portrayed as that of an eternal family. Scriptures describe this family relationship in two ways. First by the use the analogy of a wedding depicting Jesus Christ as the groom and the Christians as His bride. As in a marriage both agree to this relationship as depicted in the New Covenant terms. The relationship in actual fact will always be Christians as siblings, with God their Father and Jesus their elder brother. Let's next turn our attention to a closer look concerning the terms of the marriage covenant that Christ and His bride must agree to in order to consummate the wedding.

3

The Mystery of the New Covenant

It seems today that the New Covenant is not expounded on much in church services. It is amazing that such an important topic as the New Covenant is so rarely spoken of. Most every Christian is well acquainted with the Old Covenant, which is the Ten Commandments. Chances are, you can recite most, if not all, of them. But how much do you know about the New Covenant?

Let's have a little fun and take a short test with each answer worth ten points if you want to grade yourself. Please don't panic; no one but you need know how well you do. Let's see just how much you know about the New Covenant (I will give you the correct answers shortly):

I. What was the New Covenant?

II. When was it established?

III. When was it inaugurated?

IV. What is the purpose of the New Covenant?

V. What does God says He will do in the New Covenant?

VI. What does the New Covenant state Christians will no longer do?

VII. What law(s) contained in the New Covenant will Christians keep?

VIII. The Old Covenant was written by the finger of God in stone. What is the New Covenant written on?

IX. Without God's help, which Covenant is more difficult to keep, the Old Covenant or the New Covenant?

X. How is it possible for a Christian to perfectly keep the "new law" of Christ?

You can find the answers to these questions in the remainder of this chapter. Each answer will be identified in sequential order with a superscripted Roman numeral corresponding to the number of the question. The Roman numerals will be placed at the beginning of each sentence that contains the answer.

Our Agreement With God

What is our agreement or covenant with God? "In simple terms, it is a formal agreement. It may be an agreement between two people, a treaty between nations…, or a relationship between God and a human individual or nation."[1] As far as Christians are concerned our covenant is an eternal agreement with God, the terms of which neither party will ever break. God said of Jesus, "I the LORD have called thee in righteousness, and will hold thine hand, and will keep thee, and give thee for a covenant of the people …" (Isa. 42:6a, KJV). [I]The New Covenant, which is Jesus Christ (see Isaiah 42:6-7), is at the heart of our relationship with God. [II]The New Covenant was established when our Savior died, shedding His blood on the cross. At the Last Supper with His disciples, Jesus offered wine, saying, "This cup is the new covenant in my blood, which is poured out for you" (Luke 22:20b, WEB).

Notice what this verse says about the covenant: "But now hath he obtained a more excellent ministry, by how much also he is [now] the mediator of a better covenant, which was established upon better promises" (Heb. 8:6, KJV). "The Greek verb for "established" is *nomotheteo*, which means 'to give or to establish a law' (Louw-Nida lexicon). It is in the perfect tense, indicating that something was completed in the past and it continues to have an effect."[2] [III]Although the covenant was "ratified" when Jesus died, it was not inaugurated or "administered" for the first time until the Day of Pentecost, when the Holy Spirit entered the hearts of Christians for the first time, establishing the Church or Bride of Christ.[3] I like Joseph Prince's explanation of the Covenant. [IV]This Covenant or agreement between Christ and the Church defines the relationship that is to exist between them. It defines what each promises to do for the other in their relationship.

The Old Testament Scriptures foretold the coming of the New Covenant:

> Behold, the days come, saith the LORD, that I will make a new covenant with the house of Israel, and with the house of Judah: Not according to the covenant that I made with their fathers in the day *that* I took them by the hand to bring them out of the land of Egypt; which my covenant they brake, although I was an husband unto them.... ~ Jeremiah 31:31-32, KJV

God adds, "And I will make an everlasting covenant with them, that I will not turn away from them, to do them good; but I will put my fear in their hearts, that they shall not depart from me." (Jer. 32:40, KJV). God means what He says. Those who enter the New Covenant will never turn away from Him. God will do wonderful things for them that will never cease. What we have is an eternal Covenant, which, once agreed upon and entered into, will never be broken by either party. Did you get that? God said in the New Covenant agreement that He entered into with you, that you will never turn away from Him. How awesome and wonderful is that?

We know that we have in Christ: a most precious eternal gift of life from God that will never be taken away from us. We will never turn away from God. God again says:

> "I will also give you a new heart, and I will put a new spirit within you; and I will take away the stony heart out of your flesh, and I will give you a heart of flesh. I will put my Spirit within you, and cause you to walk in my statutes, and you shall keep my ordinances, and do them." ~ Ezekiel 36:26-27, WEB

God adds more clarity when He tells us when and how this will happen:

> "A Redeemer [Jesus] will come to Zion, and to those who turn from disobedience in Jacob," says Yahweh. "As for me, this is

my covenant with them," says Yahweh. "My Spirit who is on you, and my words which I have put in your mouth, shall not depart out of your mouth, nor out of the mouth of your seed, nor out of the mouth of your seed's seed," says Yahweh, "from henceforth and forever" ~ Isaiah 59:20-21, WEB.

ᵛThrough the prophet Jeremiah, God expounds on the New Covenant and beautifully explains—clearly and simply, using several "I will" statements—what the conditions of the New Covenant are:

But this *shall be* the covenant that *I will* make with the house of Israel; After those days, saith the LORD, *I will* put my law in their inward parts, and write it in their hearts; and will be their God, and they shall be my people. And they shall teach no more every man his neighbour, and every man his brother, saying, Know the LORD: for they shall all know me, from the least of them unto the greatest of them, saith the LORD: for *I will* forgive their iniquity, and I will remember their sin no more. ~ Jeremiah 31:33, 34 KJV, emphasis added

God speaks of this covenant that He will make in the next chapter of Jeremiah also. There, He adds a couple more "I wills," which I think we covenant people need to be aware of and rejoice in. These last two are very encouraging.

I will make an everlasting covenant with them, that *I will not turn away* from following them, to do them good; and *I will put* my fear in their hearts, that they may not depart from me. Yes, *I will rejoice* over them to do them good, ~ Jeremiah 32:40-41 WEB, emphasis added

Did you notice the joy God expresses in doing good things for His saints? ᵛᴵThe New Covenant also states, "and they shall teach no more every man his neighbor, and every man his brother, saying, Know Yahweh; for they shall all know me, from the least of them to the greatest of them, says Yahweh" (Jer. 31:34a, WEB).

The Old Covenant contained Ten Commandments written in

stone for the people to keep. [VII]The New Covenant requires us to keep only two laws: "This is his [God's] commandment, that we should believe in the name of his Son, Jesus Christ, and love one another, even as he commanded." (1 John 3:23, WEB). Jesus said, "A new commandment I give to you, that you love one another, just like I have loved you; that you also love one another" (John 13:34, WEB). These two statements show that the New Covenant commands us first to believe in Jesus and then to love others as God loves us. Because of God's great love, all other required actions in the New Covenant are performed by our heavenly Father.

We do not have to keep these two commands on our own, for God supplies us with the supernatural ability to abide by both laws. As Paul states, "For it is God who works in you both to will and to work, for his good pleasure" (Phil. 2:13, WEB). However, although God supplies us as Christians with the ability to do both of the things that He desires, He will not force us to do them. God's Holy Spirit gives us total freedom to search after the things of the Spirit or after the sinful desires of our flesh. That is something we must choose to focus on according to our free will.

Regarding the matter of believing, it is important to note that some people can believe, yet not repent. The prophet Isaiah said that those the Redeemer has forgiven need to repent of their sins (see Isaiah 59:20). Repentance simply means changing your attitude toward God. Repentance entails more than just believing. It denotes an effective change in attitude, embracing (by faith) the New Covenant through the sacrifice of Jesus Christ for the forgiveness of all your sins, just as was granted to the thief on the cross beside Jesus (see Luke 23:39-42). Then you must let God write His law of love on your heart with His Spirit. When this takes place, you will be able to express God's love back to not only Him but also to yourself and your fellow mankind.

Let's stop and ponder for a moment the loving laws that a God who cannot lie guaranteed us and bound Himself to. [VIII]First, "...*I will* put my law in their inward parts, and in their heart *will I* write it..." (Jer. 31:33b, WEB, emphasis added). This is not a case of "maybe" or "I will try" or "I will if you obey me." God simply said, "I will!" These should be comforting words to each of us who have accepted Jesus as our Savior.

God is saying to you and me, "I will be in you and lead you to follow My will." Remember, He said, "A new commandment I give to you, that you love one another, just like I have loved you; that you also love one another" (John 13:34, WEB). The only laws that God writes on our heart simply command that we believe Him and let His love pour back out to Him and to others as Christ did.

Think about the new laws of God. [IX]Humanly speaking, without God's help, the new laws are more difficult to keep than the first laws written in stone. [X]However, through the grace of Christ, who has washed all past, present, and future sins away, this New Covenant provides the way for us to keep it perfectly. We don't have to rely on words written in stone. God lives in us and guides us daily. God says He will show us His way: "The LORD *is* my shepherd; I shall not want. He maketh me to lie down in green pastures: he leadeth me beside the still waters. He restoreth my soul: he leadeth me in the paths of righteousness for his name's sake" (Ps. 23:1-3, KJV). We can read God's Word for nourishment and we can also rest assured that God is in our hearts and minds, leading us and ready to comfort us, no matter how we may feel to the contrary at any given moment. All we need do is focus on Him and hold tight to His promises concerning us.

Next, God says in the same fashion, "I will put my law in their inward parts, and write it in their hearts; and will be their God, and they shall be my people. And they shall teach no more every man his neighbour, and every man his brother, saying, Know the LORD: for they shall all know me, from the least of them unto the greatest of them, saith the LORD" (Jer. 31:33b-34, KJV). This promise is astounding. The Creator of all things loves us, and He claims us as His own. He will lead us and teach us personally with His Spirit in us. He will put His thoughts into our hearts and help us walk peaceably with Him down life's difficult road.

As a child, did you ever dream of finding a magic lamp with a genie in it who would grant you any wish you asked for? Well, the reality of what we have in God is far beyond the greatest magic genie you could ever imagine. Jesus said, "I tell you, all things whatever you pray and ask for, believe that you have received them, and you shall have them" (Mark 11:24, WEB). The classic magic genie gives only three wishes. Our great

God gives us an endless number of wishes! Some people misinterpret this verse to mean that they can ask God for whatever they want (often material things, or for plans to go according to their own desires) for selfish reasons. No, it does not mean that. God knows what we really need and only that is what He will allow. So, we can rest assured that even when we ask for something that is not good for us, our great God will filter our requests and deliver only that which is good for us. Even in our darkest hours of trial, we can take comfort that God will make the worst of it to turn out for our advantage (Rom. 8:28; James 1:2-4; 2 Pet. 2:9). Our loving Creator says, "I will not turn away from following them, to do them good…. I will rejoice over them to do them good" (Jer. 32:40a-41a, WEB). God promises He will only do good for us, all the days of our lives.

In our darkest hours on this earth as Christians, we need to recall this and take heart, knowing that whatever great trials we face, our loving Father will turn them into something good for us. How encouraging and soothing this should be to us. God is with us from now on, for all eternity, and He will never leave us or forsake us! Praise God, for remember He also says, "…I will put my fear in their hearts, that they may not depart from me…" (Jer. 32:40, WEB).

Our Eternal Desire for God

Even though today you may stray temporarily from God due to the trials and temptations of your flesh and of this world, God knows that those who are truly His will eventually return to Him, having learned the lesson that all they really want, desire, and need resides only in Him. Those impregnated with the love of God may try to hide it for a while, but deep down they will never lose the love for Him that God instilled in their hearts. This is so, though they may temporarily wander away. Today, in our deepest trials and darkest hours, we can take comfort in the ironclad promises of God that He is with us and will deliver us from all evil. Know this for an eternal certainty, no matter what you've done; no matter how far you have strayed from God, you can return to His loving embrace.

Don't let Satan trick you into believing otherwise. No matter what your distress is now or ever will be, be encouraged, for God's Word says, "For I am confident of this, that He [God] who began a good work in you will continue to perfect it until the day of Christ Jesus" (Phil. 1:6, BSB).

If you have strayed away from God, take comfort in these words: "I will forgive their iniquity, and their sin will I remember no more" (Jer. 31:34b, WEB). This is the most comforting news of all. We are clean of all sin through our Savior, Jesus Christ. The God of all creation looks at us and loves us just as much as He does His righteous Son, Jesus. Jesus said, "You [God] sent Me and have loved them just as You have loved Me. " (John 17:23, BSB). What a loving and forgiving God! God forgives and permanently forgets our sins each day we commit them, and therefore, so can we! We are free to walk forward each day, unburdened by the mistakes of the past, with a clear conscience. Although, not required for righteousness and eternal life, depending on the circumstances, it may or may not be appropriate to apologize and/or make restitution for our transgressions or offences toward others. God has already forgiven you, however, even if others will not. If you have repented (change of heart and attitude) of your sins and have accepted the invitation of God the Father to accept Jesus Christ as your personal savior, you have been born against and are now a son or daughter of God. No matter what you have done or will do, you already have eternal life and you will be given a new eternal body at the coming resurrection. Christ's sacrifice has paid the price for all our sins past, present, and future and we are now and forever forgiven. We need only recall this truth and faithfully claim it each and every time we feel condemned for our sins. Doing so will thwart Satan's favorite way of making us feel fearful, condemned, and alienated from God. We then can rest assured and expect, as King David did, "Surely goodness and mercy shall follow me all the days of my life: and I will dwell in the house of the LORD for ever." (Ps. 23:6, KJV). You know, forever is a pretty long period of time!

God speaks very lovingly of His purpose for the New Covenant, His new mutual relationship with mankind: "And I will give them an heart to know me, that I *am* the LORD: and they shall be my people, and I will be their God: for they shall return unto me with their whole heart"

(Jer. 24:7, KJV). God has accomplished the great mystery He set out to do before the beginning of time. At last, God has a people who serve Him because they choose to do so out of their free will. They are not robots, doing what God wants with no real love or feelings. Their service is out of great love and a desire to serve Him with their whole heart.

The Joy of the New Covenant

The "marriage" of Jesus and the Church was the very purpose of and driving force for all of God's creations, both spiritual and physical. Jesus was the focal point of God's mysterious secret plans. The prophets of the Old Testament foretold this, and John the Baptist prepared the way for it: "Behold, I will send my messenger, and he shall prepare the way before me: and the Lord, whom ye seek, shall suddenly come to his temple, even the messenger of the covenant, whom ye delight in: behold, he shall come, saith the LORD of hosts" (Mal. 3:1, KJV). This marriage covenant that is embodied in Jesus Christ was the genesis of God's coming spiritual and material creations and is at the core of the gospel.

This New Covenant mystery of God was to be heralded to mankind in the far distant future, long after God had devised it. God knew that by then mankind would have fallen into the depths and depravity of sin and death, enslaved under the darkness and rule of the devil's kingdom. The New Covenant would be "good news" to mankind. Good news, indeed! Through the New Covenant, God's grace is revealed by the granting of unearned, undeserved, unmerited forgiveness of all the sins of mankind, and the requirements of God concerning righteousness for mankind is met through Christ's blood. Through the New Covenant flows all the gifts and blessings of God, including grace, the heavenly kingdom, love, joy, peace, and eternal life.

The subject of the New Covenant is pretty important to God in both the Old and New Testaments. Of course, it should be, for this is the reason for the creation of time and space to begin with, and God died to make it happen! It has been on His mind for possibly billions of years, and at last the time has almost come for His bride to rejoice in a sublime, loving relationship with Him. She is preparing herself now with beautiful finishing touches to meet Him soon with great love, excitement, and joy. Notice the incredible joy and peace of the New Covenant that was foretold in the Old Testament:

> Sing, O daughter of Zion; shout, O Israel; be glad and rejoice with all the heart, O daughter of Jerusalem. The LORD hath taken away thy judgments, he hath cast out thine enemy: the king of Israel, *even* the LORD, *is* in the midst of thee: thou shalt not see evil any more. In that day it shall be said to Jerusalem, Fear thou not: *and to* Zion, Let not thine hands be slack. The LORD thy God in the midst of thee *is* mighty; he will save, he will rejoice over thee with joy; he will rest in his love, he will joy over thee with singing. ~ Zephaniah 3:14-17, KJV

God literally sings with excitement and joy over our New Covenant relationship with Him. May we also learn to sing with Him daily with great excitement and joy! May we now learn to rest peacefully in His loving arms. Let's now turn our attention to why there was a need to replace the Old Covenant for a New Covenant.

4

WHY A NEW COVENANT?

The Old Covenant, which was the Ten Commandments or Deca-logue, was first spoken by God to all Israel and later written in stone by the hand of God and given to Moses (see Deuteronomy 4:13, 5:22).[1] Exodus says, "And the LORD said unto Moses, Write thou these words: for after the tenor of these words I have made a covenant with thee and with Israel. And he was there with the LORD forty days and forty nights; he did neither eat bread, nor drink water. And he wrote upon the tables the words of the covenant, the ten commandments." (34:27-28, KJV). The covenant written in stone by God is all that Scripture reveals that Moses brought down from Mount Sinai. Later, Moses declared to Israel, "And the LORD spake unto you out of the midst of the fire: *ye heard* the voice of the words, but saw no similitude; only ye heard a voice. And he declared unto you his covenant, which he commanded you to perform, *even* ten commandments; and he wrote them upon two tables of stone." (Deut. 4:12-13, KJV). God clearly calls the laws He wrote in stone for Is-rael the "Covenant," which was the "Ten Commandments." These Com-mandments were later elaborated on in the Torah.[2] According to the Babylonian Talmud they were written by Moses on Jewish parchment made of unsplit cow-hide.[3] The Torah constitutes the first five books of the Old Testament.[4]

This distinction of the covenant being the Ten Commandments written in stone is important. It was from them that the rest of the laws and statues were drawn up to administer Israel's affairs. If God were to destroy the covenant written in stone, then all the rest of the laws and statutes based on it would crumble also. The Old Covenant and the resulting laws and statutes were perfect and beautiful. The problem was, only God could keep this agreement. This highlighted the need for a New Covenant that not only God but also Israel could keep. The Old Covenant administered only death to the imperfect Israelites. Paul explained that the Old Covenant was glorious, but it was flawed, and its flaw was corrected in the New Covenant. Paul said:

> And He has qualified us as ministers of a new covenant, not of the letter but of the Spirit; for the letter kills, but the Spirit gives life. Now if the ministry of death, which was engraved in letters on stone, came with such glory that the Israelites could not gaze at the face of Moses because of its fleeting glory, will not the ministry of the Spirit be even more glorious? For if the ministry of condemnation was glorious, how much more glorious is the ministry of righteousness! ~ 2 Corinthians 3:6-9, BSB

A Better Agreement Needed

The main purpose of the Old Covenant was to expose and demonstrate the need for a better Covenant in Christ. Hebrews 8:7-8a says, "For if that first *covenant* had been faultless, then should no place have been sought for the second. For finding fault with them [not the commandments], he saith, Behold, the days come, saith the Lord, when I will make a new covenant..." (KJV). The Old Covenant exposed the flaw that was in mankind: that man does not have the heart to obey God. The heart of mankind is as hard as the rock that God wrote the Ten Commandments on. The Ten Commandments exposed man's sins and demanded the death penalty for them. Thus, the Old Covenant could only bring death to mankind. It was called "...the ministry of death, which was engraved in letters on stone..." (2 Cor. 3:7, BSB). It was the Old Covenant, the Ten Commandments, which contained "letters on stone," written by the hand of God, that condemned Israel. A New Covenant that mankind could keep was needed to replace the Old Covenant. This is exactly what

Christ, our New Covenant from God, did on the Cross of Calvary. A New Covenant was needed, and God said He would provide one:

> But when God found fault with the people, He said: "Behold, the days are coming, says the Lord, when I will make a new covenant with the house of Israel and with the house of Judah. It will not be like the covenant I made with their fathers when I took them by the hand to lead them out of the land of Egypt, because they did not abide by My covenant, and I disregarded them…" ~ Hebrews 8:8b-9, WEB

The Old Covenant was good and perfect, because it came from a good and perfect God, but He was the only one who could keep it. A better New Covenant would solve the problem. In the Bible God explains His solution: "For this is the covenant that I will make with the house of Israel. After those days," says the Lord; "I will put my laws into their mind, I will also write them on their heart. I will be their God, and they will be my people." (Heb. 8:10, WEB).

God removed the Old Covenant marriage agreement with the death of Jesus Christ and established the New Covenant, which paves the way to marriage between Christ and the Church. The blood of the Lamb removed the Old Covenant and forgave all the sins of mankind. Salvation was then offered to all of mankind who would accept the Lamb's sacrifice and believe in Christ. Prior to repentance and accepting Jesus as Savior, Paul said, "When you were dead in your trespasses and in the uncircumcision of your sinful nature, God made you alive with Christ. He forgave us all our trespasses, having canceled the debt ascribed to us in the decrees that stood against us. He took it away, nailing it to the cross! And having disarmed the rulers and authorities, He made a public spectacle of them, triumphing over them by the cross." (Col. 2:13-15, BSB). In spite of the fact the blood of Christ has released us from the Old Covenant and all its rules and regulations which hang from the Ten Commandments, most of Christianity seems ignorant of Christ annulling their necessity to still keep any of these laws in order to be righteous. As a result Satan has rejoiced over Christian's vain beliefs that righteousness is produced by keeping the Old Covenant laws. These beliefs have produced only self-righteousness and sins which Satan has used to hammer Christians continually with guilt, fear, and death.

A Better Love

The Old Covenant called for the keeping of the Ten Commandments, namely as summed up in the two great commands, which told us we were to love God with all our hearts and to love our neighbor as ourselves. As good and perfect as these commandments were, the New Covenant called for the keeping of a better and even more difficult set of commandments. Love was the essence of both the Old and the New Covenants. However, the main difference between the love described in the Old Covenant and that described in the New was that the Old Covenant required us to love others as much as we love ourselves while the New Covenant requires us to perform the humanly impossible task of loving others as God loves us. The New Covenant also calls for God to write His laws in our hearts. God's new laws are summed up in the word "love," just as with the Old Covenant. However, the love of the Old Covenant and that of the New Covenant are as different as night and day. It is worthy to note that in the New Covenant, God gives us only two commands. John briefly combined them saying "…we should believe in the name of his Son, Jesus Christ, and love one another, even as he [Christ] commanded." (1 John 3:23b, WEB). John first stated the need to believe in Christ and then referred to what Jesus said about the next command. Christ expounded clearly on the second this way: "A new commandment I give to you, that you love one another, just like I have loved you; that you also love one another" (John 13:34, WEB).

Although loving as God loves is humanly impossible, God provided a way for us to keep this commandment through Jesus Christ's Spirit dwelling in us. As Paul said, "I can do all things through Christ, who strengthens me" (Phil. 4:13, WEB), and, "I have been crucified with Christ, and it is no longer I that live, but Christ living in me. That life which I now live in the flesh, I live by faith in the Son of God, who loved me, and gave himself up for me" (Gal. 2:20, WEB). That is why Jesus said, "I have told you these things, that in me you may have peace. In the world you have oppression; but cheer up! I have overcome the world" (John 16:33, WEB). Christ living in us can and will overcome the world, and in Him we will keep God's New Covenant perfectly!

New Covenant Was Before the Old

Since the time of Adam and Eve, every word written in the Bible has had to do with the mystery concerning the prophecy about Christ made by God in the Garden of Eden. Understanding this mystery of the gospel has been veiled over the centuries even though its story has been foretold in the Scriptures from Adam to its fulfillment in Christ. Yes, I mean God has hidden this mystery from the vast majority of mankind since the days of Adam and Eve. Only a few throughout the Old Testament were given understanding of it. "The Scripture foresaw that God would justify the Gentiles by faith, and foretold the gospel to Abraham: 'All nations will be blessed through you.' So those who have faith are blessed along with Abraham, the man of faith" (Gal 3:8-9, BSB). It is interesting that the gospel spoken of in Galatians is referred to as a covenant in Acts 3: "You are the children of the prophets, and of the covenant which God made with our fathers, saying to Abraham, 'In your seed will all the families of the earth be blessed.'" (vs. 25, WEB). This shows that the New Covenant and the gospel were one and same thing that was given to Abraham.

The words "gospel" and "covenant" are thus interchangeable. Jesus Christ was the Gospel and also the New Covenant! Throughout Abraham's life and that of Isaac and Jacob, a broader and better understanding of the mystery of God began to unfold for them and all saints to follow. Hebrews 11 gives some very interesting insight about all of those from Abel to the apostle Paul who heard about the gospel. It speaks of Abel, Enoch, Noah, Abraham, Isaac, Jacob, Joseph, Rahab, Moses, Gideon, Barak, Samson, Jepthah, David, and the prophets. In the summation of their stories, in verses 39 and 40, it says, "These all, having had testimony given to them through their faith, didn't receive the promise, God having provided some better thing concerning us, so that apart from us they should not be made perfect" (WEB). These people undoubtedly knew of the gospel about the coming Christ, and they will be in God's Kingdom. Moses, as an example, is stated to have specifically "…valued disgrace for Christ above the treasures of Egypt, for he was looking ahead to his reward [God's Kingdom]" (vs. 26, BSB).

The prophet Isaiah, "saw Jesus' glory and spoke about Him" (John 12:41b, BSB). All the Old Testament spiritual patriarchs and matriarchs knew that their heavenly reward was coming though Jesus Christ. As the Scripture says, "Salvation exists in no one else, for there is no other name under heaven given to men by which we must be saved" (Acts 4:12, BSB). The saints of the Old Testament scriptures and we of the New Testament will all be granted bodily entry into God's kingdom at the same time when Jesus returns. Hebrews goes on to say that the many saints of the Old Testament are great examples of faith for those of us who strive for the kingdom of God just as they did: "Therefore, since we are surrounded by such a great cloud of witnesses, let us throw off every encumbrance and the sin that so easily entangles, and let us run with endurance the race set out for us. Let us fix our eyes on Jesus, the pioneer and perfecter of our faith, who for the joy set before Him endured the cross, scorning its shame, and sat down at right hand of the throne of God." (Heb. 12:1-2, BSB).

5

GOD'S SEVEN STAGES

The mystery of God required complex detailed plans that have been in the process of being implemented in successive stages through eons of time. From the Scriptures, I have observed seven major events that act as platforms or stages on which God's glorious plans for mankind will be executed. In short, these stages supporting God's mystery called for: (1) the creation of the angelic realm; (2) the creation of the physical universe; (3) the creation of all living plants and animals; (4) the creation of the first man, Adam; (5) the incarnation of Jesus Christ; (6) the manifestation of the sons and daughters of glory; and (7) the coming of the new heavens and new earth. The first five of these events are now history. The sixth stage is when the actual manifestation of God's love mystery will occur. This will be God's grand design and ultimate purpose for all of history, which is the revealing of His glorified children.

The first five stages were deemed vital to prepare for God's supreme creation in the sixth stage, that of the glorified man. After the glorification of those who choose Jesus Christ as their savior, then comes a breathtaking event setting the stage for the rest of eternity. The existing physical universe will be purified with fire as Peter said (2 Peter 3:12). Then next as Peter said in verse thirteen, we will see the Holy City of New Jerusalem will descend down out of heaven to the new purified earth to dwell as one with the children of God for all eternity! But let's not get too far ahead of our story. In this book we will review the first five stages planned by God. We will also see how the devil has tried to sabotage God's plans and how his efforts have negatively affected our lives, no matter whether or not we are Christian. The sixth and seventh stages are briefly touched upon in the closing chapter of this book. Let us now look at the first five successive stages of God's plan to produce His children.

The Creation of Angels

God's love mystery, which is expressed in the good news or gospel, first called for the creation of angels. This was the first stage in God's master plan. The full purpose and mystery of God's master plan was probably kept secret even from the angels, though God may have revealed some of it to them, which may have been a factor in their eventual rebellion against God. God also revealed some of it to the righteous saints of the Old Testament. Scripture, however, indicates that although they knew of it, they may not have understood it fully. Peter said:

> Concerning this salvation, the prophets, who foretold the grace that would come to you, searched and investigated carefully, trying to determine the time and setting to which the Spirit of Christ in them was pointing when He predicted the sufferings of Christ and the glories to follow. It was revealed to them that they were not serving themselves but you, when they foretold the things now announced by those who preached the gospel to you by the Holy Spirit sent from heaven. Even angels long to look into these things. ~ 1 Peter 1:10-12, BSB

One of the major reasons why angels were created was to support God's great plan for the creation of His children. "Are not the angels ministering spirits, sent to serve those who will inherit salvation" (Heb. 1:14, BSB)?[1] God created the angelic hosts according to various ranks and types of angels. Only Michael is specifically mentioned as an archangel of God.[2] "Archangel" in Greek means "chief angel."[3] Daniel states that Michael was one of the "chief princes" (Dan 10: 13, WEB), indicating the possibility of other archangels.[4] Prior to the creation of the earth, another very powerful angel of high rank by the name of Lucifer existed. Only one other angel is named in the Bible, and that is Gabriel. He undoubtedly is one of high rank as well. These three may all have been "chief angels" or archangels of God in the beginning. They existed in God's kingdom along with other angelic hosts referred to as cherubim and seraphim, with most simply referred to as "angels" or as "elect angels."[5]

Prior to the existence of the physical creation, there was perfect peace and harmony. Indications are that the angels may have been let in on God's plans for the next phase of His creation, which was that of the universe. No mention of discord among the angels is made at the creation of the universe. To the contrary, they were extremely joyful about it (see Job 38:4-7). God is a God of order, perfection, and beauty. He is not the author of destruction, chaos, and confusion (see 1 Corinthians 14:33). Isaiah said that "the God who formed the earth and made it, who established it and didn't create it a waste, who formed it to be inhabited" (Isa. 45:18b, WEB). When God creates anything, it is the epitome of exquisite perfection. When the physical universe was created, it was perfect, orderly, and very beautiful.

Satan's Rebellion

God had created the angels to worship Him and eventually assist Him in His grand design for Adam and Eve and their descendants. God knew when He gave the angels free will that a portion of them would fall away. Most likely, God gave them free will when He created them; however, it could have been later. Apparently, Lucifer had preeminence among most of the other angels. If he, Gabriel, and Michael were all archangels together, they each may have had command over one-third of the millions of angels serving God. Satan was the first angel to exercise his free will to refuse to obey God's truth and light, creating sin and its dark side with his jealousy, hate, lies, and pride. The apostle John said, "He was a murderer from the beginning, refusing to uphold the truth, because there is no truth in him. When he lies, he speaks his native language, because he is a liar and the father of lies." (John 8:44, BSB).

It may have been that God revealed to the angels His plans to create an eternal new heaven and earth someday, but first He would create mankind lower in status and power to them. He may have told them that the purpose of mankind was to be immortal and in a supreme position over them as actual sons and daughters of God, to rule all things under His guidance. The Bible tells us, "For it is not to angels that He has subjected the world to come, about which we are speaking." (Heb. 2:5, BSB). Three thousand years ago, David mused about the purpose of mankind, saying, "When I consider your heavens, the work of your fingers, the moon and the stars, which you have ordained; what is man, that you think of him? What is the son of man, that you care for him? For you have made him a little lower than God, and crowned him with glory and honor. You make him ruler over the works of your hands. You have put all things under his feet (Ps. 8:3-6, WEB). Everything has not yet been put under our feet, but one day God will give all that He has created to His children to rule.

It is possible that God revealed to Satan that the very purpose for his creation as well as that of all the angels was to assist God in the supreme creation of mankind yet to come. To help mankind to eventually become his own ruler may have insulted Lucifer's prideful thinking. This knowledge may have added insult to injury and been a factor he used to justify going in a negative and dark direction. God's plans, if declared, probably did not sit well with Lucifer. The thought of mortal mankind being given such a lofty position may have been more than he wanted to contemplate. His thinking may have jelled into this:

> After all, if anyone deserved such a position as a son of God, it should be me. For that matter, I think God's thinking and plan is ridiculous and shows a weakness in Him. Why would He make lowly mankind into His children? I could have devised a better plan than that. I should be made at least co-ruler with God. As a matter of fact, I think I could do a better job of ruling the universe than God!

However it all came down, we can only speculate from what the Scriptures reveal. We do know that Lucifer allowed vain thoughts and imaginations to permeate his mind. He eventually acted on these imaginations, creating the dark side. As we can see in Isaiah, Lucifer suffered from pride, lust, vanity, and a desire to become ruler of all that God had created, rather than be ruled by it. This led him to rebel.

As Satan began to fill his mind with wicked thoughts, he undoubtedly began to speak to and infect the other angels with rebellion against God's plans for them. Over a period of time, he convinced one-third of the angelic host to rebel with him against their creator. Every angel had free will to choose to remain loyal to God or become a follower of Lucifer. Eventually the battle lines were drawn. Lucifer assembled a massive army against God and attacked Him and His loyal angels. Ezekiel describes what happened:

> You were the anointed cherub who covers: and I set you, [so that] you were on the holy mountain of God; you have walked up and down in the midst of the stones of fire. You were perfect in your ways from the day that you were created, until unrighteousness was found in you. By the abundance of your traffic they filled the midst of you with violence, and you have sinned: therefore I have cast you as profane out of the mountain of God; and I have destroyed you, covering cherub, from the midst of the stones of fire. Your heart was lifted up because of your beauty; you have corrupted your wisdom by reason of your brightness: I have cast you to the ground; I have laid you before kings, that they may see you. ~ Ezekiel 28:14-17, WEB

We have in Genesis 1:1 the creation of the universe; then it jumps forward possibly millions of years to verse two where God is ready to repair the chaos and confusion that existed immediately after the angelic rebellion prior to the creation of Adam and Eve's new world. Now, let's turn our attention to the next stage preparing the way for God's love mystery to be revealed.

6

CREATION OF TIME AND SPACE

Now, what I am about to tell you is an interesting account of God's creation of the universe and all life on earth. The traditional account of creation says that God did all this approximately six thousand years ago within a seven-day period. I have no problem with this traditional teaching. It does, however, run contrary to existing scientific evidence, which shows that the material universe has existed for billions of years. But, God is God and can do anything. He could have made everything to appear billions of years old and still have created it all in six days just exactly as we have traditionally been taught. It really doesn't matter to me which story is, in reality, the truth. Whichever way God created the universe is all right with me and does not affect or shake my belief in God.

Only Speculation

Please allow me to present a possible scenario that harmonizes existing scientific evidence and biblical truth. I believe the Bible in Genesis chapter one, verses one and two allows for such a possible explanation. I personally believe in the creation account I will give. It is certainly all right for you to believe in another. My belief allows for the creation of the present world as we now know it in a seven-day week six thousand years ago. It also allows for a pre-adamic world existing for hundreds of millions of years as science claims existed. Whichever belief is true does nothing to affect the salvation of our souls, so you can take or leave either explanation as you desire. However, the account I'm giving you helps merge the Bible and science to strengthen and support each other. True science does not contradict God! It only supports His existence!

In the Beginning

Genesis 1:1 tells us about the moment when the second stage of God's love mystery burst forth in the creation of the universe, time, and space. Scripture simply states, "In the beginning God created the heavens and the earth" (WEB). The Hebrew word for God used here is *"Elohim."* It is a plural noun that allows for the existence of the Trinity consisting of God, Word, and Holy Spirit.

This momentous and grand event is interestingly not expounded on much in the Bible. It seems as though there is a lot God has not revealed to us, and thus much of it is mysterious to us. For now we have to rely on hints from the Bible and scientific evidence we see in the universe. Psalms gives some interesting insight: "By the word of the LORD were the heavens made; and all the host of them by the breath of his mouth" (Ps. 33:6, KJV). Scientists' latest guess as to the age of existence tells us that the universe exploded into being approximately 13.8 billion years ago.[1] True or not, it is reasonable to believe that when God breathed the universe into existence, it was not in chaos and confusion but was beautiful and perfect in every way. However, when we come to verse two of Genesis, it says, "the earth was without form and void."

About fifty-three years ago, I heard an account of how God created a perfect universe only to have it destroyed by Lucifer and his fallen angels. I read this story from the publications of the Radio Church of God (later known as the Worldwide Church of God or WCG). I suspect the church's "apostle," Mr. Herbert W. Armstrong, came up with his teaching on earth's creation from the Scofield Bible's commentary on the first two verses of Genesis. Scofield speculates that the destruction of the pre-adamic world resulted from Lucifer's fall from heaven to earth. I believe WCG's account is correct and it forms the bases of what follows concerning it. The first two verses of the first chapter in the book of Genesis allow for billions of years to have elapsed between the perfect creation of verse 1 and the utter chaos that is described in verse 2. Verse 2 states, "And the earth was without form, and void; and darkness was on the face of the deep. And the Spirit of God moved on the face of the waters" (Gen. 1:2, KJV). The Hebrew "*hā·yə·ṭāh*"[2] is the word translated "was" in most Bibles. However, Barnes' Notes on the Bible says that the Hebrew word had three possible meanings. All of them are closely related in meaning. In one case the Hebrew word "was" shows a change from something to something else. Barnes said the word could, "… be, as a change of state, 'become'. This is applied to what had a previous existence, but undergoes some change in its properties or relations… [For example] 'and she [Lot's wife] became' a pillar of salt Genesis 19:26." The word "was" is translated "became" in many other places in the Bible. The Hebrew words for "form" and "void" are "*tohu*" and "*bohu*," meaning utter waste and confusion.[3] Clarke's Commentary on the Bible said these Hebrew words "convey the idea of confusion and disorder."[4] That being the case, Genesis 1:2 could read, "The earth became wasted, mixed up, and confused."

If this is so, how could the earth, after God created it perfect and beautiful, become destroyed, full of utter waste and confusion? And how long was the earth in it pristine state prior to this terrible state described in verse 2? Could it be that something terrible happened between the time that God created the universe perfect in verse 1 and it being described as descending into a state of utter destruction and confusion in verse 2? Could billions of years have existed between the time of verse 1 and that of verse 2 of Genesis? If so, this could explain science's estimated 231 million years of the existence of a beautiful prehistoric earth filled with dinosaurs, plants, and animals prior to the devastation of the earth and all prehistoric dinosaurs some 66 million years ago.[5]

Science tells us that approximately 65 million years ago, an object, which was most likely an asteroid six miles wide, slammed into the earth, killing all life with the exception of small creatures such as turtles, birds, and small mammals.[6] It is believed that the comet or asteroid created a crater about one hundred miles wide, which created a cloud of debris blocking out the sun, killing off 75 percent of all species on earth.[7] Of course, this would take care of all of the dinosaurs, which had roamed the earth for about 166 million years. They all would have become extinct. This would also explain the discovery of prehistoric dinosaurs, plants, and animals dating back prior to 65 million years ago.[8] It is possible that the large object that hit the earth 65 million years ago was not an asteroid or comet at all. Jesus may have described the demise of the prehistoric world when he said, "I saw Satan fall like lightning from heaven" (Luke 10:18, BSB). God threw Satan from heaven and cast him to the earth after Lucifer led one-third of heaven's angels in rebellion against God. If Satan was cast to the earth along with millions of his co-conspirators, they could have been the cause of the destruction of the prehistoric world.

Humanoids?

It is possible that after the destruction resulting from Satan's rebellion God created a new world with plants and animals that would thrive for the next several million years. During this time God also could have created humanoids, whose existence scientifically dates back as far as nearly two and a half million years ago. These "earliest documented members of the genus *Homo* are *Homo habilis* which is said to have evolved around 2.3 million years ago; the earliest species for which there is positive evidence of use of stone tools."[9]

The biblical account of Adam and Eve is the first time where Scriptures show us God dealing personally with mankind. There is a lot God has not revealed to us in His Word about all that He has done throughout eternity. Much of it will remain a mystery for now, but He probably will reveal it to us when we join Him in eternity. He has, however, revealed to us the most important things we need to know now, and those things that are most pertinent to us are those things concerning our eternal salvation in Christ. We should be careful about saying that God did not or could not have done something. The existence of humanoids and dinosaurs are prime examples. Could God have created them? The answer is "Yes!" He did not have to tell us about them. We have only come to know of them through archaeology. Fossils found in various strata of the earth have proven their past existence, so, obviously, God created them at some time during the past, whether it was millions of years ago or at the time of Adam and Eve.

If there was a pre-adamic world, we do not know how long it existed between Satan's rebellion and Adam and Eve's creation. Isaiah tells us that Satan was "cut down to earth" (Isa. 14:12, YLT), so we know that the earth existed at the time of Satan's rebellion. If this account is true, then Genesis 1:3 picks up the account of God's reconstruction of the earth from its destroyed, chaotic state as a result of Satan being hurled to earth. It is possible that the next seven days of creation did occur exactly as Christianity has traditionally taught. If so, God created in one week the oceans, the land masses, the plants, the animals, and Adam and Eve. Soon after God created Adam and Eve, Satan tempted Eve, so it is evident that Jesus' account of seeing Satan cast to the earth indicates that occurred prior to Adam's world. It is most likely that Satan and his fallen angles had been cast down and bound to the earth for millions of years prior to Adam. I think God may have wanted Satan and his fallen army, for a long period of time, to sit and stew in the chaos and confusion on earth that resulted from their rebellion.

During the period between Satan's rebellion and the creation of Adam and Eve, there could have been several cataclysms, including more asteroids, devastating ice ages, and worldwide floods, impacting all life on the planet. At some point during or after these events and prior to Adam and Eve, God may have created plants, animals, and even humanoids. It is possible that after millions of years another cataclysmic event destroyed all life on earth as God prepared to create Adam and the world as we now know it. Whatever the case may be, the creation of Adam took place after verses one and two of the first chapter of Genesis.

Whether or not there were humanoids in the pre-adamic world is unimportant to us today for salvation. However, if these humanoids did exist, some questions naturally follow. Could these humanoids have been self-conscious and intelligent? If so, how smart were they? Why did God allow them to exist? Why did God allow the dinosaurs and all the prehistoric plants to exist? The Bible is silent on these questions. If there was a pre-adamic world, I think one obvious answer for why is that God created and allowed it to exist in preparation for His greatest creation yet, the post-adamic world. Much of what accounts for mankind being able to have a comfortable lifestyle in our world today is drawn from the residue of the vast resources deposited in the pre-adamic period. From that we enjoy valuable items like copper, iron, coal, oil, gold, diamonds, minerals, and so on, which are so vital to our economy today. There is scientifically a fairly solid basis for showing that the earth existed for billions of years prior to the time of Adam and Eve. Could God have done all of His creation six thousand years ago, exactly as traditional Christianity has taught? Yes, He could have! Could He have done it the way I have described, over billions of years? Yes, He could have. Scripturally, God gives us the freedom to believe either way.

In the next chapter we will briefly discuss God's third stage creation and then look more deeply at the next stage, the creation of Adam and Eve. Present-day plants and animal were first created, completing the third stage of God's love mystery, His supreme creation of mankind. The possibility of a pre-adamic world is interesting speculation. However, all we really need to know now for sure is that Adam and Eve were the epitome of God's special creations done for a grand purpose. It was to be through their linage that the prophesied Messiah was to come. It was through them that the modern races have been derived.

7

WHY LAW? WHY SIN?

Now God was ready for the third stage in His plan. God refashioned the destruction described in verse two of Genesis one, creating again a perfect and beautiful world filled with wonderful plants and animals. He created a gorgeous paradise, the Garden of Eden. It was time for the special fourth stage of God's creation, Adam and Eve. God created them and gave them the world to rule and the luscious Garden of Eden to live in. The gospel of man's redemption, which had been kept secret from the foundation of the world, was about to be revealed for the first time to Adam, Eve, and even Satan. The only law that God gave Adam and Eve was that they were not to eat of the fruit from the tree of the knowledge of good and evil. God warned them that if they did eat of this forbidden fruit that they would die. All was peaceful and harmonious until Satan twisted God's truth and caused Adam and Eve to sin. Sin then entered the world, along with fear, shame, guilt, and death. The universe and mankind came under sin's curse. Adam, who had been given absolute rule of the earth earlier by God, was driven from the Garden of Eden. Satan grabbed control and became ruler of the earth, establishing his kingdom of darkness that still rules today.

It was in the Garden of Eden that it became evident that mankind and the universe somehow would need to be redeemed from sin, death, and the power of Satan. It was at this point that God revealed "the good news," the "gospel" to Adam and Eve, and the "bad news" to the devil. God said to the devil, "I will put enmity between you and the woman, and between your offspring and her offspring. He [Christ] will bruise your head, and you will bruise his heel" (Gen. 3:15, WEB). God here prophesied that a savior would come to redeem all that was lost and finally eradicate all sin. It was probably a fearful shock for Satan to hear this "bad news" from God. It undoubtedly gave some comfort and hope to Adam and Eve. Satan got the "bad news" and Adam and Eve got the "good news" that all was not lost and that there would come a redeemer from Eve. The gospel they received was simple and short. There is no record of it being expounded to Adam any further in Scripture. The gospel simply said that in the future a man would be "bruised" by Satan, but that the devil, in turn, would be "crushed." When Christ died on the cross, Satan undoubtedly was relieved. The Messiah had died, not just been badly bruised, as God had told him. Jesus was dead and buried in the tomb! Satan surely rejoiced at the thought that the prophecy given him by God had failed. Satan probably thought that since God's prophecy had failed, he (Satan) was the victor and would remain ruler of the world forever and perhaps even defeat God's plan. Yes, indeed, his thinking was twisted, but what would you expect from the father of lies and twisted minds?

Law and Sin

No matter when life began on earth, no matter whether humanoids existed or not, no matter whether they were intelligent or not, sin did not enter the human heart until Adam and Eve. The Bible is clear about that: "...where there is no law, there is no transgression." (Rom. 4:15b BSB). There was no law given prior to Adam and Eve to be broken. Therefore, no sin would have been imputed in a prehistoric world. God's command to Adam and Eve not to eat of the forbidden fruit is the first recorded law given to mankind. They ate of the tree and they became conscious of their sin, transgressing the one and only law God had given them. The Scripture says, "...the Law merely brings awareness of sin" (Rom. 3:20b, BSB). The reason God gave a law to Adam and Eve was to give them true liberty by which they could choose to walk in faith with Him or walk by sight and according to their own human reasoning. That is God's purpose for any of His laws. Adam and Eve chose to walk after what they thought was right rather than what God told them. Once any of God's laws are broken, then the resulting sin exposes man's need for a Savior.

As a result of exercising their free choice to disobey God, they were conscience-stricken and tried to hide their sin from God. It is interesting to note here that Satan used the words of God given to Adam and Eve and twisted them just enough to confuse Eve and cause her to doubt God. This led her, Adam, and all mankind into Satan's darkness. Throughout the ensuing millennia, the words of God have been continually perverted by Satan in an effort to control people and events in history, endeavoring to destroy God's plans and His people.

Two thousand years ago, when God revealed the culmination of His love for us in His Son, Jesus Christ, Satan tried to kill Jesus as a baby and again hide the truth of the gospel. Satan actually partially accomplished his goal of distorting the truths of God. He did so just enough to send most of Christianity into a life of self-righteous works rather than allowing God's spirit do the works of true righteousness in them. Using and perverting God's truth is Satan's greatest weapon of attack! This is a technique that Satan still uses against us today. He has used it against mankind to hide the truth and meaning of God's words from Eve up until the present. As a result, individuals, organizations, churches, and nations have suffered countless divisions, wars, horrific guilt, pain, and death.

God Knew Sin Would Happen

God was not surprised by the sin of Adam and Eve. He knows and controls the future in advance. He is not limited by time and space. He knows the end from the beginning. He states, "'I am the Alpha and the Omega,' says the Lord God, who is and was and is to come—the Almighty" (Rev. 1:8, BSB). This Almighty One is also described by the apostle John this way: "In the beginning was the Word, and the Word was with God, and the Word was God. He was with God in the beginning. Through Him all things were made, and without Him nothing was made that has been made.... The Word became flesh and made His dwelling among us"

(John 1:1-3, 14, BSB). This Word who created all things became the man Jesus Christ, the promised savior of the world. He, in His pre-incarnate God position, knew prior to His creation of the physical universe and mankind that both would fall under the power and darkness of the devil through sin. Therefore, before God created the universe, He formulated a plan to redeem it and mankind as well.

Why Sin?

You may be wondering why God would allow sin into existence if He knew about it in advance. The answer is that God is love and God wants His creation to serve Him out of free will, love, and desire, not out of forced duty as a mindless robot. In order to accomplish this, God had to allow sin to be born, and he deemed it necessary. He knew the price would be the death of His Son. God knew that there could be no joy for Him or His creation in a forced servitude of Him. Not only that, God wanted His created beings to be able to participate and enjoy the inexplicable love He is. If God's creations could not choose to serve Him, there could be no true exchange of love given out of free will between His creation and Himself. Worship of God would be only a hollow and mechanical exercise. In this scenario, the created would have no choice to love or worship God. Also, His created beings could not express true love to each other. Their relationships would be as hollow and mechanical as that which would exist with God.

The only way in which the love of God could be shared by His creations was if He gave them the dangerous and precious gift of "free will," the ability to choose to love or hate. This was dangerous because it meant that God's created beings would have the capability of rejecting Him and His love. Free will is the only thing that God cannot control. However, it is the only way God's love could be born in a created being. It was because of this and God's great desire to share His love with more than just Himself, the Word, and the Holy Spirit that He chose to formulate and implement His grand seven-stage building project that would eventually produce Him multiple billions of children to share His love for all eternity. It was out of God's great desire to share His love with billions of others that He was willing to allow the emergence of His opposite, which is evil and darkness. God, however, allowed sin and therefore only He could redeem that which was lost and ultimately totally obliterate it. God did not create sin; the devil did.

God's Plan

God devised His plan to deal with sin before anything was created. It is called the "mystery," "good news," or "gospel," kept hidden, to be revealed only in God's good time and place (a little here and a little there) throughout the ages. That mystery was the fact that God would allow sin into the universe and this would require no less a sacrifice than the Creator of all things, Jesus Christ. Christ was worth infinitely more than all of God's physical creations, which would need redemption. Randy Alcorn's book "Heaven" speaks eloquently of this redemptive process. Christ's supreme sacrifice will eventually restore all things to the perfection in heaven and earth that existed prior to the sin of Satan's kingdom and mankind. Yes, God was willing to do all this in order to usher in His love to billions who would joyfully and willfully share it with one another through the remainder of eternity. The sharing of God's love to His creation was and is just that important to God! This is so even though it meant the sacrifice of Jesus Christ, whose life and existence was worth far more than all of God's creations. This perfect, priceless sacrifice would be more than sufficient to redeem mankind and the physical universe from sin and restore them to their original state of perfection. All that I have said in this section bursts forth in the most famous verse in the Bible, "For God so loved the world that He gave His one and only Son, that everyone who believes in Him shall not perish but have eternal life" (John 3:16, BSB).

Before the physical universe existed, God knew that Lucifer would rebel and turn one-third of the other angels against God's Kingdom. He knew that Satan would form a new kingdom of darkness and it would become an adversary to God and mankind. God knew that Adam and Eve would sin, ushering in the darkness of Satan's kingdom to re-place them as ruler of the world. Although great battles would rage for thousands of years, God determined He would eventually utterly crush Satan and his fallen angels. In the meantime, God would make this great disaster Satan had wreaked turn out for the good of mankind and the universe. As a result, mankind would have the opportunity to become love as God is love. God can make all bad things, even Satan and fallen mankind, turn out for the eventual good of those who He redeems. God is using the bad things Satan has done to help mankind join Him in His kingdom as eternal beings to live with Him forever in peace and joy. To do that, God formulated His grand plan to redeem and restore all that the devil and his angels wrecked. He would redeem and then reconcile all of mankind who were willing to repent and embrace their savior, the Messiah. This, indeed, was a grand plan and unbelievably astonishing good news. Summing up, God so loved the world that He was willing to allow sin, which would be redeemed and destroyed by the sacrifice of His only begotten Son. This made it possible for those who accept Christ as their Savior to be able to serve God and do so out of love, desire, and free will. It was so important that God was willing to die in order that it might happen! Now we are ready in the next chapter to look directly at the greatest gift God has or could ever offer give to us. It is the fifth and most crucial stage on which the stability and viability of all the platform stages hang, the birth of the Messiah.

8

THE MYSTERY IS INCARNATED

Next in our story is the fifth and most important piece in God's plan, the birth of the second Adam, Jesus Christ, Redeemer of mankind, heaven, and earth. He existed in the beginning with God. God created everything through him (John 1:2-3).

> He [Christ] was in the world, and though the world was made through Him, the world did not recognize Him. He came to His own, and His own did not receive Him. But to all who did receive Him, to those who believed in His name, He gave the right to become children of God— children born not of blood, nor will of the flesh, nor will of man, but born of God. The Word became flesh and made His dwelling among us. We have seen His glory, the glory of the one and only Son from the Father, full of grace and truth. ~ John 1:10-14, BSB

The apostle John's inspired words thus beautifully describe the greatest event that will ever occur. God, who created the universe and everything in it, stepped out of eternity to be born into mortal human flesh for the express purpose of dying for His creation that they might join Him, the Holy Spirit, and the Father in eternity. This is the great love mystery in a nutshell! As John put it, "Look, the Lamb of God, who takes away the sin of the world" (John 1:29, BSB). God's priceless gift, the Savior and very expression of His love to mankind was born fully human and fully divine. "From His fullness we have all received grace upon grace. For the Law was given through Moses; grace and truth came through Jesus Christ" (John 1:16-17, BSB).

Jesus came to give many blessings to the world, but contrary to what most people believe, Jesus Christ did not come to reveal and explain all the mysteries of God while he walked the earth. He did not come to make the Scriptures easily understood for everyone. He came to keep the Old Covenant laws of God perfectly, never sinning even once in his thirty-three years of life on earth. Furthermore, he came to be the sacrificial Lamb of God for the sins of the world. Although He laid the groundwork for it, He did not come to establish His Church during His life on earth. He came to prepare the way for it. The Church was not established until the day of Pentecost, a couple months after His resurrection. He did come to make disciples of those predestined to become Christians, those whom he knew in advance would believe in him, but even there the disciples had only a shallow understanding of the things Jesus told them. He came as a witness of God to the world, not to condemn the world but to save it and all who would come to believe in and embrace His name. He came preaching the good news concerning the mysteries of God and their coming blessings for mankind. However, Jesus never intended His preaching to give the people who heard Him any more than a superficial understanding of their true meanings. He intentionally masked the mysteries' meanings by speaking them in parables. The disciples were perplexed at this and asked him, "'Why do You speak to the people in parables?' He replied, 'The knowledge of the mysteries of the kingdom of heaven has been given to you, but not to them'" (Matt. 13:10b-11, BSB). Even so, the understanding of the disciples was quite shallow, for they time and again showed an inability to grasp the revelations Christ gave them.

Jesus Cloaked the Mysteries

Jesus preached about the mysteries of the coming kingdom of God, but intentionally cloaked even his disciples' understanding of them. This kingdom of which Jesus spoke actually was not new news to the Jewish nation. Nearly every Jew in Israel knew of the prophecies about the coming of the Messiah and that he would set up God's kingdom on earth. However, none of the Jews understood certain vital truths about the kingdom they were expecting. They had their own ideas of what to expect and how it would be set up. All of which were wrong.

They expected that when he came, the Messiah would raise an army, throw out the occupying Roman army from Israel, and set up the physical kingdom of God in Jerusalem. Jesus was just one of a long line of Jews in Israel's history who claimed to be the Messiah preaching of the coming of God's kingdom; so they did not see him as different from the other false messiahs. They certainly did not expect the Messiah to die and be resurrected! They did not know that the kingdom Christ was preaching about would first be set up in their hearts and minds, and would not come physically to the earth to rule for another two thousand plus years. Jesus simply did not fit the mold of their expected Messiah! They looked at Jesus like we might look at the guy today who stands on a street corner holding a Bible and a sign saying, "Repent, for the end of the world is near!"

Well, why didn't Jesus make the mysteries of God plain to them so they could understand the truth about them? Could he have done so? Certainly he could have! Why didn't Jesus make it plain to them that He was the mystery of God who could eventually be in them and who would be their "hope of glory" (Col. 1:27)? The answer is simply a matter of timing! God's plan called for Jesus to come and be a living expression of God's love, grace, and truth. He did not come to judge, condemn, and destroy. He came to live His life perfectly under the laws of the Old Covenant. Those laws were not to be done away with until He died on the cross. The New Covenant could not be established with the Church until the Old Covenant died with Christ on the cross. The Old Covenant marriage agreement had to die before spiritual Israel would be free to marry a new husband, Jesus Christ. As Paul explains it, "a married woman is bound by law to her husband as long as he lives. But if her husband dies, she is released from the law of marriage.... Therefore, my brothers, you also died to the Law [Old Covenant] through the body of Christ, that you might belong to another [New Covenant], to Him who was raised from the dead, in order that we might bear fruit to God" (Rom. 7:2b-4, BSB). Jesus explained it this way: "Do not think that I have come to abolish the

Law or the Prophets; I have not come to abolish them, but to fulfill them" (Matt. 5:17 BSB). Jesus came to do what no human could. He came to keep them perfectly in order to be a perfect sacrifice for mankind. Jesus continued, "For I tell you truly, until heaven and earth pass away, not a single jot, not a stroke of a pen, will disappear from the Law until everything is accomplished" (Matt. 5:18, BSB). The "everything" that the Old Covenant law required of mankind was accomplished through Jesus Christ keeping it perfectly. All the requirements of the Law for mankind was satisfied through Jesus' sacrifice on the cross and that is why he cried out, "It [the Old Covenant] is finished" (John 19:30, KJV). The books of the gospels were about the completion of the Old Covenant age, preparing the way for the New Covenant writings, which began after the death of Jesus. The age of the new eternal Covenant had begun.

Jesus Came to be a Sacrifice

Jesus came to be the loving Lamb of God to be sacrificed so the sins of mankind would be forgiven and the world would thus be reconciled to God. Jesus could have saved Himself if He had so chosen. When Peter drew the sword to prevent Jesus' arrest in the garden of Gethsemane, Jesus told him to put away his sword, warning that, "For all who draw the sword will die by the sword. Are you not aware that I can call on My Father, and He will at once put at my disposal more than twelve legions of angels? But how then would the Scriptures be fulfilled that say it must happen this way" (Matt. 26:52-54, BSB)? Jesus said concerning His life, "No one takes it from Me, but I lay it down of My own accord. I have authority to lay it down and authority to take it up again" (John 10:18, BSB). Jesus' death was a part of God's plan, and Jesus was not going to short-circuit the timing or plan of His Father! None could have killed Jesus unless He allowed them to. Jesus willingly laid down His life so that all who would believe in Him might have access to God's love and gain eternal life. This was the plan of God, and no man or the devil himself could have stopped Jesus from giving His life to redeem heaven, earth, and mankind from the curse of Adam's sin.

If the Jews and the Roman army had known Jesus was indeed the Messiah, they would not have allowed His crucifixion; thus we'd have no sacrifice for sins. Jesus said on the cross, "Father, forgive them, for they do not know what they are doing" (Luke 23:34, BSB). He said his killers were ignorant that they were killing their Savior! Jesus was more than able to get across understanding of all these things to them if He had so desired. It is obvious that He did not want to at that time. Jesus intended to lay down His life as their sacrifice and refused to give them spiritual understanding of the mysteries of God concerning the fact that He was indeed the promised Redeemer and Son of God! God's master plan called for this revelation to come a few days after the resurrection of Jesus. Also, what good was it to preach the gospel of salvation in its spiritual fullness when it was not yet possible for the people to have it? The necessary sacrifice to forgive their sins had not yet occurred. It would be only after Jesus' death and resurrection that the world would have forgiveness of all their sins and thus access to the key that would open the door (Jesus Christ) to grant entry into God's kingdom.

Did Jesus Preach the Kingdom?

You might ask, "Didn't Jesus preach and make plain all the meanings of the mysteries concerning the gospel to the Jews when the Scripture says Jesus came into Galilee, preaching the gospel of God, and saying, 'The time is fulfilled…and the kingdom of God is near. Repent and believe in the gospel' (Mark 1:14-15, BSB)? Doesn't that clearly state that Jesus preached the gospel?" Technically, that is true, but again Jesus did not open up the minds of his hearers to a spiritual understanding of the gospel and how they could get into that kingdom. Even the disciples, though He had told taught them about it, did not understand it and deserted Him when He was arrested. If the disciples didn't get it, what makes you think anyone else who heard Jesus preach got it? The disciples did not grasp it until after his resurrection, when Christ had to come and personally put it all together for them.

Spiritual Ignorance

The spiritual ignorance of the people who heard Jesus preach of the kingdom of God is clearly demonstrated best by none other than Jesus' own disciples. Jesus had spoken to them about the kingdom of God throughout His ministry, so one would think they would surely have gotten the message. However, the very night before Jesus was crucified, Jesus said to them concerning the kingdom of God, "'In My Father's house are many rooms. If it were not so, would I have told you that I am going there to prepare a place for you? And if I go and prepare a place for you, I will come back and welcome you into My presence, so that you also may be where I am. You know the way to the place where I am going.' 'Lord,' said Thomas, 'we do not know where You are going, so how can we know the way?' Jesus answered, 'I am the way and the truth and the life. No one comes to the Father except through Me'" (John 14: 2-6, BSB). The way to what? The kingdom of God!! Jesus was the gateway to the kingdom of God, all truth, and eternal life. But notice, Jesus stated this in response to what Thomas had just asked Him. Stop and think about this: after three and a half years of Jesus preaching about the kingdom of God and the need to repent and believe, none of the eleven disciples, the elite of Christ's followers, had understood the gospel message of Jesus.

The answer He gave to Thomas still was not understood by any of the disciples until after His resurrection from the grave. Understanding did not come until Jesus suddenly appeared to his disciples after His resurrection. It is stated, "Then He opened their minds to understand the Scriptures. And He told them, 'This is what is written: The Christ will suffer and rise from the dead on the third day, and in His name repentance and forgiveness of sins will be proclaimed to all nations, beginning in Jerusalem'" (Luke 24:45-47, BSB). It was only then that the disciples' mission became clear to them. That crucial most important spiritual knowledge and the teaching of the true gospel mysteries had been reserved for the apostles and disciples to preach after the resurrection of Jesus. Did the disciples understand all the mysteries of God at that time? Of course not! They understood the mysteries of the scriptures concerning Christ, but all the mysteries of God to be known were not fully disclosed to them yet. God would at His appointed times in the future continue to unfold more of His mysteries to His Church. For instance, they were totally ignorant of the fact that eternal salvation was not meant just for Israel, but for all mankind. It would be years later that Peter and Paul would have this mystery revealed to them by God.

The Gospel Christ Commanded

Jesus did not reveal much understanding of the mysteries to anyone on earth during His ministry. Just before Jesus rose to meet His Father from the Mount of Olives, Jesus again gave the commission to preach the gospel this way: "Go ye into all the world, and preach the gospel to every creature. He that believeth and is baptized shall be saved; but he that believeth not shall be damned" (Mark 16:15-16, KJV). Mathew adds, "All authority in heaven and on earth has been given to Me. Therefore go and make disciples of all nations, baptizing them in the name of the Father, and of the Son, and of the Holy Spirit, and teaching them to obey all that I have commanded you. And surely I am with you always, to the very end of the age" (Matt. 28:18-20, BSB). After Jesus said these things to them, the apostles then watched Jesus ascend into the heavens right before their eyes.

Concerning these instructions from Jesus, it is important to note that He did not specifically command them to preach the gospel of the "kingdom of God." The preaching of the gospel that would bring about entry into the kingdom was what was commanded. This points out that, at last, the missing key to entering the kingdom was now in their hands. They were now equipped, replete with spiritual understanding, to carry the gospel of salvation through Christ to the world. If you want to parse the issue, which is more important? Is it the gospel of the kingdom or the gospel about the key (Jesus) that opens the door so you can enter? What good is the kingdom to you if you can't get into it? If I had to choose between the salvation or the kingdom part of the gospel, I'd want the gospel of salvation part. That would let Christ come into my heart, saving me and giving me automatic entry in to the kingdom part, which I suspect will be pretty good. The point here is that the two parts work together and both are absolutely necessary in the Gospel of God.

Ten days later, after Christ ascended to the Father; the day of the Feast of Pentecost came. It was on this day that the Holy Spirit was given, filling the faithful disciples. They then were born again, given eternal life, and became a new creation in Christ. At that event the Church was established. They entered into the marriage Covenant and kingdom with God. The bride of Christ (the Church) was purified, made virginal, and firmly established. The Church was filled with the Spirit of God. The apostles began to preach the gospel of Christ with great courage and power. They began expounding on the mysteries as much as the Spirit of God revealed to them. They progressively began to better understand Christ, the kingdom of God, grace, salvation, and many other mysteries of the gospel.

Even at this point in time there was a lot about the various mysteries or facets of the diamond [Jesus Christ] called the gospel that God had not yet revealed to the saints. The apostles' journey in viewing the various facets of the mysteries of Christ had just begun. For instance, the disciples believed that salvation was only for the Jews, and to them only was the gospel to be preached. It would be a few years yet before Peter was to learn through the miraculous conversion of the gentile Cornelius that salvation was for all mankind on earth. And, as seen earlier, the very purpose of Paul's ministry was to present in its "fullness" the mystery hidden by God before time began. Salvation coming to the world and not to just Israel was a part of that mystery. A lot of unveiling was yet to be done! The "fullness of the mystery" the apostle Paul was to explain was not presented until sometime after he was converted, which was about five years after Christ was ascended to the Father.

Importance in Understanding the New Covenant

If you preach Christ crucified, what difference does it make about the rest of the mysteries of the gospel? It makes a great deal of difference. It is the difference between happiness and despair in the remainder of our Christian walk here on this earth with God. About the only consistent thing about Christianity from the days of the apostles until now is that, for the most part, Jesus Christ was preached as being crucified for our sins. After that vital bit of knowledge, which most of Christianity has shared, almost everything else concerning Christian worship and conduct differs a little and sometimes a great deal among the churches. Satan wasted no time in trying to repair the breaches in his crumbling walls in order to protect his worldly kingdom when the gospel began to blast them apart. He attacked the revelation of the love mysteries of God and strove to destroy understanding of these mysteries in the minds of Christian converts. The end result was that many times churches were, and many are still today, diametrically opposed to one another regarding the meaning of the mysteries of God.

Christ crucified, of course, is the most important part of the "good news" to mankind, but that is not all there is to the good news that God wanted preached to mankind. The good news is about not only salvation but also love, grace, the kingdom of God, the children of God, resurrection, heaven, hell, the New Covenant, the new heaven and earth, and on and on. Proper understanding of these mysteries gives peace, hope, purpose, and joy to the saints. If you do not understand what the rest of the good news is, then you can't know and enjoy the many blessings and promises to be bestowed on you. It is Satan's mission to try to hide and distort as much as is possible about the good news God's plan has in store for us. If the gospel has to be delivered, then Satan wants it to be as perverted and disruptive as possible.

Understanding the good news of the mysteries in Christ is critical to your spiritual health and well-being. The truth concerning the gospel or good news is a glorious message about the Savior of the world who brings grace, the New Covenant, and eternity in the kingdom with God. You have heard Jesus described as the Messiah or Savior of the world, but how many times have you heard Him described as the New Covenant? God said that Jesus was the messenger of God's covenant and that He was the covenant of God (Isa. 42:6)! The New Covenant was crucial to God's plan of salvation. At the heart of Salvation resided the New Covenant. Its understanding is crucial for Christians. It can mean the difference between a Christian's life being miserably burdened or their life being filled with peace, hope, and joy even in the mist of the most severe trials. God said of Jesus, "I, Yahweh, have called you in righteousness, and will hold your hand, and will keep you, *and make you a covenant for the people* [emphasis added], as a light for the nations; to open the blind eyes, to bring the prisoners out of the dungeon, and those who sit in darkness out of the prison" (Isa. 42:6-7, WEB).

Our True Rest

Jesus Christ was the New Covenant of God. It is only in understanding the New Covenant with God that we can truly rest and have the peace, joy, and excitement that God intends for us in our walk with Him. Jesus came to set us free from captivity from our sinful works and enslavement to the devil. He came to release us from death to eternal life and rest with Jesus in his spiritual kingdom, now on this earth and at its literal coming at His return. Jesus said we would suffer tribulation in this world. Even though in our remaining earthly journey we will have to endure trials, Jesus sandwiched His statement between two of the most comforting sentences in the Bible, stating, "I have told you these things so that in Me you may have peace. In the world you will have tribulation. But take courage; I have overcome the world" (John 16:33, BSB)! And so will each and every one of us who are properly residing in Christ!

You can receive salvation and eternal life and still remain locked in past chains of sinful habits that make your life miserable. The key to having the peace that Christ spoke of lies in our understanding and having faith in the new agreement, the New Covenant of God. Christ was and is the New Covenant, and we can find in Him the rest we need in the midst of the worst trials Satan can throw at us. Rather than focusing on our fears, focusing on the realities of the New Covenant (Jesus Christ) promises to us can bring peace to our weary souls and teach us to be able to say, as did Paul, "I have learned to be content regardless of my circumstances…I can do all things through Christ who gives me strength." (Phil. 4:11b, 13, BSB). Every Christian who wants the peace of God that passes all understanding must, as Paul did, "learn how to be content" in Jesus. The simplicity of eternal salvation is joyous, comforting, and breathtaking. Why would anyone try to make it unnecessarily complex and burdensome as it seems to have so become in Christianity? In the next chapter we will look more deeply into the simplicity of the gospel and God's wonderful gift of grace.

9

THE GOSPEL TRUTH AND THE SIMPLICITY OF GRACE

There certainly are a lot of "true" gospels that differ widely from one another in various churches of Christ around the world. It is amazing that there is so much confusion and division over what the true gospel is, when, in fact, the true gospel is very easy to grasp from the Scriptures. Satan's primary task in the first-century Church was to pervert the true gospel. This has led to the many divisions we have in the Church today. The gospel was Satan's worst nightmare, because its message heralded the doom of his kingdom and offered entry into God's kingdom to all who would hear and accept God's offer of salvation. This definitely is not the message Satan wanted heard, much less understood.

When Christ was born of the virgin Mary in Bethlehem, the angels came to the shepherds in a field and announced the true gospel: "I bring you good news [the gospel] of great joy that will be for all the people: Today in the City of David a Savior has been born to you. He is Christ the Lord" (Luke 2:10-11, BSB)! At last, the mystery of the ages was manifested in the flesh. The long-awaited Savior and Redeemer of fallen mankind, earth, and the entire universe had been born. He was the New Covenant that God had promised to send (see Isa. 42:6; 49:8). This was the good news or gospel of which the prophets had spoken.

Speaking of the gospel to be preached, the prophet Isaiah said, "How beautiful on the mountains are the feet of him who brings good news, who publishes peace, who brings good news of good, who publishes salvation, who says to Zion, 'Your God reigns'" (Isa. 52:7, WEB)! Here, you have a summation of the glorious gospel that John the Baptist, Jesus, and the apostles brought to the world. This is the good news the angels proclaimed to the shepherds—the promised Savior of the world, the Messiah, was born. He was the covenant of God that brought redemption and the many eternal blessings of God for all who believed. As Isaiah proclaims, God in the flesh, Jesus Christ, has come, and He is bringing His kingdom to reign first in the hearts of His disciples and eventually over all the earth at His return as King of kings. Because God reigns, we can enjoy the good news of all these promised blessings of God.

Jesus Is the Gospel

The gospel was the good news about the coming Savior of mankind, Jesus Christ. Notice how Paul put it:

> Now to Him who is able to strengthen you by my gospel and by the proclamation of Jesus Christ, according to the revelation of the mystery concealed for ages past, but now revealed and made known through the writings of the prophets by the command of the eternal God, in order to lead all the nations to the obedience that comes from faith. ~ Romans 16:25-26, BSB

The gospel about Jesus Christ has revealed [God's] plan about salvation for all mankind, not for just the Jews. The gospel is synonymous with Jesus Christ, and in Him is hidden all the wisdom and secrets of God and in Him is revealed the plan of God for all mankind.

Let's delve a bit deeper into these two verses. The King James Version of the Bible phrases Romans 16:25 in this way: "Now to him that is of power to establish you according to my [Paul's] gospel and the preaching of Jesus Christ ..." (Rom. 16:25, KJV). So, what is the gospel that Paul taught? Of the various commentaries on Romans 16:25-26, I like *The Pulpit Commentary* the best, which states: "The phrase ['and the preaching of Jesus Christ'] seems to be added as declaring what Paul's gospel was, rather than as referring back to Christ's personal preach-

CHAPTER 9: THE GOSPEL TRUTH AND THE SIMPLICITY OF GRACE

ing...."[1] In other words, Paul's gospel was about Jesus Christ, "according to the revelation of the mystery, which was kept secret since the world began" (Rom. 16:26, KJV). Jesus Christ was the mystery kept secret, and that secret was the good news or gospel that would be revealed to the world someday. *Pulpit* continues:

> We have seen throughout the Epistle how the Scriptures of the Old Testament are referred to as foretelling the revelation in Christ of the long-hidden mystery (cf. also Romans 1:2); and it was through showing them to be fulfilled that, in all the apostolic preaching, the mystery, now manifested, was made known to all the nations; and this according to the commandment or appoint-merit of God, that the mystery should thus be now at last made known.[2]

From other Scriptures mentioned in *The Pulpit Commentary* on these verses, we can conclude the following. Paul's gospel was about Jesus Christ and what was being revealed in Him. Paul was "called to be an apostle, separated unto the gospel of God, (which he had promised afore by his prophets in the Holy Scriptures,) concerning his Son Jesus Christ our Lord" (Rom. 1:1b-3a, KJV). Paul also said that he "...had been entrusted to preach the gospel to the Gentiles, just as Peter had been to the Jews" (Gal. 2:7b, BSB). This gospel that Peter and Paul preached was the same one that had been kept secret from before the beginning of time in heaven.

Jesus came preaching about His coming kingdom. The job of preaching about the good news of salvation in Christ was left to the apostles and to God's Church. Many facets of the gospel were progressively revealed in the early Church over a number of years. Many Christians did not understand that they were no longer bound to the laws of the Old Covenant until Paul revealed it to them years later. One major facet of the gospel was that salvation would be offered to the Jews first; later, it was revealed that the Gentiles also had access to salvation. To Paul was committed the ministry to the Gentiles concerning the revelation of this new facet of the gospel mystery. Paul's ordained ministry was not only to preach to the Gentiles but also to reveal more facets of the mysteries contained in the gospel. The gospel that Paul taught was the same as that eventually taught by the other apostles.

  The very reason God called Paul and the very reason Paul suffered the many beatings and trials that he did was for preaching of the gospel about Christ. The Scripture can't make it much plainer as to what the gospel was than Paul declaring this:

> Remember Jesus Christ, raised from the dead, descended from David, as proclaimed by my gospel, for which I suffer to the extent of being chained like a criminal. But the word of God cannot be chained! For this reason I endure all things for the sake of the elect, so that they too may obtain the salvation that is in Christ Jesus, with eternal glory. ~2 Timothy 2:8-10, BSB

Paul clearly declared the supreme importance of understanding that the true gospel mystery was contained in Jesus Christ when he said that it was his desire, "…that they may be encouraged in heart, knit together in love, and filled with the full riches of complete understanding, so that they may know the mystery of God, namely Christ, in whom are hidden all the treasures of wisdom and knowledge. I say this so that no one will deceive you by smooth rhetoric." (Col. 2:2b-4, BSB). The gospel that Paul preached was Christ, and he obviously knew there would be false or uninformed ministers who would preach an errant gospel through which Satan would try to obfuscate that the true gospel was Jesus Christ. These errant and often well-meaning gospels have been constantly dividing the congregations of Christ since the first century.

  If you separate one facet of the gospel, like that concerning salvation, and make it the totality of the gospel, then you run the risk of neglecting other vital aspects of the gospel of Christ. Undoubtedly the most wonderful good news in Christ was that eternal salvation as sons and daughters of God was now possible for Jew and Gentile alike.

  The gospel of Jesus Christ, God's Love, faith, grace, peace, salvation, New Covenant, and eternal glory in the kingdom are all synonyms, in that they are all about the same thing. They are all beautiful, brilliant facets of the same covenant diamond, which is Jesus Christ, the epitome of God's love offered to all mankind. This multifaceted nature of Christ is not original with me. A few years ago I read a similar statement which

I thought was profound and thought provoking. I'm sorry to say I do not have that source material and would most certainly cite it if I knew who the author was. In spite of this I think it necessary to recognize and expound on the concept which I believe is true and has profound implications for all Christians. I suppose, actually, the original source material is not from any one individual, but from the very three in one nature of God Himself. God the Father, Jesus Christ, and the Holy Spirit are one. It is from them that all love, liberty, faith, grace, peace, salvation, the New Covenant, eternal glory and anything else good originates. I suppose that if there is any one person that should be cited as originating this multifaceted model of the nature of Christ and the need to understand His many facets, I would state it is the apostle Paul. Remember he said he wanted the Church to be, *"filled with the full riches of complete understanding, so that they may know the mystery of God, namely Christ, in whom are hidden all the treasures of wisdom and knowledge"* (Col. 2:2b-3, BSB, emphasis added). The multifaceted nature of Christ being our covenant reflects the various aspects of what Christ did and does for us, and all are necessary in explaining what the good news is about. You can't have one without the other to understand the totality of the true gospel !

There is one proper interpretation of what the gospel is in a nutshell, and that interpretation can be none other than it is Jesus Christ. Jesus Christ came bearing many gifts for mankind, and each one is a wonderful, mind-boggling blessing in increasing measure by which the children of God will be continually dazzled throughout eternity. Now, let's look more closely at just one of these gifts from Christ, that of grace.

The Simplicity of Grace

God kept the good news about the coming work of Jesus simple and short at its first revelation to Adam and Eve. That simple statement is true, but it was only a glimpse for Adam of God's mysterious plan to redeem creation.

Today, we understand God's plan much more clearly than Adam did. I think the simplicity of God's grace—the undeserved gift of His love and mercy to mankind—was clearly and potently demonstrated when the thief on the cross looked to the Savior of the world in believing faith and said, "'Jesus, remember me when You come into Your kingdom!'

And Jesus said to him, 'Truly I tell you, today you will be with Me in Paradise'" (Luke 23:42-43, BSB). That was pretty simple, wasn't it? The thief did not have to get baptized, return what he had stolen, give all that he had to the poor, go to church, tithe, confess all his sins, speak in tongues, quit smoking, serve in any soup lines for the poor, or do anything for anyone. He just had to have believing faith that Jesus was his savior! No works would have saved him; only the unmerited, undeserved, loving grace of God could have saved him and given him eternal life. That is the simplicity of grace in Christ!

It is interesting to note at this point that the thief had precious little time after Christ granted him salvation to offer up any demonstrated righteous fruit to God. However, God's purpose in the thief's short life had been accomplished, just as it had been accomplished in the long life of King David: "For when David had served God's purpose in his own generation, he fell asleep. His body was buried with his fathers and saw decay" (Acts 13:36, BSB). The thief was used by God to make this statement. Grace brings salvation to all to whom it is granted, whether or not fruit is produced in their lives. God has called each of us for a special purpose, and once His purpose is fully accomplished, our earthly bodies die. As long as God gives us breath after our salvation, we should strive to walk in faith each day, open to God's direction. Our desire should not be to please others or ourselves but to strive to become all that God designed and wants us to be. That should be our prayer. This will bring us to the epitome of joy and satisfaction.

As we have just seen, the simplicity of salvation in Christ is much less complicated than what many of us have been taught to believe. It is God's plan and desire that all mankind enters the door that Christ will hold open for each of them. When Jesus spoke of His crucifixion, He revealed his Father's great desire that all would be saved and not just a few:

Just as Moses lifted up the snake in the wilderness, so the Son of Man must be lifted up, that everyone who believes in Him may have eternal life. For God so loved the world that He gave His one and only Son, that everyone who believes in Him shall not perish but have eternal life. For God did not send His Son into the world to condemn the world, but to save the world through Him. Whoever believes in Him is not condemned, but whoever does not believe is already condemned, because he has not believed in the name of God's one and only Son. ~ John 3:14-18, BSB

You've likely heard John 3:16 (the second sentence in the passage above), which is the most famous and most quoted scripture in the Bible. I grew up being taught that its meaning was something akin to:

All mankind are dirty, rotten sinners in need of salvation. God stepped in and because He loved mankind so much He was willing to sacrifice His Son Jesus to offer forgiveness if one repented. So, you had better repent of all your dirty, rotten sins and give your heart to the Lord to get saved. After that, you had better work hard keeping the Ten Commandments and every word of God. Keep on repenting of your daily sins to get your slate cleaned each day so you don't end up in hell for an unforgiven sin you committed that day. Most people are going to hell. Getting to heaven will be hard work, but maybe you'll just make it by the hair of your "chinny chin."

Many Christians today are concerned about dying in a sudden car crash before having time to ask God for forgiveness of that day's sins, thus going straight to hell to burn for all eternity. What a relief it be to those Christians if they knew that their sins—past, present, and future—died on the cross with Christ. When I see sin rising up from the "old man" today, I simply recognize it and hand it over to God for destruction. In doing so, He (not me) by His Spirit replaces the residue of my sinful nature with His righteousness. I trust He will gently correct me if I stray off His righteous pathway now or in the future. One thing is for sure, I have learned the importance of not dwelling on past sins, but do as Paul said, "one thing I do: Forgetting what is behind and straining toward what is ahead, I press on toward the goal to win the prize of God's heavenly calling in Christ Jesus" (Phil. 3:13b-14, BSB).

Let's delve a little deeper into John 3:14-15 to see what it tells us about the love, mercy, and kindness of God: "Just as Moses lifted up the snake in the wilderness, so the Son of Man must be lifted up, that everyone who believes in Him may have eternal life" (BSB). Just prior to Israel entering the Promised Land, the people began to gripe, as they had been prone to do during their forty years of wandering in the wilderness; notice:

> And the people spoke against God and against Moses, "Why have you brought us up out of Egypt to die in the wilderness? For there is no food and no water, and we loathe this worthless food." Then the Lord sent fiery serpents among the people, and they bit the people, so that many people of Israel died. And the people came to Moses and said, "We have sinned, for we have spoken against the Lord and against you. Pray to the Lord, that he take away the serpents from us." So Moses prayed for the people. And the Lord said to Moses, "Make a fiery serpent and set it on a pole, and everyone who is bitten, when he sees it, shall live." So Moses made a bronze serpent and set it on a pole. And if a serpent bit anyone, he would look at the bronze serpent and live. ~ Numbers 21:5-9, WEB

This prophesied about and pictured the story of Christ's crucifixion for all of us. These passages show what is required of us today to be healed of our sins and saved. The Israelites bitten by the deadly serpents only had to "look" at the snake on the pole to be healed and not suffer death.

Now, stop and think about this. Let's say you are on a summer camping trip and have just seen two people bitten by snakes. They both died near you. You run for your life, but are bitten by a deadly snake too. You know you're as good as dead, but someone rushes up to you with good news—you are told you will not die if you will just look at a serpent wrapped around a pole fifteen feet away. What would you do? You would be looking in a flash, intently, with great hope and anticipation; you'd probably continue staring intently, uttering a prayer along with it until you were healed! I'm sure this is the kind of look the people of Israel gave their snake on the pole.

The mystery of Christ formulated by God billions of years ago was pictured in Israel's story of being saved from death by looking at the serpent on the pole. The Scriptures have shown us that all sins of mankind were forgiven at the time of Jesus' sacrifice on the cross. Your sins and all of mankind's sins have already been forgiven. The only question now is have you accepted—or will you accept—the forgiveness that the sacrifice of Christ made possible for you? John said, "...There is a sin that leads to death..." (1 John 5:16b, BSB). If you are called by God and offered that sacrifice and then you refuse and never thereafter accept Christ prior to your death, then this is the one and only sin that would require eternal punishment at the end of your physical life on earth.

If you have not already accepted that sacrifice, and God is calling you to repentance in Christ, you are now being offered at this very moment salvation and entry into God's eternal kingdom. If you will only heed God's call and "look" expectantly to Christ, embracing His loving sacrifice in faith and asking Him to come into your heart, He will then come and unite with your spirit, creating in you a new man or woman with eternal life in His kingdom. You don't need me, any minister, or person to be with you when you make this act of repentance. Repentance means to change your mind about your way of life and embrace God's way accepting Jesus Christ as your savior. When this is done, you will be instantly saved from eternal damnation and given eternal life in God's kingdom.

This is the "simplicity in Christ" that Paul spoke of! May God remove your blinders and grant you the eyes to see, grasp, and lovingly behold the beauty of God's boundless unbelievable love and grace! Why would anyone want to complicate the simplicity of eternal salvation? There are many reasons that I will discuss with you in the next few chapters. The fact of the matter is the history of Christianity is strewn with Christians having to suffer unnecessary burdens of fear, guilt, doubt, depression, and even death because they were malnourished in the truth concerning the gospel and grace; not to even mention the countless individuals who refused to become Christians because of the distortions by Satan concerning the true gospel and simplicity of grace. I will next turn to my story which will demonstrate in the next two chapters what can happen to a Christian when deprived proper understanding of the gospel and grace.

10

FOLLOWING A TWISTED GOSPEL

At the age of twenty I was introduced to a skewed gospel at best, which I accepted. In the next chapter we will see the dire consequences I suffered following after this twisted gospel. My story is probably your story, too, in varying degrees. It is certainly the story of countless other Christians during the last two thousand years who did not grasp the meaning of the gospel's New Covenant. It is the story of trying to mix Old Covenant oil (required law keeping) with the New Covenant living waters of Grace (unmerited and undeserved forgiveness of sin). That mixture of oil and water has drastically inhibited the production of God's righteousness. It does, however, produce a great deal of "self-righteousness." There is a difference between man's righteousness and that of God. This effort to mix oil and water in Christianity was Satan's great deception during the early Church and polluted the true gospel of Christ.

God's Righteousness vs. Mankind's

I believe the famed psychiatrist and Holocaust survivor Victor E. Frankl was correct when he saw "the prime motivating force in human beings to be a will for meaning."[1] People do indeed search for meaning. They are not born with knowledge of how to satisfy that meaning. The true meaning of mankind, apart from God, is unfathomable. A person's meaning resides solely in the hands of his or her Creator. It is only when God reveals to mankind his meaning and how to achieve it that their soul will begin to be satisfied. This knowledge is contained in God's love mystery, which has been hidden from most of mankind since the beginning of time. The love mystery is only revealed through the gospel. Saint Paul succinctly capsulized that mystery, which explains what mankind's "will for meaning" is, when he said it is "Christ in you the hope of Glory!" The answer to satisfying mankind's desire and solving all of his problems does not reside within but without. Rather than looking to inward drives and instincts to solve mankind's problems, he must look to God. God created our desire for meaning to assist in His ultimate supreme creation of an eternal superhuman race called the children of God. This is God's intended destiny and desire for mankind; and this is the only way in which mankind's search for meaning can be achieved.

Isn't it interesting to note that this inborn need is incessantly displayed in mankind's very nature? Probably the most widely exhibited characteristic of mankind is his desire to be right, or shall I say righteous. This aspect of human nature is blatantly expressed by mankind's striving to live a life that he can justify and not feel guilty about. Mankind makes up his own laws defining and supporting what he deems is right and wrong. Scripture puts it this way: "All the ways of a man are clean in his own eyes…" (Prov. 16:2a, WEB). This is mankind's attempt at fulfilling his basic need to be right or righteous in what he allows. Paradoxically, at the same time this also can be an effort by the individual to atone for past sins. If he can join a movement considered a righteous cause by a segment of society (such as "global warming," "gay rights," or "a woman's right to choose"), then he can hold up a "banner of being righteous" in an effort to expiate his past failings and justify his future transgressions and actions.

Why a Conscience?

God also created in mankind a conscience, which demands he or she do what they believe is right. Without a conscience there can be no freedom of choice. The intent of our conscience is to expose to us when we fall short of the law(s) we accept to be true. A conscience gives us the ability to choose between two or more pathways for our thoughts, feelings, and actions. We have the freedom to be the final judge which path we will take. This enables us, once God opens our minds to the gospel, to have a free choice to embrace or reject it. When we do something contrary to the truths or laws we accept to be true, our conscience condemns us. This encourages us to live by that which we justify (make right), which is often based upon selfish reasons. Just because a man's conscience doesn't condemn him does not mean the man is right. There is often a huge difference in what man accepts as true versus what God does. For instance, man and God both use the same words for love, peace, joy, truth, freedom, and the like, but they often define them differently. As humans we judge ourselves and others based on what we believe is right and wrong and not necessarily by what God says is right and wrong. Guilty feelings and judgmental attitudes, be they right or wrong, are dictated by the standards we have accepted from the world around us.

No one likes to feel condemned, so each of us naturally strives to live within the boundaries of our conscience. Our consciences condemn us when we don't live within the standards or laws we accept to be true and we thus feel guilt. Just because we may feel guilty doesn't necessarily mean we really are, and on the contrary, just because we don't feel guilty doesn't mean we aren't. Guilt tends to urge us into obedience to what we accept or think is right. The only problem is that what a person thinks is right is often determined by what is in that person's own selfish interests.

If an individual desires something enough, there is nothing that he or she can't eventually rationalize, and thus feel no guilt for doing. People are constantly seeking to avoid condemning themselves for what they allow. They often will modify their values and laws in an effort to free their minds of guilty feelings and thus allow themselves to do whatever they wish. When one begins to believe truth and freedom are the abolition of what one considers to be restrictive laws, the ultimate end of this pathway is a mind devoid of conscience, with no feelings of guilt. This is so because any truth or law outside one's own selfish interest is not recognized or accepted. In the extreme, you end up with what psychologists call an antisocial personality disorder.[2] You can have, in essence, an individual totally self-absorbed, for whom right is determined entirely by what is convenient for that individual.

What is Truth?

God is the only one who has total correct knowledge of truth and righteousness. Any truth that a person holds that is contrary to God's truth is wrong. It is to God that we must go to determine what is true and righteous. Human reasoning establishing our righteousness will not satiate our needs; only God's truths can. Adam and Eve rejected God's righteousness and thereafter mankind was left to decide for themselves what was right and wrong. We have evolved various standards of righteousness, depending on the nations, cultures, and societies we live in. Some individuals rebel against these societal standards or laws and thus become lawless, or a law unto themselves. These individuals develop their own rules and laws that define what makes them feel happy or sad. The bottom line here is that God put a desire in mankind for "righteousness" that can only be truly satisfied by that which God made mankind to need, and that is His righteousness.

Putting on God's Righteousness

The first step in being able to experience God's meaning for us, which will lead to the peace and rest Christ promised, is for us to come to recognize our self-righteousness versus God's. Only then can we see that the answer to our most basic drive is not our filthy self-righteousness rags but God's righteousness. We then can view and judge ourselves and our world as God does. This kind of insight can only come when we hear the gospel of Christ, and only then if God the Father opens our minds to give us insight into His truths. It is at this moment in time that we are given an opportunity to see the unseen and to choose eternal salvation and entry into God's kingdom. This is granted if we agree to repent, recognizing and repudiating our self-righteousness and seeking God's righteousness by accepting His Son Jesus Christ as our Savior. Our agreement with God at this time is the New Covenant agreement (see chapter three). If we accept Christ's sacrifice, we are granted the righteousness of God and eternal salvation. From this point on in our lives, we agree to let God change our old ways of thinking and doing to His ways. As the New Covenant says, "I will put my law in their inward parts, and in their heart will I write" (Jer. 31:33, WEB). It is through understanding the Covenant of God with His saints that the righteousness of God enables growth and maturation in His newborn sons and daughters. Paul capsulized how this is done:

> Therefore I urge you, brothers, on account of God's mercy, to offer your bodies as living sacrifices, holy and pleasing to God, which is your spiritual service of worship. Do not be con-formed to this world, but be transformed by the renewing of your mind. Then you will be able to discern what is the good, pleasing, and perfect will of God. ~ Romans 12:1-2, BSB

To say the least, Satan hated this knowledge which, if under-stood and followed, would destroy within each of us the works of Satan's de-structive character, to be replaced with the divine character of God. Satan immediately began attacking the understanding of God's trans-formation process among first-century Christians. His purpose was to pervert the understanding of this process for God's children contained in the New Covenant. Satan's corrupted the transformation process by simply teaching that a Christian must do the work of writing God's laws into his or her heart rather than allowing God to do it. The end results of this perverted transformation process was and is that a great deal bur-densome works by Christians being done which produces a great deal of self-righteousness rather than God's righteousness. Satan's efforts began on day one, when the first Christian Church was established on the Day of Pentecost, just days after the ascension of Jesus to heaven.

The three thousand converted that day were all Jews and quite used to equating law keeping with righteousness. It was quite natural that Satan would strive to keep them believing that. The apostles fought this works righteousness heresy within the Church. However, eventually, despite Paul's preaching to the contrary that our works do not produce righteousness, by the third century the Church was solidly enmeshed in the belief that righteousness was produced by rituals and law keeping. Satan seized upon people's basic desire for meaning and their proclivity for equating righteousness with their law keeping, rather than with letting God do the work of creating His righteousness in them. In doing so, Satan greatly minimized the spiritual maturation process of the saints. Rather than God creating His righteousness by His works in us, we strive to create God's righteousness by our legalistic works apart from God.

The Church's Vital Role

As born-again children of God, if we understand the New Covenant, our eyes have an ability to begin distinguishing between our remaining self-righteousness and the righteousness of God. If we as Christians focus on the things of the Spirit, then God will begin to open our understanding concerning the righteousness of God as displayed in the glory of Jesus. However, if we focus on and seek the things of the flesh, the righteousness of Christ in our eyes is diminished. God will not force us to focus on Him; we must daily choose to do so. God will never take away our freedom of choice as a sinner or saint. Each of us must choose what we focus on. Whatever we choose, we will tend to move in that direction. Yes, Christians have eternal life no matter which way we choose, but only focusing on Christ will mature us in His mind and truth. Being a Christian is the first step that affords us the opportunity to know and grow in the measure and stature of the fullness of Christ. If a Christian allows this maturation process, then the fruits of God's righteousness will be borne in his or her life. These are the fruits of God that are pleasing to Him. To the degree that we allow God to transform our minds, this is the magnitude of the reward that we shall receive in God's kingdom. The transformation process into the likeness of Christ continually increases our joy and peace. We are therefore maturing in the likeness of Christ and proportionately decreasing our fears and unhappiness as we let God rid us of ungodly thoughts, feelings, and character.

Although a Christian has access to the righteousness of God, this does not mean he will allow God to transform his thoughts. God will not force a son or daughter to mature in His righteousness. A vital role of the Church is to properly feed its congregation the truths taught in the Covenant of God. This encourages members to grow in that which God made them to need, His thoughts and feelings. This proper feeding gives understanding to the saint as to how to mature in the very mind of Christ and produce the fruits God wants. Paul makes this plain, stating:

> And it was He [Christ] who gave some to be apostles, some to be prophets, some to be evangelists, and some to be pastors and teachers, to equip the saints for works of ministry, to build up the body of Christ, until we all reach unity in the faith and in the knowledge of the Son of God, as we mature to the full measure of the stature of Christ. ~ Ephesians 4:11-13, BSB

Satan's Deception

Satan could not stop eternal life from being granted to the new converts, but he could pervert the knowledge of how the newborn children of God were to mature in the righteousness of Jesus. It is this knowledge that Satan attacked by distorting proper understanding of the New Covenant of God. Instead of allowing God to do the work of creating righteousness in Christians, Satan taught that saints were to create God's righteousness through law keeping. This heresy caused a severe lack of spiritual growth in Christians. Satan doesn't want us to have access to the truth of how Christians are to mature in God's mind. Early on in the first-century Church Satan perverted and obscured this knowledge as much as he could. He did so by appealing to the basic human desire of man to be able to achieve his own righteousness without God's help. With Christianity beginning among Jews born and raised in the "righteousness" of Old Covenant legalism, Satan's sell to Christians that law keeping was the way to build righteousness was not difficult.

Effects of Legalism

I believe that to the extent the slavery of legalism is practiced in today's churches, it is responsible for the many Christians who avoid involvement in church worship and activities. Many pay only lip service to Christ and rarely attend church. They may have had an inspired moment in the past when they responded to God's call to salvation, recognizing their sins and need for salvation. They then accepted the salvation offered by Christ. However, after a period of time their enthusiasm and dedication waned. Their Christianity, which at first was exciting, wasted away due to a dearth of proper spiritual feeding of the New Covenant by God's ministers. Soon the weight of their inability to keep the "laws of God" and the ensuing guilt began to press down upon them and drive them away from their faith. No one likes to be reminded of and condemned in their sins week after week. Rather than being a place of peace, refuge, encouragement, and protection for the saint, the sanctuary of the church became a morgue. It is human nature to avoid that which condemns one to hell each week. Eventually due to continual reminder of their failures, the joy and enthusiasm intended by Christ dwindles away through guilt and sorrow to not much more than a hope that somehow, in spite of their sins, they'll make it into heaven. All of this is the result of not knowing how to experience the rest and joy that comes in understanding our New Covenant in Christ!

The New Covenant teaches that once we are born again, we have eternal life and the righteousness of God, never to be lost. Yes, I know most protestant Christian churches proclaim they are living under the New Covenant! However, if they don't correctly understand and properly teach this to their flocks, how can the members appropriately deal with the sin in their lives, produce righteous fruit, and at the same time rest peacefully in Christ?

How did you do on the quiz about the New Covenant I gave you in chapter three? Please don't feel bad if you did not do well. I dare say most church members and many pastors as well could not have passed the test. It is no wonder to me so many Christian lives are burdened and unhappy! Those who do not know how to rest in the New Covenant and yet are zealously dedicated workers for the Church often do so not because they are living in the peace and joy of the New Covenant but because they believe it is through their works for God that they will gain heaven. These servants of the Church often become burned out and quite unhappy. Although ministers and members are driven to serve out of a desire and love for God, many also are driven out of a fear of going to hell because of their inability to keep the commandments of God. I know, because that used to be my story. Some feel they are being continually redeemed from their past or their daily sins through their efforts at law keeping. This lack of understanding of how we can be sinners and yet rest in Christ has been the main cause for the frustration, pain, and unhappiness of God's children since the time of the first-century Church. It is the Devil who has obscured the truth about how to be a sinner and at the same time a saint in the New Covenant.

The question now is how should saints view and deal with their sins? If we do not understand God's answer to this question, it may seem that the Scriptures condemn us in our sins, something that no one likes to face. We then will naturally draw away from God's Word, which is meant to set us free rather than enslave us. This reality only causes us fear, tears, frustration, and misery! Yes, you can have born-again Christians who have accepted the forgiveness of Jesus, yet don't know how to deal with the remaining sins in their lives by resting in the New Covenant. Therefore, alas, without the knowledge and joy that can come only from a correct understanding of the New Covenant, it is just more comfortable to profess Christ but simply ignore or refuse to hear the condemning words of the pastor. In this atmosphere, little spiritual growth can be experienced, and certainly not many fruits will bear witness to the glory of God. If most of what we see and hear in church services leaves us feeling condemned, it is impossible to rest in peace and joy in our daily walk with Christ.

The Righteousness of Self

It is critical to know the difference between "self-righteousness" and

"God's righteousness." If we do not, we can live our Christian lives falsely thinking we are producing the righteousness of God, when in fact we are primarily producing "self-righteousness," which God rejects. In short, this understanding can be the difference between a joyful and a depressed Christian. To the degree you are burdened down with depression, fear, worry, guilt, and every other negative human emotion, you are not resting in our New Covenant in Christ. You are works-conscious and not resting in Christ-consciousness. Chances are, there is something you think you should have done or still have to do to please God and stay in His good graces. These beliefs produce only a self-righteousness. In short, self-righteousness is anything you do that makes you feel righteous. God's righteousness is anything Christ does in you that you acknowledge is His righteousness. Yes, both will make you feel good. However, one is produced through your works and the other is God's works produced in you. All you have to do is believe and rest in the Lord's covenant with you! As I heard Pastor Joseph Prince say, "When you work, God rests! When you rest, God works!" Your work produces only self-righteousness; God's work produces His righteousness in you. In varying degrees the delusion of our attaining godly righteousness through our "good works" has befallen all Christians who have been without proper understanding of the New Covenant of God.

My Self-Righteous Legalistic Past

I in no way would want to compare myself with the apostle Paul, but after I spent decades bound in the extremes of legalism, producing self-righteousness, I can certainly understand and identify with Paul's assessment of himself in his past life as a "religious Pharisee of Pharisees." He summed it up this way:

> I count all things [his self-righteous legalistic past] as loss compared to the surpassing excellence of knowing Christ Jesus my Lord, for whom I have lost all things. I consider them rubbish, that I may gain Christ and be found in Him, not having my own righteousness from the Law, but that which is through

faith in Christ, the righteousness from God on the basis of faith. I want to know Christ and the power of His resurrection and the fellowship of His sufferings, being conformed to Him in His death, so that I may somehow attain to the resurrection from the dead. ~ Philippians 3:8-10, BSB

In my life's story contained in the next chapter I will give you my extreme example of being a modern-day Christian "Pharisee" who spent the better part of my life as Paul did, and as maybe some of you have, building what I thought was the righteousness of God, only to find that my activities were primarily self-righteous attempts at law keeping, which were not God's righteousness and thus did not satisfy my soul.

In the next two chapters, I will expose the misuse of the love mystery of God contained in a defective gospel perpetrated by both the right (legalist) and left (licentious) Christian factions. We will see the resulting disastrous effects in the lives of well-meaning Christians. It is my desire to help free Christians to enjoy the sublime happiness and rest that can come only from Christ.

I suspect you also may not have experienced the peace, faith, love, and joy God meant for you to have. The reason I say this is because very few churches, from the time of the apostle Paul to the present, have taught the correct gospel of Christ, which must be understood if we are to gain the peace God wants for us all. It is because of many churches' failure to present the complete gospel that the dark side of the Christian Church's history has occurred. History is strewn with horrendous stories of abuses and perversions of the gospel perpetrated by Christians. I am speaking here about all of the horrible things that have occurred in the name of Christ throughout the last two thousand-plus years: the countless religious wars perpetrated, including the Crusades; the persecution of other religions; the persecution of fellow Christians (the Inquisitions); and many other godless acts of persecution done in the name of Christ.

I submit to you that these atrocities occurred because a proper understanding of the true gospel was nearly lost during the first two centuries after the death of the last apostle John. The only part of the gospel that is necessary for salvation is the revelation to you from God that Jesus is His Son and that you change your attitude and believe in and accept

Jesus as your Savior. Thankfully, this part of the gospel message has not been lost during the ages since Christ's crucifixion; however, major distortions marred the rest of the gospel's story for most Christians and hid from them how to rest in the Lord.

A vital part of the beginning of the restoration of this gospel truth came through Martin Luther. Knowledge of the true, complete gospel has been in the process of being slowly restored ever since. However, even today, too few churches fully understand the full gospel that Paul spoke of two thousand years ago. The vast majority of Christians today do not rest in the full knowledge of this gospel because the gospel taught in many churches today is incorrect because it is incomplete!

People like to think they can earn by their efforts and works the righteousness God wants us to have. This was the perverted form of the gospel that I was introduced to. It was a legalistic, works-based gospel. This perverted gospel did not even teach us that we were living completely under the New Covent agreement. With that critical bit of knowledge missing, no wonder in the ensuing thirty-six years I did not experience the peace promised by Jesus, though I fervently sought it. This caused me untold grief, wreaking havoc in my life. Countless stories of ongoing abuse and misery could be told of Christians today striving to be "righteous" by keeping the laws required by their church. My story is just one of many millions; however, it is my story, one with which I am intimately familiar. I believe it has the power to teach many who are now laboring under law keeping how to find the rest and peace in Jesus that has evaded them throughout their Christian lives.

After decades of striving to please God, I was exhausted and worn out simply because I did not understand the truth of the gospel concerning the New Covenant. My heart and intent was right in striving to please God. However, I had spent my entire Christian existence striving to accomplish that by keeping Old Covenant laws. Mostly it produced self-righteous feelings and poisonous fruits, all of which were un-acceptable to God. Time and again when I fell short of keeping those laws, I felt guilty, fearful, and depressed.

I had the vain notion that I, not God, was the one who was supposed to do the changing in me. Most of my time was spent trying to create God's righteousness in me by my own power. Little did I know that all of my personal efforts to keep God's laws did not produce one ounce of His righteousness. I desperately needed to learn what the New Covenant taught, which is that only God can create His righteousness in me. No amount of effort on my part could accomplish that. I needed to learn how to rest in Christ and let Him do the work of creating His righteousness in me.

Once you give your heart to the Lord, aren't you generally supposed to be spiritually satisfied, peaceful, and joyful? My joy, peace, and satisfaction throughout my Christian life suffered a great deal for reasons I did not fully understand until a few years ago. I attributed my struggles and misery to my sinful nature and spiritual warfare with Satan and his kingdom, and thought this misery was normal for a Christian. I was terribly wrong. After all, Jesus said, "Peace I leave with you; My peace I give to you. I do not give to you as the world gives. Do not let your hearts be troubled; do not be afraid" (John 14:27, BSB). Pondering this, I wondered why my Christian walk with God had filled me with more pain, guilt, sin, and sorrow than the peace of mind that He intended for me.

Although I knew enough of the gospel to be saved, the real joy and peace offered by God eluded me because there was something in the gospel message that I was not taught and could not see. This was the devil's doing. If he can't keep you in darkness about the Covenant that will bring the peace of mind that Christ spoke of, then he will try to hide and distort it to keep you from the joy it can give.

Looking back over the last six decades of my life as a Christian, I feel that the story of my life is pretty much summed up in a humorous little sign I once read: "Don't feel worthless; you can always be used as a bad example!" I could get discouraged and even angry at all those seemingly wasted years of slogging through the slime pits of legalism, an activity that brought me only pain and sorrow. However, I believe "…God works all things together for the good of those who love Him, who are called according to His purpose" (Rom. 8:28b, BSB). Rather than feeling worthless, I greatly rejoice that God allowed me to learn the message of the true gospel and to deliver it in this book.

I am certainly not the only one who preaches this true gospel message. However, my experiences in coming to understand what the true gospel is might add a voice that may reach and enlighten some who do not yet know this truth. I believe that maybe one of God's purposes in letting me walk with an incomplete understanding of the gospel for forty-four years was to allow me to deliver to you the true gospel message that will set you free to enjoy your life as God intends. As cowboy pastor Butch Bruton says at the end of each of his "Living The Good Life" television programs, "If you're not having fun serving Jesus, you're doing it wrong." One thing is for sure: if your gospel understanding is limited, so will be your joy, peace, and rest in Christ! Only the true, full gospel of Christ will set you free from unnecessary pain and suffering caused by a well-meaning but misguided and fractional understanding of it.

The part of the gospel that most Christians do not understand is the New Covenant relationship we have with God. Yes, many Christians have understood and relished the blessings of our salvation in Christ that the gospel brings. But many, like I was, are still struggling to find the peace that Christ promises His children in our daily walk with Him. This book is for those of you who may be struggling to find peace and happiness in Christ. God wants to show you that when His New Covenant is not understood or followed—whether due to willful neglect, ignorance, or otherwise—the pain, burden, and suffering of either legalism or its opposite extreme, licentiousness, will rain down into your life. Your suffering will be proportional to the degree that the New Covenant message is veiled in your Christian worship.

Though it's difficult to tell my story, I know it is unique, and in it lie important, major keys for us all in understanding what the true gospel's covenant message is for us. My life story in this next chapter reveals the pitfalls of all churches that indulge in any degree of legalism and shows how I finally came to a full understanding of the gospel. Later in the book, I will also discuss the pitfalls of opposite extreme: the licentious abuse of grace.

Let's begin my story. Hopefully you will learn from it and avoid the mistakes I made. If you are enmeshed in legalism, enslaved to works-righteousness, I pray this book will help you find your way to the freedom, love, joy, and peace that God intends for you. If this book helps set you free, then the spiritual misery I experience over 50 years will have been worth it!

11

ROAD MAP INTO AND OUT OF LEGALISM: MY STORY

I had the fear of God and eternal hellfire put in me at an early age by my Pentecostal preacher grandpa when I lived with him from the ages of six to eleven. Being a Christian meant going to church every Sunday, "getting the Holy Ghost," and doing things such as speaking in tongues. Women's clothes covered nearly every square inch of their skin, and they wore long hair for a covering in church. Sin was going to the movies, dancing, watching TV, wearing jewelry or makeup, playing cards or dominoes, wearing shorts or swimming suits, playing basketball, and on and on it went. I learned a lot about the Devil, and also about the horrible sin in me and in the world. Oh yes, and I also learned, "Jesus may come tonight, so come down to this altar and give your heart to the LORD and get saved while there is still time to save you from going to hell for ever and ever!" Since the age of six, there have been many bloody spiritual battles in my Christian journey.

When I was eleven, I moved from my grandpa's home to live with my mother. It was then that I joined the Baptist Church and was "liberated," in the sense that I could enjoy movies, TV, and in short, most all of what I had been taught was sinful in the Pentecostal Church. But, of course, any good Baptist was not to dance, gamble, or drink alcohol.

After I graduated from high school, it was during my sophomore year in 1962 at a nearby college in Weatherford, Oklahoma, that I first heard the religious radio broadcast of the Radio Church of God (later called the Worldwide Church of God). It was my understanding at the time hat the broadcast was the largest religious radio program in the world. It was supposedly on more radio stations than any other religious program.

The Radio Church of God

I heard the broadcast by chance one evening. I was a young, impressionable twenty-year-old and I was captured by the charisma of the Radio Church of God's two dynamic leaders, a father (Herbert W. Armstrong) and son (Garner Ted Armstrong). The program that night was expounding on the prophecies of the book of Revelation. I was immediately intrigued and by their promise of receiving a free booklet that would provide "the key to unlock" this mysterious book. I sent in for it and thus began my journey toward joining the Radio Church's membership a few months later. I continued to be fascinated by their other broadcasts on prophecy, which seemed to be correct according to Scripture.

I received the free booklet, "1975 In Prophecy," and also began to receive their monthly magazine, *The Plain Truth.* I also began regularly attending the Radio Church of God's worship services. At that time, there were only two Radio Church of God congregations in Oklahoma; one was in Oklahoma City and the other was in Tulsa. I attended the church in Oklahoma City, which was seventy miles away. I believe there were about two hundred or so in attendance at the time.

I soon came to believe this was the one and only true Church of God and that God was calling me into it. It didn't take long before I was brainwashed into their brand of ultra-legalism. As a result, I became so far to the legalistic right that all other "so-called Christian" denominations (as we liked to label them) seemed wanton and hedonistic by comparison! The father and son Armstrong team seemed infallible in their teachings, and I hung on their every word. They saw their "end-time work" as one of understanding prophecy and proclaiming it around the world. I was in awe of these two men of God.

The Radio Church of God taught that it was a direct descendant of the apostolic Church and was the only "true Church of God" on the face of the earth. Its leader, Herbert W. Armstrong, was referred to as God's "end-time Apostle." Armstrong had absolute control of the church and formed any doctrine taught by it. There was some confusion among many in the church as to our Old and New Covenant relationship with God. There were arguments about which we were under. The matter received a clarification of sorts when Mr. Armstrong settled the issue: "In 1978 Herbert Armstrong wrote an article intended to clear up the confusion. He wrote that while it was correct to say we were no longer under the Old Covenant, we were not yet under the New Covenant either, and that wouldn't begin until Christ returned. So where were we? We were 'between' the two covenants."[1] This certainly was a convenient position for Mr. Armstrong to take; he therefore was free "to pick and choose which items from the Old Covenant and which items from the New would apply to us…. Whatever we were commanded to obey, however, we were commanded to obey in no uncertain terms."[2]

So the "Apostle" Herbert W. Armstrong had somehow construed we were somewhere in a no-man's land between the two covenants. This understanding, though biblically difficult to justify, proved propitious for Mr. Armstrong. He was free to cherry-pick from either covenant that which he believed was required of us by God. Armstrong had long ago drug in many of the Old Covenant requirements, making them necessary in our worship of God. For instance, the church taught that we were to keep the Saturday Sabbath; the Holy Days given to ancient Israel; and first, second, and third tithes, plus offerings. Incidentally, it just so happened members were required to send all tithes and offerings directly into the church's Pasadena, California headquarters, where they were administered as the apostle saw fit.

We adhered to the clean and unclean food laws of the Old Testament and many other Old Covenant teachings that I now know are not necessary for salvation. We did not celebrate any of the "pagan"-inspired customs of birthdays, Christmas, Easter, Halloween, and the like. Our women were forbidden to wear any lipstick or makeup on pain of being suspended from church. Smoking, dipping, and chewing tobacco were not allowed. We did not believe in medical doctors or drugs. It is sad to note that babies died in childbirth because of this teaching. Furthermore, many others died of various illnesses because we did not believe in drugs and medical care.

Those in the ministry were considered the royalty of the Radio Church of God and were treated with great awe and respect. The members thought that the ministers were next to infallible. They surely knew about everything in the Bible and God's will for the local church members. Most ministers thought this too; they were the considered experts and authorities on the Bible and on how church members should live their lives. Many members went to the ministers for advice about major events (and oftentimes, minor events as well) in their lives, from buying a car to whom to marry and when to have a baby.

The ministers had almost absolute dictatorial power over the lives of the members they pastored. Divorce and remarriage was not allowed unless approved by the ministry. Couples who had been married to others prior to becoming members of the Radio Church had to separate if the ministers decided their present marriage was invalid. This was a sad travesty wreaking devastation and untold misery on the lives of many who came into the church. I heard that some pastors checked members' kitchens to see if unclean meats or other banned foods were being eaten. I even heard of one pastor who, while visiting the homes of members, would slip on a white glove so he could run it over the furniture for dirt to see how well the wife was performing her duties.

Members were subject to suspension from church attendance for committing any "sins." There were many different sins a Worldwide Church of God member could be suspended for, a few of which were smoking cigarettes, not attending church, or not paying tithes and offerings. (Tithing was so important to the church that if someone was being considered for a position as a deacon or minister, the church authorities checked the headquarters tithing records of these individuals prior to their ordination.) If a member's sins became habitual enough that he was considered incorrigible, then he was "disfellowshipped" and was an anathema to all church members until, hopefully, after Satan was through with him, he would come to his senses, completely repent, and overcome his sin. He could then return to our fellowship.

We did not believe that when we accepted the sacrifice of Jesus Christ we were saved. The church taught that we were only begotten or conceived by the Holy Spirit as a "fetus" with immortal life and not yet born again as sons and daughters of God. We held that "at the resurrection the believer would be raised up and finally be born again. 'We are begotten sons of God if we have the Holy Spirit. And therefore we are impregnated with immortal life, to have it when Christ comes, which will be in the Family of God.'"[3]

This sounds like a contradiction in terms. How could we be impregnated with immortal life and yet not receive eternal life until Christ returns? However you figure it, this position allowed the church to teach that prior to the resurrection, it was possible for the begotten fetus to "miscarry," so to speak, in the "womb" of the church and therefore not be given eternal life. Thus, one was not saved eternally until the resurrection at the return of Christ.

The fear of not being saved when Christ returned tended to keep you working hard to keep all the laws enforced by the Church. "We taught that only those who obeyed all the commandments—including those portions of the Old Covenant law that Herbert Armstrong believed and taught to 'still be in effect'—could achieve salvation. In other words, while salvation was a gift, one had to qualify to receive this free gift."[4] (Let's see now … let me get this straight. We will receive this "free gift" of eternal life if we keep the commandments? Doesn't sound all that free to me, if you have to work for it!) We taught that when we died, we would not regain consciousness until the resurrection at Christ's return. We would then join the family of God as members of the godhead.

We rejected the Trinity, "claiming that it was a pagan doctrine. Although we upheld the deity of Christ, we understood Him to be a separate God from the Father; while we said He had always existed with God Almighty, we also taught He did not become the Son of God until He was born into the world through the Virgin Mary. And the Holy Spirit? We denied His personality and taught that 'He' was really an 'it.'"[5] We maintained that the Holy Spirit was only the Spirit power of the godhead sent to do their will.[6] We believed the godhead was a family, which now consisted of only the Father and the Son.

"We taught that God was literally reproducing Himself through mankind. Our destiny was not to remain merely human, but to become God—born again as members of God's family. Just as human children are fully human, so (we thought) God's children will be fully God."[7] At the return of Christ, we would be resurrected as God beings. Jesus Christ would be our elder brother and thus God would have reproduced many sons and daughters into the God family.[8]

The church taught a form of British Israelism, which held that the "lost" ten tribes of Israel had migrated to Western Europe, England, and the United States. We held that England was populated primarily by the descendants of the tribe of Ephraim, and the United States was populated by descendants from the tribe of Manasseh. This teaching helped distinguish us from just about every other church denomination in the world and made us feel privy to knowledge that God had revealed especially to Mr. Armstrong.

British Israelism helped support Mr. Armstrong's interpretations of biblical prophecies and our position as God's unique church on earth. British Israelism was a major teaching at the core of the church. It was vital to our understanding of prophecy. "In many ways this doctrine of British Israelism shaped our major beliefs and practices."[9]

I remember being taught with detailed calculations made from the Scriptures that Christ's return would most likely be in 1975. This probably would occur on the Feast of Trumpets (a Jewish holy day). The church would be spared the "great tribulation" that would come on the world by being taken to and protected by God at the historical ancient city of Petra. Petra is nestled in a basin surrounded by sandstone mountains in the kingdom of Jordan. This event would supposedly occur three and a half years prior to the return of Christ.[10] The journey to Petra looked to me like it might be a long one in desert-type surroundings. I remember buying a new pair of combat boots specifically for the expected trip, which at that time was only about four years away.

We did not believe in buying life insurance. What need did we have of insurance when we believed that Christ would return in just a few years? However, 1975 came and went. Oops, looked like Mr. Armstrong missed the return of Christ by a few years!

When Christ didn't show up on Mr. Armstrong's timetable, that should have told me something, but there was plenty of waffling, recalculating, and excuses made by the church for why Christ did not come back when expected. I maintained the faith, however, and remained ready at a moment's notice for the call to Petra, which we still expected would come in a few years. I believe I kept those combat boots for at least the next thirty years, waiting for the journey to begin.

It was not until recently that I learned 1975 was not the first time Mr. Armstrong had been wrong about predicting the year of Christ's return. According to Mr. Joseph Tkach's book *Transformed by Truth*, Mr. Armstrong also predicted that the church's journey to Petra would occur in 1936. After that failed, it was rescheduled for 1943.[11] Would it have made a difference to me had I known about Mr. Armstrong's previous failed predictions? Looking back, I doubt it. I had a good set of blinders hung on me by then that prevented me from seeing anything that would shake my thoroughly indoctrinated faith in the church. If only I knew then what I know now.

Perhaps worst of all, the Radio Church of God did not preach the great commission Christ commanded His disciples to carry to the world when He ascended to His Father after His resurrection. We preached a gospel all right, but it was not primarily about the saving grace of Jesus Christ. We replaced that with a gospel about the coming kingdom of God at the return of Christ. We thought that was the gospel Christ wanted us to preach. Of course, salvation by grace is the most important truth and gospel message any church can preach. In spite of this, it seems as though that message was only a secondary afterthought to the WCG. We believed our primary gospel commission was to warn the world of the coming Kingdom of God. Our job was not to save the world, but to witness to the world.

We also believed that just as John the Baptist was called by God to prepare the way for Christ's first coming, we were the prophesied "end time," one and only true church of God who were to prepare the way for Christ's return. We believed we were fulfilling the prophecy that stated the "gospel of the kingdom shall be preached in all the world for a witness unto all nations; and then shall the end come" (Matt. 24:14, KJV).

It is sad to say, but I believe we were wrong on almost all religious doctrines we taught, except the truth that salvation through faith in the sacrifice of Jesus was necessary. Thank God, at least we understood enough about Christ's sacrifice to be saved in spite of being buried up to our eyeballs in weird doctrines and the legalism of the Old Covenant. I think a shallow understanding of the gospel is all too often about as close to the true doctrines of Christ that most of the estimated 1,500 different U.S. Christian faith groups get.[12]

Attending the Church's "West Point"

The Radio Church of God established two colleges, both named Ambassador College: one in England and one at the church's headquarters in Pasadena, California. Later, one was also established in Big Sandy, Texas. These colleges were considered by all members worldwide to be what we called the "West Point" of God's educational system for the church. Only the elite of the Church's young people were allowed to attend. If I remember correctly, the year I entered the freshman class of 1965, out of 1,500 who had applied, only about 100 were admitted.

The college was so strict in its teaching and discipline that only about half of those entering could expect to graduate. In college, we referred to the many trials we faced there as God's "pressure cooker," in which only the best of the elite managed to survive and graduate. As a result of this intense pressure cooker, when we graduated and received our diplomas we were considered good and faithful servants of God. Despite all the difficulties faced there, young people from all over the world applied to the colleges.

Two years prior to being admitted to the college, I applied for admission and was turned down with a comment by one of the members of the admissions team that fairly well summed up why I was not accepted. He simply stated, "Too much football!" At that time, I was finishing my sophomore year at Southwestern State University in Weatherford, Oklahoma. My academic career from grade school through two years of college was barely average. I had not valued good grades and was interested in only sports and girls. I was so proud of being stupid that I used to brag as a senior in high school, "I haven't yet taken a book home from school to study." Well, duh! Just looking at my academic achievements to that point clearly reflected that bit of wisdom.

After my application was rejected by Ambassador College, I figured I did not have "too much football"—rather, I had enough! One thing football had taught me was to never give up: "the bigger they are, the harder they fall!" I determined I would buckle down and not only do better the last two years in college, but also apply again to Ambassador College again upon graduation.

I decided to choose a major that would make me more attractive to "God's college" (as it was also called) the next time I applied. I also hoped the degree might help the efforts of the church in proclaiming the gospel of the coming kingdom of God. Because the main outreach of the church's ministry was through a worldwide radio program (and later, a television program), I chose radio and television broadcasting as my major. I pulled a 3.3 grade point average during my remaining two years of college and graduated with a bachelor of science degree from Oklahoma State University in 1965.

I was then well armed to apply again to Ambassador College. This time, I was accepted. At the age of twenty-three, I boarded a train in Clinton, Oklahoma, and headed to the West Coast. I was ecstatic and most thankful to God to be one of the chosen few attending the college. The college campus in Pasadena was absolutely gorgeous, rivaling and probably excelling that of any college on earth. It prided itself on the beauty and refined culture it presented to the students.

I had achieved the pinnacle of my dreams. At last I would be immersed in the center, the heartbeat of what God was doing on earth. At the time, I thought it was His only work on earth. I believed that God had called me to help preach to the world the return of Christ and His kingdom. I did not know what part God would have me play in preparing for Christ's return, but I had totally committed myself to the church and to God's will.

I hoped to become a minister after completing my studies at Ambassador. Nearly all of the ministers in the church came from its two campuses, and nearly all married one of the college's women. That sounded pretty good to me.

"God's West Point" rivaled the army's West Point in strictness and discipline. The rules were clear and strictly enforced. For instance, you could escort a coed to church services and other activities, but you could not steadily date or become engaged to a young lady until your senior year. You certainly were not allowed to kiss or even hold hands with them. Fornication would most likely have caused immediate expulsion. We were not to become "unequally yoked" with unbelievers, which meant we were to date and marry only those who were members of the church. Breaking these rules could get you immediately expelled from not only the college but church membership as well. Being removed from both college and church would have crushed me emotionally, along with all my hopes and dreams.

During my second year at Ambassador College, at the age of twenty-four, I faced one of the greatest traumas I have ever struggled with. Its aftermath plagued me for decades. At the time I was forced to come to grips with one of the greatest transgressions I could commit against Herbert Armstrong's church and college. What I am about to tell you now was so devastating to me at the time that I have not talked about it with anyone but my wife.

The summer after my first year, I went home to Cordell, Oklahoma, to spend a couple of weeks visiting family. While there, I made a date with an old girlfriend. Prior to moving to California we had a physically intimate dating relationship, so I should have known I would be throwing gasoline on the fire if I were alone with her again. However, it was a beautiful full moonlit night and I drove her out into the country and parked so we could "see how beautiful the moon and star-filled sky was." One thing led to another and as I sat with one arm around the back of her car seat, I leaned over and kissed her a few times as passions began to rise. I then pulled her much closer to me than I should have in a full-body embrace.

My conscience was deeply stricken at that point and I did not go any further. I managed to finally pull myself away and I took her back home. However, it was too late—I had crossed the line!

Driving back home that night, I was devastated. Yes, I know this story may sound trivial compared to today's standards. However, I had broken my moral values and the college's dating code. Not only did I kiss the young lady, she was not even a member of the Radio Church.

In my mind, I had utterly failed God and His college. I tried to rationalize it away during the remainder of my stay in Cordell. However, my heart was in great turmoil as to what to do now. I could see that my career at Ambassador College would probably be cut short if any administrator of the college knew what I had done. Several had been kicked out of the college for similar incidents. Over the remaining few days before I returned to college, I did a great deal of soul searching and spent many hours of serious repenting before God.

I returned to Ambassador with a very troubled and heavy heart. What was I to do? 'Fess up or keep it quiet? I spent many hours praying for the right answer to that question in the next few weeks. By this point, I had spent an entire year at the college in its self-absorbed culture of seeking and confessing personal sins, trying to be the model student the college taught I should be. Mr. Armstrong taught that the "heart was deceitful above all things and desperately wicked" and that we needed to be continually on guard against its sins, searching for and removing all sin in our lives. I was a believer now in the importance of that job. I buried myself in self-deprecation, pity, and remorse repenting of my summer's moral failure; but now it was too late. My self-confidence and image speedily crumbled to dust, and I could no longer trust my wicked self.

After agonizing over the matter, I finally went to two high-ranking officials (also high-ranking ministers) of the college and confessed the evil I had done. I fully expected I could be kicked out of the college. I was hoping against hope I would be allowed to stay. One of the officials did want me kicked out. As I remember, he asked me a few probing questions. For instance, he wanted to know if I also had been involved with any of the girls at the college in an inappropriate way. I told him I had not and that I had not even held hands with anyone.   Fortunately or unfortunately, as the case may be, the other official was the higher-ranking member of the two and he did not want me thrown out. My fear and guilt were finally eased and I felt joy and thankfulness return when I was told I would be allowed to stay.

I felt that God had been merciful to me. However, that experience had so shaken my faith in my ability to fight sin that I had little confidence left. Prior to my great sin, I had already been trained by the college to focus inwardly to find sin. Now, I was really on the hunt with laser-like focus, searching every nook and cranny of my heart. I felt somehow I had been unjustly pardoned for my moral failure and really didn't deserve to remain in college. From that point forward, it seemed I continually was trying to redeem myself to God and the college by destroying my sinful self. I felt if either of the Armstrongs knew what I had done, they would have kicked me out! I lived as though I would be found out eventually and receive what I deserved, which was to be kicked out of the college and church for what I had done.

I stayed in college and I was thankful, but my mind kept going back over and over again to the sins I had so horribly committed against God. Then, I remembered something else that I had failed to tell the two college officials. I feared they still might kick me out of the college if they knew about it. Fear and guilt returned with a vengeance. My conscience drove me back to the official who had said I could stay, and I confessed the new information to him: "It was not just a kiss," I told him, "it was a full-body embrace!" He told me not to worry about it and that I could stay in college. My conscience again was cleared, and I felt great relief. Unbeknownst to me at the time, a vicious cycle had begun to emerge. It was a negative, dangerous pattern, which Satan would use to haunt me for the next several decades.

My summer's sin had so deeply and emotionally scarred me that it left me feeling undeserving to be at the college. I withered in fear that my just punishment would eventually come. I felt like a fraud. My already sensitive conscience now kicked into hyper drive. My "forgiven" sins morphed into other real or imagined sins in the future that also needed to be forgiven. I would review the ever-increasing list of sins with sorrow and regret. I was not able to leave them at the feet of Jesus Christ and accept His total forgiveness. I did not trust myself and I did not have the faith to trust that Christ had accepted my repentance without confessing it to a human being, a minister of God.

The destructive pattern was now set. In order to expiate and cleanse perceived sins and gain peaceful relief from a guilty conscience, I felt a compulsion to confess to a minister to gain assurance of forgiveness and find an uneasy temporary truce with God. With each confession, the pattern became more entrenched. This confession would only bring me temporary relief from my pains of conscience. Soon after, I once again would be focused inward, searching for sin to rid myself of. I was like a volcano. After each eruption the need for confession would slowly build up to another explosion, erupting real or imagined sins into a minister's lap. The periods between these confessions varied from a few months to maybe even as long as a year or two. But eventually, sooner or later, I would do it again. So goes a religion focused on works and inward self-examination and not on Jesus and His New Covenant brilliantly displaying His grace.

I was constantly looking back over my shoulder at my past traumas and not looking forward to Christ. My past haunted me, and I feared it would soon catch up with me and I would receive the tragedy I thought I deserved. I guess I felt a bit like Job when he said, "For the thing which I fear comes on me, That which I am afraid of comes to me" (Job 3:25 WSB). I kept expecting it would for me, too.

Life in the Ministry

Over my remaining two years at Ambassador College, I worked twenty to thirty hours a week in the church's radio studio to help pay for my education there. The summer between my junior and senior year, I worked in the "field ministry" under a minister pastoring two churches in the Long Beach, California, area. Only those who were being considered for the ministry after graduation were given that privilege. At that time, churches were growing rapidly around the world and there was a great shortage of ministers to pastor them. To make up for this shortage, most ministers pastored at least two churches and sometimes more.

In 1968—the year the Radio Church changed its name to the

Worldwide Church of God—I graduated with a Bachelor of Arts degree in theology and speech. I married one of the ladies from the college, and we were sent to Nashville, Tennessee. I was a ministerial trainee under a pastor-ranked minister. There were several ranks of ministers. Next to being an apostle, came the rank of an evangelist and the next in rank was that of a pastor. Then came the rank of a local elder, and lastly that of a local church elder. There were very few holding the rank of an evangelist or pastor. These men were considered to be the elite ministers and thus the most coveted positions. There was, of course, only one "Apostle," Herbert W. Armstrong, and there would never be another.

After about a year assisting in Nashville, I was ordained a local elder, which was the starting ministerial position for college graduates. Soon after that, I was transferred to assist a pastor who was in charge of two churches in Kentucky. in Louisville, Kentucky. Under him I was given basically the responsibility of pastoring the church in Louisville while he pastored the other. My wife and I had two girls during this time. Both were born at home, one with a midwife and the other with the help of a chiropractor. This was in line with the church's anti-medical stance. Thankfully, there were no complications with either delivery. Both were born beautiful, healthy girls.

The Bitter Fruits of Legalism

So, here I was, a graduate of "God's West Point," Ambassador College, and in effect pastoring one of His churches. I had reached the pinnacle of what most people in the Worldwide Church of God (WCG) would have equated with rare and great success by pastoring a church and driving a new church-owned car. I had a wife and two baby girls. I had it made! My climb to the top of the ministerial ranks had begun. To others, it looked like I was on top of the world. However, that was not the case.

You see, although I preached a great deal about grace, the forgiveness of sin, the coming kingdom of God, how to be a good Christian, and the like, I was miserable! My mind was still racked by my past sins from college and my current new sins, which were piling up. I did not understand how I could still carry so much past and present sin. I felt like I was a fraud to be found out. I was living in fear, guilt, and misery. Something had to be wrong with me. Every other minister seemed happy and sin-free. I thought my problems were unique, so I felt alone. I wondered, "Why am I living in such misery? Is this what God wants for me?"

I had labored hard to do this and do that—all that Mr. Armstrong and the WCG said I should be doing to be righteous. I had totally dedicated my life to God and worked hard to please Him. And all those works I had done brought me no peace and happiness. They only brought me a ton of guilt and shame, a load I could no longer carry!

I had come out of Ambassador College, but the hang-ups of the college had not come out of me. I knew about grace, but its full meaning had not been taught to me and therefore I did not know how accept it. I knew I was not the perfect minister I thought I ought to be. I felt like a hypocrite. My mind was in constant turmoil, warring with myself. Satan was having a field day with me.

I found myself wanting to run away from it all and move back home to Oklahoma. However, I was caught between the proverbial "rock and a hard place." Of all who had been called into the ministry of that church, I knew of none who had dared to leave the ministry. At that time, there had never been even a divorce by any couple that had graduated from the college, much less a minister turning his back on his godly calling! We had been taught that, "No one who puts his hand to the plow and then looks back is fit for the kingdom of God " (Luke 9:62, BSB). I believed I was in God's church and that He had called me into an elite position in His ministry and it would be tantamount to an act of heresy to leave it. I knew the other ministers and local church members would look at it that way.

In spite of this, I had come to the breaking point mentally. I could no longer carry my legalistic burdens and function as a productive minister in God's church. I called headquarters in California and told them I wanted to take a break, a sabbatical, and get away for a while from the duties of the ministry. To make a long story short, they not only gave me a break they defrocked me from the ministry and send me packing back home.

I returned home to Oklahoma in a large U-Haul truck, disgraced and ashamed. Years before, I had left as one of the few WCG members from Oklahoma who not only was accepted to "God's college" but graduated there and joined the top echelons of the vaunted royal ministry of the church. Whereas before I had been regarded as a celebrity of sorts, now I was an oddity, an enigma.

Though disgraced, I was allowed to remain a member of the church. To attend, we had to drive one hundred miles from Cordell to Oklahoma City. This was the church I had attended before going to Ambassador College. I had been a favorite native "son" prior to my downfall; now, the local church did not know what to do with me. I was a pariah to them of sorts. Essentially where one month earlier I had been giving sermons and performing all the normal pastoral duties such as visiting members, counseling them, conducting Bible studies, men's speech clubs, and church singing; but now all I was allowed to do was to attend church. I was never even asked to be an usher, hand out songbooks, lead a song, give an opening or closing prayer, or sweep the floors.

I had two college degrees, a wife, two children, and no job. What I had feared had indeed come upon me! Out of desperation, I went to work at a local chicken processing plant for a few months, earning minimum wage, until I found a sales job with Motorola Communications and Electronics, selling business band two-way radios.

Rising from the Ashes

Over the next four years, I slowly began to heal from the burdens I had been carrying. Being responsible for just my family and me helped ease the load I had been carrying. Also, I was an immediate success with Motorola. I became one of the top salesmen in the entire country. Financially, God prospered me greatly. I built a new home at Lake Latonka near Lawton, Oklahoma, in 1972. There was a WCG congregation just fifteen miles away, and we started attending there. The local pastor and I got along well and I found myself trying to help him serve the church in any way I could. He began allowing me to lead songs and even give short sermons. Being called on to serve showed me that God had not abandoned me, and I was pleased to serve. After a year, I was restored to my position as a local church minister (not employed by the church) supporting the pastor. In spite of this, I felt like I had failed God's calling by leaving the full-time ministry four years earlier. Although the compulsion to confess sins had lessened, from time to time I'd still have my little "clearing of the conscience" confession sessions with the local pastor.

It was in 1974 that I got a call from the pastor of the Oklahoma City church. He wanted to know if I'd consider coming back into the ministry full-time as an associate with him. I felt this was God's call for me to redeem myself for leaving the first time. God was offering me a chance to return to the "plow" I had left a few years earlier, and I was determined not to fail Him again. "Yes!" I said to the call. I gave notice to Motorola of my intention to leave.

Two weeks later, just prior to returning to work full time in the ministry, it seemed all the fears and emotional trauma I had left in Louisville came flooding back into my mind all at once. I panicked and became very fearful. I'm sure Satan was laughing and having a field day, seeing my paralyzing panic set in. However, this time I was not quitting. I walked forward in faith, trusting God knew what He was doing with me.

We moved to Midwest City, Oklahoma, where the church was located. Not only did the fear and panic not leave me, it intensified! However, I stayed quiet, keeping it between me and God. I did not want to spread it to my wife and I definitely was not going to tell headquarters or the church pastor. I knew God had given me talents to preach and help others, so I threw myself into my work.

A few months after moving to Midwest City, I remember feeling at the breaking point mentally. I was fearful and felt hopeless. The thought came to me that the only way out of my mental anguish would be suicide. The Devil agreed with me, I'm sure. He was hard at work at that point in my life. I pondered suicide, but then did as David did in 1 Samuel 30:6— I prayed to God and strengthened myself in the Lord. I told God, "You called me back to climb this mountain and in spite of my great fear, I will not turn back from your calling again; you have a plan and a purpose and I will follow you one day at a time from now on until the end." I stepped forward in faith. I studied and prayed constantly for stability and strength during the first year after coming back. I struggled to grow in faith and mental strength and slowly I made encouraging progress.

A year later, I was raised in rank to that of a preaching elder and was immediately transferred to Ada, Oklahoma, to pastor the church there, and a little later, added another one in Lawton. God did provide me with increasing strength to do the job He gave me. I clung to His promise: "No temptation has seized you except what is common to man. And God is faithful; He will not let you be tempted beyond what you can bear. But when you are tempted, He will also provide an escape, so that you can stand up under it. " (1 Cor. 10:13, BSB).

With this faith, I slowly began to climb the mountain He had set before me. I had come to see that my way out of this mess was to build the mind of God. Paul had said, "Let this mind be in you, which was also in Christ Jesus" (Phil. 2:5, KJV). This was a beautiful, encouraging revelation to me. I longed for the mind of Christ and strove toward it. As I did, I made slow but steady progress in handling my problems. I noticed Paul's statement that "For God hath not given us the spirit of fear; but of power, and of love, and of a sound mind" (2 Tim. 1:7, KJV). Since I believed God wanted to build His mind in me, I worked very hard at capturing wrong thoughts and replacing them with God's as revealed in His Word. My big mistake was that I was doing all the work. I didn't leave much for God to do. I thought God's job was just showing me the "works" I needed to do.

In my new pastorate in Ada, I began preaching a great deal about the importance of thoughts and our need to build the mind of God. I taught abundantly about the "being forgiven" part of grace. I needed it and I knew the congregations needed it, too. I preached more on positive thinking and the forgiveness of God than on any other subject. I preached much of it for my benefit as well as for that of the church members. I even wrote a couple of articles of encouragement that were published around the world in the church's magazines.

In spite of the fact that the church frowned upon members reading any secular or even Christian sources other than their Church literature, over the next several years I studied a great number of self-help books on mental health. Tim LaHaye's book, *How to Win Over Depres-*

sion, was the first of these forbidden books I read. It was a godsend to me and was particularly helpful. Going to secular colleges was forbidden for ministers, but I did secretly want to go back and get my master's degree in counseling. I thought this would not only be a help to me in building the mind of God but would also help me help the church members.

In 1979, I faced a new, life-changing challenge: my wife was diagnosed with paranoid schizophrenia. She decided to leave our home and travel in an attempt to get away from her real or imagined problems. In these attempts to escape, she left me and our two daughters a couple of different times the first year as I recall. I began to realize I was losing complete control of what was becoming a dire situation. She ended up in a hospital's mental ward on one occasion. I tried to calm her fears and reason with her, but to no avail. She left a third time as I recall leaving me with nothing to say about it. I did not know if she was coming back. I had been in consultation with church headquarters concerning the situation over the last two years. After struggling to keep the marriage together during these years, I did not take her back the last time she left on the advice of church headquarters. I realized it would be useless to try and keep the marriage together any longer, so I filed for a divorce and was awarded custody of my eleven- and twelve-year-old daughters. I remained single for three and a half years. I then met and married the love of my life, Cindy. She was as close to being an angel on earth as humanly possible. She was a Proverbs 31 wife to me and was a blessing beyond what words could possibly describe of her!

In 1985, the year after Cindy and I married, we were transferred to Colorado. There, I pastored three churches located in the cities of Colorado Springs, Pueblo, and Alamosa. It was there, a couple of years later, that I was elevated to the lofty, coveted position of pastor-ranked minister. Only evangelists were higher in rank (and of course, the "Apostle," who was ranked highest of all).

Embracing the New Covenant

In January 1986, the "Apostle" and head of the Worldwide Church of

God, Herbert W. Armstrong, died at the age of ninety-three. Prior to Mr. Armstrong's death, he had appointed Joseph Tkach Sr. as the heir to his position as pastor general of the Worldwide Church of God and had told him that changes needed to be made in the WCG.

"Mr. Armstrong never detailed everything that he meant, but it was clear even then that the Church's stance on medicine and use of doctors was at the forefront of his mind. At that point in our history, it was commonly believed that people of real faith had no need of doctors and medicine."[13] At that time, considering the illness of Mr. Armstrong and his use of doctors be-fore his death, some questions arose about the Church's medical beliefs. "Within a year of Mr. Armstrong's death, Church leadership began an intensive study of the WCG's practice and doctrine [concerning medicine and doctors]. No one had any particular agenda in mind, nor did anyone have any specific goals in view other than to identify, if possible, what changes Mr. Armstrong might have had in mind before his death."[14]

This study paved the way for the first major doctrinal change on healing in 1987.[15] The church's booklet, "The Plain Truth about Healing" was rewritten and now "made it clear that it was OK to go to doctors. Visiting a physician wasn't a sign of lack of faith in God."[16] This change lead to questions from church members about other doctrines.[17] The next doctrinal change allowed women to wear makeup.[18] The time had come for the legalistic curtain of the WCG to begin to open. As it did, the glory of Christ's grace began to shine proportionately more brilliant-ly. The floodgates of change were beginning to open in the church.

In 1990, Cindy and I were transferred to North Carolina, where I pastored another three churches in the cities of Lenoir, Boone, and Mar-ion. We lived in Boone, where my wife taught at Appalachian State University. This was another change in the church; prior to this, the wife of a minister was not allowed to work outside the home. Furthermore, pastors now were allowed to attend college programs that might be useful in their ministry. I decided to pursue my dream of obtaining a counseling degree by applying for acceptance into Appalachian State's counseling program, ranked as one of the best in the nation. I was accepted into their counsel-ing program and graduated with my master's degree in December 1994.

It was in 1994 that the WCG's biggest doctrinal changes happened. Study papers on the Old and New Covenants were sent to the ministry worldwide showing the error of our ways in legalism. They proclaimed the true gospel of Christ was not about the kingdom of God coming, but the forgiveness of sin by the blood of Jesus Christ. I studied them carefully, and the scales of legalism began to fall off my eyes. I greatly rejoiced and over the next several months led my three churches into the wonderful new understanding. I don't remember any member having a problem with the dramatic changes in the church. Sadly, that was not the case for a number of other congregations.

Once the dam of legalism burst wide open in the church, the doctrinal changes flowed like a raging flood through WCG congregations around the world. J. Michael Feazell and Mr. Tkach's son, Joe Tkach Jr., were the right-hand men supporting Mr. Tkach Sr. during these trying years of the church. Mr. Feazell had grown up in the WCG and served Mr. Tkach Sr. as his executive assistant and editorial adviser.[19] He and Mr. Tkach Jr. were deeply involved in and had a great deal to do with the transformation of the church.[20] Mr. Feazell wrote eloquently about this period of time in his book, *The Liberation of the Worldwide Church of God*:

"How did all this [WCG's changes] begin?" I have been asked this question scores of times, but I have to pause and reflect anew every time I hear it. How did all this begin? I cannot point to a single starting place either for the transformation of the Worldwide Church of God or for myself. I cannot isolate a particular moment, a particular place, or a particular thought. Many things came together like tiny brooks and rivulets, bubbling up from here and there and nowhere in particular but little by little joining with others and growing steadily to form larger streams and finally cascading together into a mighty river. How did all this begin? It began in the hearts of men and women who heard the voice of their Savior. It began in the testimony of Scripture. It began in the pain and frustration of unforgiving moralism. It began in the agonizing disillusionment that comes from failed predictions and fallen heroes. It began in the idealism of youth and the simple wisdom of old age. It began when the angel spoke the timeless words of hope and redemption to the shepherds: "Today in the town of David a Savior has been born to you. He is Christ the Lord."[21]

Mr. Feazell went on to explain the significance of the sweeping changes the WCG experienced:

> The Worldwide Church of God made evangelical history…with its leadership-driven abandonment of the unorthodox doctrines of its founder, renowned radio and television evangelist Herbert W. Armstrong. The radical changes in the small Pasadena-based Christian denomination have been heralded by mainstream Christian leaders as "miraculous," "astounding," and "unprecedented." No other Christian Church in our modern experience has rejected its founding sectarian roots in a return to the essentials of historical Christian doctrinal orthodoxy.[22]

The reactions of ministers and church members were just as dramatic. Worldwide losses of ministers and members, as well as income to the WCG, were staggering. For example, in the United States alone, during the eleven years following 1989, church income dropped from "$168 million a year to only $31.2 million. Weekly [church] attendance declined from 87,000 to 18,200, membership declined from 66,000 to 37,500."[23] "By 1997, the massive drop in income "the church had ended its World Tomorrow television program, closed both campuses of Ambassador College, virtually ended its publishing ministry, and spun of The Plain Truth magazine into Plain Truth Ministries, an independent para-church organization.[24] led to the closure of both campuses of Ambassador College and the end of The World Tomorrow television program. The church's publishing ministry also ended, though The Plain Truth magazine was turned into Plain Truth Ministries, an independent para-church organization.[25] The number of career pastors dwindled from 458 to 120.[26]

Several years earlier, after the death of Herbert Armstrong, some dissenting pastors of the WCG left to form new churches purporting to be remnants of Armstrong's one and only true church. During and after the major doctrinal changes of 1994, many more WCG pastors did the same thing. Most continued on teaching the Old Covenant legalistic doctrines that Herbert Armstrong taught. There seemed to be a cascading effect: a new church would be formed after breaking off from the WCG. Soon thereafter, that church would have a pastor splitting off, forming yet another new church. During the ten years after the death of Mr. Armstrong, there were about twenty-two direct splits from WCG and fifteen other churches that branched off from the original splits.[27] This seems to have been the case throughout history, though—just look at what Martin Luther started when he left the Catholic Church.

Many of those who broke off from the WCG to form new churches may have thought that Satan himself had taken control of the leadership of the WCG in an attempt to destroy the church, its end-time mission, and the truths of God. If it were the one and only true church of God as Mr. Armstrong proclaimed, then it should follow, as Jesus told Peter, "…I will build My church, and the gates of Hades will not prevail against it" (Matt. 16:18b, BSB). Mr. Armstrong believed God called him to raise up the one and only true church for a critical special calling, to fulfill the prophecy that Jesus himself made: "And this gospel of the kingdom will be preached in all the world as a testimony to all nations, and then the end will come" (Matt. 24:14, BSB). He believed he and the WCG would fulfill this prophecy and both would see the return of Jesus. He obviously was wrong. You would think that even though Mr. Armstrong died, surely the one and only true church could not be conquered and fall to the grasp of Satan and his ministers.

I believe there is another explanation to who took over the WCG. Who in their right mind would have done to a church what no other modern-day denomination of this size has done in order to reject legalism and usher in the grace of Jesus? Considering the drastic losses of membership, ministers, churches, and income; I believe the more logical answer is that Jesus Christ came to let the floodgates of his grace shine more brightly than ever before to all his people who were willing to open their eyes and accept it. I believe the burdens and chains of legalism weighed heavy on the necks and backs of most in the church, and Jesus showed great mercy and grace, saying lovingly to each of us, "Come to Me, all you who are weary and burdened, and I will give you rest. Take

My yoke upon you and learn from Me; for I am gentle and humble in heart, and you will find rest for your souls. For My yoke is easy and My burden is light" (Matt. 11:28-30, BSB).

I am now profoundly proud and grateful for what those brave leaders of the WCG did. These men were willing to walk in the new light of God's truth out of the darkness and chains of legalism into the grace of Christ. Would to God we all are willing to do that until our death or the return of Christ. Thank you, Joe Tkach Sr. (deceased 1995), Dr. Joe Tkach Jr. (current leader), Dr. J. Michael Feazell, and all the other courageous ministers that allowed God to use them for His glory. I'm no longer a member of their denomination (now called Grace Communion International; www.gci.org), but I will forever be grateful to them.

Disillusioned

In May of 1994, the year of the big changes within the WCG, Cindy and I were transferred to Lubbock, Texas, where I pastored the church in Lubbock and four other churches as far away as Clovis, New Mexico, and Abilene, Texas. It was a strange time due to the sudden changes in the church. The changes were exciting in a way, yet I was left with a sense of unease due to the sudden change in the way we had worshiped God for so many years. It was totally different from what we had been accustomed to. I applauded the changes, but questioned why the church still maintained its control from one man still at the top with all tithes and offerings worldwide being sent to church headquarters in California. I did not understand then why the authoritarian structure remained. I now believe the change in the church from legalism to grace would have been virtually impossible to accomplish otherwise.

During these ongoing changes, ministers and members were leaving and dissident groups were splitting off, forming new churches. With less money flowing to headquarters, there was a need to cut spending. The church began offering severance packages to ministers who wanted to leave. This maneuver saved a great deal of money for the church, and also got rid of ministers who were hostile to the changes or simply disheartened and desiring to leave.

Although I agreed with the radical new direction of the church, there were still some changes that were not being made within the church leadership that I thought should be made. Because these changes were not made, a crisis of conscience in my mind over them developed. I maybe should have been a bit more patient to see if those changes would be made. However, quite frankly, by then I had become disillusioned with the church and my walk with God over the previous thirty-six years. Because of these factors, I came to the point where I felt I no longer wanted to pastor a church or support the autocratic church governmental structure I believed was still extant. In 1996, a severance package was offered to ministers who wished to leave the ministry. I took the offer and resigned. The severance package contained a salary that would continue for only about five more months. There I was at age fifty-four, with no job, no retirement benefits, nothing but a few months of pay from the church for my twenty-two years of full-time service in the ministry. My wife and I continued attending the Lubbock church until we moved to Amarillo two years later. It was then that I permanently severed my relationship with the church where I had spent my youth and thirty-six years of my life.

Cindy taught at colleges in the Lubbock and Amarillo area, which kept us afloat financially while I struggled to find my new vocation. I entered what seemed to be a promising financial venture in a new home-building technology with a friend. We spent three years trying to get it off the ground. However, in spite of our valiant efforts, it failed. Now I was fifty-eight, with no job and only my wife's meager income. The church I had spent my life with had offered me no retirement. Our financial future looked very bleak. I figured I had only a few years left, if my health held up, to secure a retirement for Cindy and me.

I am sad to say it was at this juncture that I became disillusioned with religion in general. I could not believe that God would call me into a religious cult and leave me dangling there for decades. Whereas I had believed He had led me into the Radio Church of God at age twenty, now I believed He did not do that. My faith in God was greatly diminished. I had left home and family to devote decades of my life and youth following God, doing what I thought He wanted me to do. During those years in the ministry, my heart yearned to be back home with my family in Oklahoma, but I felt I was called by God to do His work. I pastored what I thought were His congregations at various cities around the country only to find that nearly every "truth" the church had taught was wrong.

At this point, I definitely was suspicious of God and of all Christian churches. I no longer trusted any organized religion, although Cindy and I did attend a local church. I did that mainly for Cindy's sake, since she wanted to go. Her faith was stronger than mine. Although I became distrustful of God, I never completely rejected Him, though I mostly stopped praying and studying the Bible for a period of about twelve years. However, a few times I found myself thinking of God during that time and actually talking to him, just a little bit.

In spite of this, I believe God was merciful to me. He brought me into the insurance business. I became a captive agent with the largest long-term care insurance company in the nation. My wife and I moved back to my hometown, Cordell, in 2000, where she became employed as a speech instructor thirty miles away at Southwestern Oklahoma State University in Weatherford. My insurance business was very successful, and I traveled all over the western half of Oklahoma. Over the next ten years, with the help of my wife, we secured our retirement.

On September 19, 2009, Cindy attended a conference for teachers in Ada, Oklahoma. I shopped in downtown Ada, waiting for Cindy to call and tell me when to pick her up so we could head back home to Cordell. I did receive a call, but it was the frantic voice of her close friend, saying, "David, Cindy has collapsed. Come quickly!"

I rushed to the hospital, where the doctors were working on her in the emergency room, and waited to hear her fate. After a while, I was ushered into a private room. "The doctor will be with you soon," I was told. My heart began to sink, telling me this was not a good sign. In came the doctor, accompanied by a nurse. They told me Cindy was dead. My lovely, precious sweetheart had died unexpectedly of a massive heart attack. I felt devastated and completely crushed. I cried the deep, gut-wrenching sobs of one whose entire world has just fallen apart.

Later, after I had gained some composure, I walked out of the hospital. With tears welling up again, I turned my eyes up to heaven and said to God, "Your will be done. Oh Lord, I am at your mercy at your feet at the foot of the cross. I am yours to do with as you wish. I know all things work together for good. You give life and you take it away. Blessed be your name. I give myself back to you. Do with me what you will. My wish is for you to take me now and let me join my sweet, lovely Cindy, but not my will, but yours be done."

The four-hour drive back home was very long by myself. I was deep in thought all the way, communing with God. A deep sorrow for my loss hung heavily over me; strangely, however, I felt great peace and resignation at living in the will of God once again.

My loving family closed ranks and gave me great support over the coming days and weeks. My two wonderful Christian daughters were invaluable in lifting me up to God. My darling saint of a sister also greatly ministered to me. She helped greatly to comfort and anchor my soul in Christ when she showed me Louie Giglio's DVD entitled *Hope, When Life Hurts Most*.

I laid my darling to rest. On her tombstone I had inscribed the essence of her life in one sentence: "Cindy shared God's love through her beautiful eyes, smile, and words: all who met her, loved her." She was the most beautiful and gentle woman I have ever known—one of the top finalists to Miss Iowa in 1966—and "Miss Congeniality" title; yet her inward beauty far exceeded the outward. She had a loving, kind, attentive, respectful, nonjudgmental way with everyone she met, and she never met a stranger. Whoever met her instantly loved her. She lit up the place wherever she walked with her gorgeous smile, shining, beautiful eyes, and gracious words.

Considering the pain I suffered during my years in the Worldwide Church of God, it was all more than worth it just to have been the husband of Cindy for the twenty-five years and four days we spent together on this earth. God brought her into my life in the church and in His love and wisdom took her to be with Him. God says He has numbered each of our days on this earth. He took her for a reason, and I was forced to accept that. I felt that Cindy was about as close to heavenly perfection as an earthly body could become. Me? That was a different story! I needed to be slapped silly and spiritually awakened. And indeed, Cindy's death did that to me. Without God coming to my rescue, my life would have been dead without her.

God has not granted my request to join her yet. He obviously is not done with me. He has a lot of work yet to do in building His character in me, and I suspect He desires for me to witness for Him in various fashions. Perhaps this book is one of them.

"The Second Blessing"

I wish I could tell you that in the years since Cindy's death, all my problems were solved. That is not the case. Although I did return wholeheartedly to God, I felt lost, so to speak, for the next two years. I struggled to find a church where I felt I fit in, and I was still mourning the loss of Cindy and searching for what God wanted me to do next. During those two years, I attempted to find and replace what I had lost, but I now feel that is impossible for me. A love like that comes around only once in your life, if you're lucky; many never experience that kind of love in their lifetime. I have finally settled down to that reality.

I have read stories of Christians who, after years of striving to follow Christ, come to a much deeper spiritual understanding and relationship with Him. It is almost like a second conversion. They experience a dramatic shift from a superficial relationship with God to a deeply personal one, which has been described as "the second blessing." I guess it could be best described as walking with, talking to, and relying on God for guidance concerning all good and bad events of life each and every day. This has certainly been my experience.

As far as my present condition, though my past has left scars, I am learning to put them into the hands of God. For many years my life was plagued from the many scares that legalism inflicted upon me. However, I feel God has been and is continuing to greatly heal me from my past. As I focus on the light of Christ, He is continually transforming me more and more into His likeness in my thoughts, feelings, and actions. I am truly learning to enjoy the "light burden" and "easy yoke" that

Christ promised. In Christ, I have at last found access to the beautiful rest promised for my weary soul (see Matthew 11:29-30). And not only that, I am now experiencing the promise of Isaiah 40:31 (KJV): "But they that wait upon the LORD shall renew *their* strength; they shall mount up with wings as eagles; they shall run, and not be weary; *and* they shall walk, and not faint."

I am continually learning how to better rest in the grace of God. What a wonderful blessing—a soothing, healing salve for my weary soul! I am profoundly grateful. If you are lacking the peace I speak of, this book is dedicated to introducing you to its glorious wonders. Hopefully this book can inoculate those of you becoming a Christian against the disasters of religious legalism and if you are enslaved in it to any depth, help release you from its unnecessary chains into the true rest that all Christians should enjoy. Please learn from my mistakes that I will now address in the next chapter.

12

LEARN FROM MY MISTAKES

My experience with the Worldwide Church of God shows how a skewed gospel can lead well-meaning believers down a path of works. As a young man, I bought into the doctrines of the WCG; as a result, I spent the next thirty-six years of my live devoted to following and preaching a well-meaning but misguided partial gospel. My whole life was dedicated to and predicated upon a false understanding of the gospel and commission Christ gave us. I completely missed the other parts of the gospel—namely, how to rest in our New Covenant relationship with God and produce righteous fruit acceptable to Him. This caused me great pain and suffering.

Believing an incomplete gospel does not exclude you from salvation, as long as you believe and embrace the part about the sacrifice of Christ and look forward to eternity with him. However, the gospel you accept—whether true or only partially true—is critical, for it will determine your degree of joy and how well you are carrying out the God-ordained commission for His Church. It will entirely define how happily you live the rest of your life in service to God. I don't know what, if any, gospel you subscribe to, but you might well want to consider changing or joining a church that not only teaches but actually spearheads its outreach programs with the true gospel containing the New Covenant messages that Jesus gave his disciples.

Many churches seem to be championing as their main mission causes other than what Christ commanded of his Church. Christ said,

"Go ye into all the world, and preach the gospel to every creature" (Mark 16:15, KJV). There are many good causes out there, but they are false gospels if they have, in effect, replaced the true gospel message that Christ wanted preached. The reason for this can be well-meaning ignorance, but probably more often, it has a self-serving or social agenda at its core.

Many errant gospels are embraced by gullible, believing hearts that are taught a very limited understanding of the gospel of Christ. Most preachers of errant gospels also correctly preach the need for accepting the blood of Christ's sacrifice for the forgiveness of sin. The Scripture says, "Everyone who calls on the name of the Lord will be saved" (Rom. 10:13, BSB). Once new converts, at God's call, accept the saving power of the blood of Christ, they are born again and receive the new nature of Christ. They desire and strive to please God; however, because they are infants spiritually, if they are not being "fed" by their church a proper understanding of the depth and breadth of the gospel, their spiritual condition will remain that of an infant and will not mature as much as God desires.

Pastors and ministers should be teaching new converts all facets of the gospel. However, they can't teach what they don't know! If a new Christian is not being taught the beauty and peace that comes through the true gospel, that convert is not able to enjoy complete rest in the grace that Christ wants to provide him or her. Sadly, it is like blind ministers leading blind flocks. Their old selves are dead and they are alive in Christ (see Romans 6:11), but together they stumble down a distorted, torturous road of varying degrees of either legalistic works or unadulterated licentiousness.

Hopefully, my story can help prevent you from falling prey to this. Through this book, it is my hope that you will come to know what the true gospel message is so you won't get mired down in a false one. This knowledge can remove the blinders from your eyes so you don't waste your precious life in frustration and vain striving to please God or in wanton self-gratification.

Once you grasp a proper understanding of the gospel, you can begin to enjoy more fully the godly fruits of peace and joy that God's righteousness can bring. Rather than being an exhausted, unfulfilled, unhappy, bewildered Christian, you will be able to cast off your frustrations, doubts, and fears. You will be able to allow Christ to build His mind in you and produce the fruits He wants in your life. You can find the peace your heart desires and learn to finally rest in the joy of God's grace in the present, while looking forward to the glorious eternity God has for us in His future kingdom. You will then become a well-armed soldier and great warrior for God, correctly marching toward the coming kingdom of God, preaching the true commission God entrusted us to take to the world.

What Was My Mistake?

Where did I go wrong in believing the Worldwide Church of God's (WCG) gospel? There are two major answers to that question. First of all, the gospel of Christ preached to me was incomplete. Second, I gave too much faith and power to the ministry of the church, especially to Herbert W. Armstrong and his son Garner Ted Armstrong.

Let's first look at the matter of the partial gospel. At age twenty, I was looking for direction, purpose, and meaning in my life. I did not know the true gospel to begin with, so I was ripe for being misled with what seemed to be convincing, infallible arguments concerning the gospel. What I did not realize was that I was given only part of the gospel message the disciples were told by Christ to take to the world. Preaching the WCG's gospel meant speaking only about the coming kingdom of God as a witness to the world so that the end would come. This made the WCG unique among other churches, which also made for a nice member-recruiting tool. After all, who would not like to be a member of the end-time remnant of "the only true church of God on the face of the earth"? I don't think that the church leaders tried to deceive me; I think they believed what they taught. However, I think Satan deceived these leaders with incorrect doctrines and an incomplete gospel message.

Since Adam and Eve, Satan's driving mission has been to prevent God's true gospel from being preached to mankind. He has succeeded for the most part. Paul tells us, "The god of this age has blinded the minds of unbelievers so they cannot see the light of the gospel of the glory of Christ, who is the image of God" (2 Cor. 4:4, BSB). In spite of Satan's efforts, however, God has revealed His gospel to some. In every case where God has given mankind the gospel, Satan has tried to prevent it from being taught by them; and if he can't prevent it from being taught, he tries to pervert or distort it as much as possible.

The devil is the great deceiver, and he wants to make it difficult and burdensome for us to have Christ in our lives. He obscures or distorts the true gospel so he can spin you, a church congregation, or an entire denomination off into self-righteous works or self-indulgence, both of which are abhorrent to God and prevent the production of the abundant fruits He wants in our Christian lives. Satan hopes to discourage us and make our walk with God miserable enough that we might even give up on God altogether. The devil can deal us a lot of misery with half-truths.

Now, let's look at how I idolized the leaders of my church. The dynamic duo of Herbert W. and Garner Ted Armstrong, via *The World Tomorrow* radio program, convinced me that they headed the one and only true church of God on the face of the earth, so it was quite easy to stand in awe of these exceptionally intelligent, talented, and gifted men. After all, they were responsible for bringing me into "the knowledge of the truth" about God and His purpose for my life. Their speaking ability and knowledge of Scriptures along with their unique religious insight seemed profound and astounding. They spoke to my young mind many marvelous things about God, prophecy, and the purpose of life that I had never heard before.

Now, let me clearly state that I believe WCG and Herbert W. Armstrong were used by God to bring many to salvation. I just believe Armstrong required many legalistic doctrines that God does not! The major mistake I made was crediting these men with too much esteem and authority beyond what God intended. In effect, I gave them power and control of my mind, which should be yielded to none other than God. As a result, I no longer was able to think independently about matters in my life. The Armstrongs and their ministers became the final diviners and arbitrators of what I was to think, believe, and feel. I unconsciously transferred what psychologists call my "locus of control" over to them. "Locus of control refers to the extent to which people feel that they have control over the events that influence their lives. When you are dealing with a challenge in your life, do you feel that you have control over the outcome? Or do you believe that you are simply at the hands of outside forces? If you believe that you have control over what happens, then you have what psychologists refer to as an internal locus of control. If you believe that you have no control over what happens and that external variables are to blame, then you have what is known as an external locus of control."[1] At this point in my life, I had an external locus of control because I gave control of my life over to the Armstrongs and their ministers, believing they were directly speaking for God.

It is really an honored, yet intimidating, position that God grants a minister or pastor. I retained that title for twenty years, leading a total of eleven churches during that time period. It is a powerful position, in which you can do incredible good or harm to the people in your congregation.

The dissemination of God's truth concerning His love mysteries is a serious matter for any pastor or even a church member. However, those God holds most responsible are those in the ministry, for they are given the authority to teach the mysteries of God. Thus, they are the ones most responsible, and the guiltiest when abuses occur. They are the ones whom God has charged to enlighten and deepen our spiritual growth, not to cover up knowledge for personal gain. Jesus told Peter, "...Feed my sheep" (John 21:17b BSB). Jesus did not say, "Beat my sheep."

There are repercussions for those who have knowingly abused their positions of authority. There will be pastors who have retained incredible power and authority over their flocks who, because of their misuse and abuse of the position that God gave them, will be doorkeepers (a lowly position) in the kingdom of God. God does and will hold them to account.

God's Instruction to Pastors

Our great Shepherd, Jesus Christ, gave the creed that all ministers should strive to live by when He said:

> Be shepherds of God's flock that is among you, watching over
> them not out of compulsion, but because it is God's will; not

out of greed, but out of eagerness; not lording it over those entrusted to you, but being examples to the flock. And when the
Chief Shepherd appears, you will receive the crown of glory
that will never fade away. ~ Peter 5:2-4, BSB

According to Strong's Concordance the Greek word Peter used
above for "shepherds" is *poimainó*. Its short definition is "I shepherd,
tend."[2] The shepherds are to lead, care, and protect the flock. "Shepherd"
is a very appropriate term that pictures what a minister or pastor should
strive to emulate. He is one who cares for and watches over the sheep. He
is an example after whom the sheep willingly follow. A shepherd does not
hold the best-paying job in the community; likewise, ministers should not
be in the ministry for the money. Ministers are not to be taskmasters lording over and taking advantage of their flock. They are to be serving them.

While Jesus was at the Last Supper with His disciples, Scripture
tells us:

A dispute also arose among the disciples as to which of them
would be considered the greatest. So Jesus declared, "The
kings of the Gentiles lord it over them, and those in authority
over them call themselves benefactors. But you shall not be
like them. Instead, the greatest among you should be like the
youngest, and the one who leads like the one who serves. For
who is greater, the one who reclines at the table or the one who
serves? Is not the one who reclines? But I am among you as the
One who serves. ~ Luke 22:24-27, BSB

Jesus clearly paints the picture for all shepherds to emulate. Jesus
was the Master Shepherd and He served all He met throughout His ministry on earth. Should a modern-day church shepherd strive to do any less?

God's Warning to Pastors

Through the prophet Ezekiel God speaks to His shepherds who abuse
their congregations. God outlines the sins of these shepherds and pro-
nounces dire retributions on them. These wicked ministers are exposed

for their greed and selfishness. God said they feed themselves, leaving their people to starve for lack of hearing the God's words. God indicts them for neglecting the weak and sick; for not seeking those who have wandered away due to their negligence and thus are scattered and lost to be prey for wild beasts. God sternly warns them:

> Therefore, ye shepherds, hear the word of the LORD; *As* I live, saith the Lord GOD, surely because my flock became a prey, and my flock became meat to every beast of the field, because *there was* no shepherd, neither did my shepherds search for my flock, but the shepherds fed themselves, and fed not my flock; Therefore, O ye shepherds, hear the word of the LORD; Thus saith the Lord GOD; Behold, I *am* against the shepherds; and I will require my flock at their hand, and cause them to cease from feeding the flock; neither shall the shepherds feed themselves any more; for I will deliver my flock from their mouth, that they may not be meat for them. ~ Ezekiel 34:7-10, KJV

Always remember that there is only one perfect Shepherd and that is your Savior, Jesus Christ. Always remember to look to Jesus for the final word on what is truth. The more the line between Christ and a pastor is blurred, the more it fosters the idea that the pastor has more wisdom, spiritual knowledge, and authority than he actually does. This tends to elevate the pastor to a dangerous status, equal to that of an "Apostle" or even equal to or above Christ. The Christian needs to know the position and responsibility of their pastor is a grave matter that God does not take lightly. Church members should respect, not idolize, their minister or pastor. The church member should realize each pastor has gifts, strengths, and weaknesses. Every pastor is fallible. None of them have a perfected theology, nor do they have all the answers to life, no matter how much they may act like they do.

A pastor should encourage the individuality of the church members, feeding them spiritually nourishing truths of God. The pastor should be teaching and encouraging each member to grow spiritually strong in the "measure of the stature of ... Christ," not that of the pastor (Eph. 4:13, KJV). Pastors need to encourage individual members to recognize their spiritual gifts from God and to allow God to use their talents for Him, a process that will produce fruit in their lives that will benefit others. Pastors should be encouraging their flock to develop mental strength in Christ, so that they can stand alone, if necessary, as soldiers for Christ during times of trial.

One thing I know for sure is that a pastor-centered—rather than a Christ-centered—church has the potential to be extremely dangerous. Furthermore, if there is an individual (often recognized as the "Apostle") at the top of the church who stands between you and Christ, that is the most dangerous of all. Your locus of control should belong only to Christ, not to your pastor.

As God admonishes, each pastor should be striving to care for his or her flock. Their congregation should be growing in the knowledge, wisdom, and grace of God under their leadership. If these things are not happening, both the shepherd and the flock suffer!

Keep Your Eyes Open

There has been an explosion of many new, nondenominational, grace-based churches all over the world that have been started up by individual pastors. This is a good thing, but therein lies a potential danger: the "checks and balances" system inherent in many of the large, well-established, denominational churches is oftentimes greatly diminished. Just like Mr. Armstrong, the leaders of these new churches can create, pick, or choose whatever doctrines they wish in order to build whatever kind of Christian faith they wish to concoct. Also, it is sad to say, but it seems that some of these pastors treat the preaching of the gospel as a business and an easy way to make a great deal of money. Whereas some of them were poor when they started, they become multimillionaires in the preaching business.

There is an important point here that needs to be made. Going into ministry is a very wonderful thing if done with the right attitude and for the right reasons. In and of itself, there is no sin in being rich. The disciple Peter was in the business of fishing in order to make a living, but Jesus told him to switch businesses, so to speak; rather than fishing for his own profit, Jesus told him to fish for the profit of God (see Matthew 4:18-20). As long as a pastor can keep this in perspective, then the organizational structure of his church is not as important.

Beware, however: the more autocratic your church governing body is, the greater the danger for spiritual abuse of its members. The most dangerous type of church governmental structure is that of a "congregational single-elder polity."[3] More on this in the next chapter. This type of church is susceptible to clerical abuse because the pastor becomes, in effect, the executive director and owner of the church. Unscrupulous pastors gather around themselves those who agree and support their positions. They accordingly hire and fire their assistants, set their own salaries, and pretty well run the church the way they want. They don't have the constraints of anyone else telling them what they can or cannot do.

Ministerial Educational Requirements

You don't have to have an education in some theological college to begin preaching. As a matter of fact, you don't have to have any formal education at all. All you have to do is get a ministerial license, which is not hard to do, and start preaching. Becoming an ordained minister of God is not as difficult as perhaps most think. I just went online and did a search for "Christian ministerial licenses." The first website that popped up read, "Become Ordained Today." I opened the website and it read:

- Guide others on the path of God
- Run your own congregation
- Perform weddings, baptisms, and other ceremonies
- Valid in all 50 US states.[4]

I checked the next website listed in my search and it stated:

> Request your ordination here and your credentials will be included in the Clergy Pack. The total cost is this one time fee of

145

$78.00 for the Clergy Pack and it includes shipping. We ordain for life and there are no additional fees or renewal fees…. Satisfaction Guaranteed- If you are not completely satisfied simply email us a request for refund within 10 days.[5]

What a deal! For $78 you, too, could get into a possible multi-million-dollar business. About the only limiting factors you have to deal with are your drive, ambition, and talent in recruiting the masses to your cause. One thing is for sure—you can find some who will follow just about anything you want to preach. I know of few other businesses that you can start so cheaply, with no education, and potentially end up making a great deal of money.

Mega-Churches

The potential for money is certainly not the reason why anyone should become a minister and start his or her own church. As a matter of fact, ministers are notorious for having a very meager income. Most are totally dedicated to a life of service to God and His people and make far less money than what they could outside the ministry. I am sure most of those who do so have a right attitude and heart. However, all of God's ministers are human and thus they are not perfect. More than a few, after having built a huge financial empire and some mega-churches, have fallen into disgrace through moral or financial corruption. For instance, in Seoul, South Korea, it took Pastor David Yonggi Cho fifty-six years to build the world's largest mega-church, which "made him one of the most respected spiritual fathers in the Pentecostal movement."[6] However, sadly, he was found guilty of embezzling $12 million in church funds.[7]

Many ministries have grown worldwide through the use of radio and television broadcasting, just like the WCG grew in the mid-1900's. Some of these ministries have congregations that are mega-churches with tens of thousands attending services. This plus the many thousands and even millions more watching their television programs each week generates millions of dollars. Many of these pastors have achieved great fame, notoriety, and wealth. They are independent of the traditional churches like the Baptists, Methodists, Lutherans, Catholics, and Pentecostals. Generally speaking, most of these are totally independent of any control by any other church. They may have only one church. Others have spread out, having "satellite" congregations in nearby or even far-flung cities connected with instant video feeds from the pastor as he preaches at the main headquarters church. Many have websites where their services can be viewed at home anytime one wishes.

Are They Christian?

Many of these new churches have names that can be quite colorful and unique. Just a few examples include "The Church of the Harvest," "First Love Christian Fellowship," "Refiner's Touch," "Prayer Ministry," "New Beginnings Family Church," "Oasis Center Church," "Covenant Life Church," and "Generations Church." Am I against any of these churches? No! Not at all. I believe most of them are preaching a wonderful grace message with which I wholeheartedly agree. My message, in a nutshell, in this book is that you, at God's call, need to understand, accept, and believe in the gospel, and definitely go to church, but don't check your brain in at the front door when you walk into any church! For that matter, never check your brain in period to anybody, anywhere, except to Christ!

With all these new independent Christian churches, one might ask are they all of God? I believe most are. Whether or not they are, however, I believe the most basic point that needs to be realized concerning them, versus the recognized major denominations, is that there is a greatly increased possibility of spiritual abuse of their membership by those in authority. This is so because, more than we'd like to think, some are accountable only to themselves. I don't necessarily have a problem with any of them, as long as they are paying close attention to God's instruction and direction. However, I am urging Christians attending any of these churches to be aware of the organizational structure of the church and to maintain an external locus of control dedicated only to God and not to the pastor or church.

The Biggest Danger

I believe that the more independently authoritarian a church is, the greater the potential there is for abuse. When the determination of doctrine and the interpretation of the Word of God reside ultimately in the hands of only one man, watch out! It matters not what authoritarian label you give him as head of your church! You can call him an "Apostle," "Pastor General," or just "Pastor." When one man rules, it can be a catalyst that can do a great deal of harm to both the pastor and his congregation. The more the reins, power, and doctrine are restricted into the hands of one minister, the more potential there is for danger. I am just saying that in these instances, if you choose to be a part of such an organization, you need to be aware of the possibilities for trouble.

Corrupted Power

Remember the saying, "Power corrupts; absolute power corrupts absolutely."[8] There has been more than one movement that was started by a Mr. Nice Guy who ended up becoming a tyrant. If Lucifer, who was one of the most beautiful and powerful beings God has ever created, could eventually become corrupted by his own power and beauty, is it any wonder that a mere man could do the same?

This generally occurs when some guy starts his own church and forms a "governing board" of directors to which he is supposedly accountable, but which in actual fact has no control over him. In order for this pastor to maintain power and control, he may stack the governing board with a few close friends, his wife, and himself. When push comes to shove, in such a situation he will most likely win any issue and vote he favors. After all, he may reason that he did all the hard work of starting the church; he sure doesn't want to get fired in a few years in a dispute with the board. In this case his governing board is in effect nothing more than a cover for the fact that all final power and authority reside in his hands.

The guy with this kind of power is not going to want to advertise this. As a matter of fact, he'll tend to obscure that fact. The more secretive the matters of church government and finances are, the more suspect I would become. I'm not saying I'd jump ship, but the matter would ring a warning bell to be alert to what's going on. A healthy church is one that has and encourages a culture of openness.[9] A vigorous, healthy church wants input from its members and values their suggestions. It doesn't mind inquiries about its financial matters. It is a good thing to request financial transparency, if it is not freely offered:

> Churches and ministries are funded by donors, and donors have a God-given right to know that their funds are being used properly. Ministry leaders also have a God-given stewardship, and they must acknowledge that the funds given to them are not for personal gain. All financial transactions of a ministry should be scrutinized by designated leaders (including an outside accountant) to prevent corruption.[10]

If your church has an unspoken attitude or even a doctrine that basically says, "Touch not My anointed"[11] (see Chronicles 16:22), then you need to be concerned. Churches that teach this are trying to manipulate members:

> In an attempt to discourage any form of disagreement in the Church, insecure leaders tell their members that if they ever question Church authority, they are 'touching the Lord's anointed' and in danger of God's judgment. Let's call this what it is: spiritual manipulation. It creates worse problems by ruling out healthy discussion and mutual respect. Church members end up being abused or controlled—or even because they dare to ask a question.[12]

In this scenario, the pastor is accountable to no man but to God. I don't think I'd like to be in that situation if I were him. In my opinion, this is the definitive definition of a cult leader. The acid test for exposing such a dangerous authoritarian structure is to ask this question: Can the board or council of elders the pastor is supposedly accountable to actually fire the church "leader" if it is deemed in the best interests of the church or if it is obvious he is abusing his position of power in the church? Another important factor is that the checks and balance of power (namely the board that controls the pastor) need to reside in the hands of local members of the church rather than in the hands of some board of "cherry-picked friends" chosen by the pastor, with the board members living in far-flung areas outside the community in which the church resides. I would suggest at a minimum that the voting majority of the board membership should be local church members elected by the members. Would this ensure no spiritual abuse of members would occur? No! But it certainly would help prevent it.

Controlling Authoritarianism

If your church's course is effectively under the control of one man, and he is the judge and jury of what goes on in your church, he then is in reality the only one at the helm of your church. If this is the case, then be aware! You have a right to know if this is the case. If you don't know, I suggest you should investigate in order to know what type of organizational structure you are supporting financially and living under spiritually. If you choose to remain in such an authoritarian church structure, then you need to be on special alert for any deviation from that which is scriptural. Are these churches Christian? I believe so if they believe in and accepted God's call to the salvation of Jesus Christ. I suggest, however, that you never allow yourself to take the pastor's word on any matter as final if it contradicts the Word of God or if you have reservations about what he or she advocates. You need to maintain a healthy amount of internal locus of control.

At times it may be difficult to know if what your pastor is advocating is of God. It would be best in that situation to discuss the issue in question with the pastor, friends, relatives, and perhaps even with ministers from other Christian denominations. Be careful in these authoritarian church structures because history is strewn with examples of horrible abuses committed by priests and pastors upon their members. Many of those abused were filled with physical and mental pain by a religious authoritarian who claimed to know the will of God for the lives of his or her followers. What is it in the human heart that would cause one to give such power to another human being? I guess I should know the answer to that question, for that is exactly what I did for thirty-six years of my life! But you know, I'm really not sure what that answer is. I have a few ideas why, but I am still pondering the insanity of it all.

Authoritarianism Run Amok

There have been many examples throughout history where churches started out in a good and godly way, only to end very tragically. Light authoritarianism can eventually lead to abusive extremism. There are many such stories that have ended in terrible disasters for church members. One of the most memorable in recent history was the Waco Massacre in 1993, where seventy-six members of the Branch Davidian Church led by David Koresh died in a fiery siege by federal, state, and military law enforcement personnel.[13] Just years prior to that, 918 church members under the direction of their church leader, Jim Jones, committed mass suicide by drinking cyanide laced Kool-Aid. This occurred in a settlement called Jonestown in Guyana, Africa, run by an American church organization.[14] Obviously, too much authority and power was given to these leaders by their church membership. Yes, these are extreme examples and unlikely to happen to you; but just be on guard anyway.

So, what about Paul's statement, "Obey your leaders and submit to them, for they watch over your souls as those who must give an account" (Heb. 13:17a, BSB)? That is absolutely true! But is Paul telling you to become a robot, to put aside your own common sense, your own free will and thinking mind, and to turn control of yourself over to another person? No, absolutely not! Paul did not say to take every word of your pastor as the inspired word and command of God. As a matter of fact, Paul cautions us to beware of false prophets and pastors who come into the Church. That's apparently what happened in the case of the Waco Massacre and the mass suicide in Jonestown. Sure, we are to respect our pastors, but we also always need to be aware that they are flawed and therefore never allow them to become the final word or arbitrator of truth for us. Christ should be the only real truth for each of us.

Our Responsibility As Church Members

Our responsibility is this: "Make every effort to present yourself approved to God, an unashamed workman who accurately handles the word of truth" (2 Tim. 2:15, BSB). And again, "you have known the holy Scriptures which are able to make you wise for salvation through faith, which is in Christ Jesus [not your local pastor]" (2 Tim. 3:15, WEB).

Finally, I suggest you double check anything preached to you by your ministers. Even the apostle Paul's words were questioned and not accepted until proven in the Scriptures: "Now the Bereans were more noble-minded than the Thessalonians, for they received the message with great eagerness and examined the Scriptures every day to see if these teachings were true" (Acts 17:11, BSB). It is interesting that God noted these guys were "more noble" for doing so!

I believe the following is good advice for all Christians. J. Lee Grady, the former editor of *Charisma* magazine, wrote:

> I'm aware that since the charismatic movement began in the 1960s, people have misused the gifts of the Spirit and twisted God's Word to promote strange doctrines or practices. Seeing these errors never caused me to question the authenticity of what the Holy Spirit had done in my life. But I knew I had to stay true to God's Word and reject any false teachings I encountered. My simple rule is based on 1 Thessalonians 5:21-22: "But examine everything carefully; hold fast to that which is good; abstain from every form of evil" (NASB). In other words: Eat the meat and spit out the bones.[15]

That advice sounds wise to me. That's exactly what sheep do when led to green pastures by the shepherd. They don't spit out the bones, but they do excrete the waste. Don't just accept everything your pastor tells you. At times it is necessary to prove its voracity by going to other sources, primarily the Scriptures, but it also may be helpful to talk to ministers from other denomination. It may be wise to bounce an issue off friends, family, and authorities You must take responsibility for any final thought you have or action you do. You need to recognize this weakness in your nature. I believe there is a law in man's nature that reads: "No one ever wants to be responsible for anything, unless it is good!" You naturally to want to be able to blame it on the other guy if anything you do turns out bad.

However, we might as well face the facts. After Christ's return, when we have been caught up to be with Him in His Kingdom for all eternity, there will come a day on which God will reward each of us for the amount of fruit we allowed Him to produce in our lives as mortals. God designed each of us with potentials and gifts that He wants us to let Him fulfill in us. It would be good to know this truth on this side of the kingdom and not after we get there. Although God created us able to become all that He wants us to be, He will not force us to let Him utilize the gifts He gave us or force us to allow Him to produce righteous fruits in our lives. God will reward us proportionately according to what we have allowed Him to use of the potential He gave us. On that day each of us will stand before God, not to be scorned or condemned but to be congratulated and given eternal rewards and positions of authority in God's kingdom. When your turn comes to stand before God, it will only be you! It won't be you and your neighbor or pastor

Even though the leaders of the Church will be held to a much greater degree of accountability, each lay member of the body of Christ is also responsible to God for striving to walk in the light He gives each one of us. Don't you believe God can write His Love Law into your heart in spite of your local pastor, when necessary? Take control of and be responsible for your daily living as best you can under God's guidance. The New Covenant clearly shows that God is directly communing with each of His children and writing His Love Law in each of our hearts. Let each of us strive to hear and follow what God has to say to us.

At this point, let's consider in the next chapter what the right church, if any, might be for you to consider joining. One might ask, what difference does it make, as long as you go to church? Yes, it does make a difference. It can make a big difference in your spiritual growth, joy, and rest as a Christian.

13

THE RIGHT CHURCH FOR YOU

Considering the thousands of Christian religious denominations around the world, it is no wonder that there are many differing church governmental structures. The spectrum varies widely from the extreme of a hierarchical church structure under the sole rule of one man to completely autonomous churches with no hierarchical structure at all. The vacuum between these two extremes is filled with various combinations and forms of governance being administered through various individuals, including deacons, elders, ministers, pastors, priests, bishops, archbishops, popes, patriarchs, and many others. All of these titles denote ranks, duties, and responsibilities within a church. Some churches use boards composed of selected members as checks and balances to monitor and decide matters concerning the church.

It can be bewildering trying to understand, much less find a church that is right for you from among the many thousands of differing Christian churches around the world. This is probably not a real big problem for most people, because I don't think most Christians give a great deal of thought to the governmental structure of the church they attend. Many just attend the denomination they grew up in with their family. Others begin attending the one in which they became "saved." Still others go with a friend to church and begin attending there. Probably few have ever sat down and considered under which governing environment they think their spiritual nourishment and growth would be best served. It really doesn't matter what circumstance in life brings you to Christ. It only matters that you accept God's offer of salvation, whether it is inside or outside of a church building. The main factor, no matter what your circumstance may be, is that as long as you grasp and embrace the spiritual reality that Jesus Christ died for your sins and is offering you eternal salvation, then you are saved!

No matter whatever circumstance you find yourself in, good or bad, when you accept Jesus Christ as your Savior, you are admonished by the Scripture, "Therefore, just as you have received Christ Jesus as Lord, continue to live in Him" (Col. 2:6, BSB). Start from there and strive to live each day of the rest of your life as Christ and the Scriptures guide you. As the next verse of Colossians encourages us to be, "rooted and built up in Him, established in the faith as you were taught, and overflowing with thankfulness" (Col.. 2:7, BSB). Your salvation does not depend on your favorite pastor or being in this or that denomination. It is a personal matter between you and God. The church is provided to assist your spiritual growth, and it is best if you find one in which you feel spiritually nourished and happy. Because of circumstances, you may or may not join a local congregation. You may join one only to find later that another will spiritually feed you much better. In reality, there is only one body of Christ. However, He has allowed it to exist under different congregations and names. It's not the church building that saves you. It is Jesus Christ, who is the true Church.

Once an individual has received God's invitation through the gospel message and accepted Christ as his or her savior, he or she is given the Spirit of God, which contains the very nature of God. A new creation infused with God's nature is then born as a son or daughter of God. This new born child of God is to grow daily more in the likeness of Christ. This spiritual growth is best facilitated in a good, Christ-centered, local, grace-based, New Covenant church devoid of Old Covenant legalistic "works of righteousness."

The Church of Christ is His body. This body of Christ is called by thousands of different names around the world. These many congregations of Christ are all a part of the one spiritual body of Christ. Rather than naming any church around the world, I will refer to all Christians, be they Catholic, Baptist, Methodist, Pentecostal, or any other denomination, as the body of Christ. I actually like that terminology, for it is a much more unifying term and more accurately describes all the Christians worldwide who make up Christ's Church.

For the purpose of making this point, I will in the next few paragraphs refer to the many local churches as "congregations" rather than "churches," no matter what name they call themselves. Are all who call themselves members of those various congregations born-again Christians? No! There generally are a few that attend that are not. They attend with the body of believers for various selfish reasons, but they are not members of the body of Christ. God knows those who have truly accepted His gospel of salvation, and I believe He will only give new birth to those who truly believe and appreciate the sacrifice of Jesus.

The Body Of Christ

The body of Christ is made up of born-again Christians attending local congregations and Christians who do not attend any local congregation for one reason or another. All of these people comprise the total body of Christ. Are all pastors of these congregations born-again Christians? No, they are not! Most are, but Jesus warned, "Beware of false prophets. They come to you in sheep's clothing, but inwardly they are ravenous wolves" (Matt. 7:15, BSB). Again Peter said, "…there will be false teachers among you. They will secretly introduce destructive heresies, even denying the sovereign Lord who bought them--bringing swift destruction on themselves" (2 Pet. 2:1b-2, BSB). And again John said, "Dear friends, do not believe every spirit, but test the spirits to see whether they are from God, because many false prophets have gone out into the world" (1 John 4:1, BSB).

Is it possible for you to be born again in one of the congregation of a pastor who is not born again? Yes, because if you accept the message of the gospel, it matters not who brought it to you. Remember John told Jesus, "'Master,' said John, 'we saw someone driving out demons in Your name, and we tried to stop him, because he does not accompany us.' 'Do not stop him,' Jesus replied, 'for whoever is not against you is for you'"

(Luke 9:49-50, BSB). The point is that your congregation does not have an exclusive corner on Christ! That may be a shock to you. It sure was to me when I finally came to this realization after twenty-some years of service as a minister for the WCG. It meant many things, but one thing for sure was that it meant I could choose to move on to a different congregation if I felt I could better serve there and be more spiritually nourished. There are many congregations that worship with thousands of different names, but there is only one body of Christ! Some congregations are more Christ-centered and spiritually nourishing than others. It may therefore be to your advantage to consider which ones those might be.

Salvation transcends the messenger. Salvation comes through believing faith in the sacrifice of Christ. Salvation is a matter between you and Christ, no matter who teaches it to you. The one who teaches you does not even have to be a born-again Christian! If you accept God's call, Christ will save you in spite of the messenger!

Do You Need To Go To A Church?

It is obvious that Christ has allowed His body to evolve into over two thousand denominations and nondenominational congregations calling themselves about every name you can think of. These many different names are not unifying in nature but divisive. It seems obvious that the many different beliefs and differences in doctrines in all these congregations will be resolved only after the return of Jesus Christ.

Can an individual come to the knowledge of Christ's saving grace and be made a member of the body of Christ in a congregation that does not spearhead with or advance the gospel of salvation? Yes! It is even possible for an individual who does not attend a congregation, to come to salvation through a friend, TV pastor, or other source. However, I would suggest that an individual find a Christ-centered, gospel-preaching congregation with whom to fellowship. It is God's intention that local congregations are to help in the maturation process of the saint. The congregation's purpose is to spread the gospel message of salvation in Christ and to provide a loving and caring environment to help promote spiritual growth and support for all Christians attending. Paul states:

> And it was He [Christ] who gave some to be apostles, some to be prophets, some to be evangelists, and some to be pastors and teachers, to equip the saints for works of ministry, to build up the body of Christ, until we all reach unity in the faith and in the knowledge of the Son of God, as we mature to the full measure of the stature of Christ. Then we will no longer be infants, tossed about by the waves and carried around by every wind of teaching and by the clever cunning of men in their deceitful scheming. Instead, speaking the truth in love, we will in all things grow up into Christ Himself, who is the head. From Him the whole body is fitted and held together by every supporting ligament. And as each individual part does its work, the body grows and builds itself up in love. ~ Ephesians 4:11-16, BSB

The task of a Christian in choosing a congregation to join can be a daunting chore. Pardon the analogy, but it is true, it seems there is about every kind of lollipop to fit the individual's desired size, color, type, and taste imaginable to choose from in a congregation. If you don't like or agree with the congregation you are attending, you can go and find one that you do like. Moving to a different church might be a good idea if and when you find out the one you are attending is not Christ-centered and is not preaching the gospel as its primary outreach. You probably could find more spiritual encouragement and nourishment in another congregation that is New Covenant Christ centered. The main criteria should be a congregation where you can best serve others and grow spiritually in the measure and stature of Jesus Christ.

It might be advisable to shop around by visiting a variety of types of congregations. After leaving the WCG's fellowship in 1998, I virtually stopped attending church for about ten years. At the sporadic times when I did go, it was for my wife's sake. She certainly was walking closer to Christ than I was during those years. Yes, I was still a Christian; however, I had become extremely disillusioned, quiet, cynical, and very disdainful of all "churches." I no longer wanted, nor felt the need, to attend any organized church.

After my disastrous experience with the autocratic rule of the WCG, I did not want any part of another church organization. It was just God and me staggering down life's road together. Just to be clear, God wasn't staggering, but I was! At the time, having walked down an abusive religious pathway that seemed to have dead-ended, I must admit I was even a bit suspicious of God as well! Did I still believe in Christ? Yes! Did I believe I had to be a part of any church organization? No. Did I grow spiritually during that time? No, not much, if any. However, the jolting death of my wife in September of 2009 woke me up. An overpowering and deep, burning need to get as close to Christ as I could overwhelmed me, as well a need to begin attending church services again. I was severely broken and shaken to the core after my lovely wife died. At that point I felt quite weak and vulnerable. I needed the spiritual strength and support that I knew could come only from God to make it through each day. I spent about two years going from congregation to congregation in order to find a church that I felt comfortable attending.

Due to my past experience with the WCG's hierarchical governmental structure, I did not want to become involved with another one with rule from one man down. [Update: The entirety of this chapter was written about three years ago. Since that time the church I speak of in this chapter was disbanded. I now co-shepherd a newly established church called the Grace and Truth Church in Cordell, Oklahoma. Now let's return to where I was three years ago.] After my time of searching, I finally found a church in which I have been continually well fed and spiritually satisfied. Ironically, as best as I can tell, it essentially is run by one man from the top down. Strangely enough, I have no problem with that, as long as he stays Christ centered. I believe my pastor and his wife are deeply dedicated to serving God and those He has entrusted to their care. Both are dynamic preachers week after week, preaching strong, encouraging, and spiritually nourishing food. Are they perfect? No. But I greatly love and respect both of them and I have been truly blessed to have them in my life.

I have come to realize that it is possible that an autocratic rule in a congregation can actually have its advantages. With it you can cut through the red tape that actually burdens many churches' ability to assist their members to "become mature, attaining to the whole measure of the fullness of Christ." In some congregations, stagnating governmental structures actually retard the movement of the gospel message forward in their communities.

I eagerly look forward to attending services each Sunday and supporting the needs of this local congregation of the worldwide Body of Christ, as Christ gives me direction. My pastor and his lovely wife have had a profound effect in helping the healing of my past legalistic wounds. The new friends I have found and the loving support I have been able to share with my newfound brothers and sisters have helped us to grow spiritually together.

If you are a Christian and are without a home church to attend, I encourage you to find a one that will love you and spiritually feed you. There are many Christians who for one reason or another are unable to attend a church. If that is the case for you, do not despair. Don't forget the thief on the cross with Christ; he never did attend a church service, but he is now in paradise with Christ. Just as the thief, when God calls and you repent and believe in Jesus, accepting His offer of eternal life and the fact that all your sins, past, present, and future, are forgiven, you are born again entering the New Covenant relationship with Christ. Whether or not you are attending a church, you will have eternal life and will be in the coming Kingdom of God. However, there is great comfort in sharing the love of Christ with brothers and sisters in a local church. God does not demand it, but that is His desire for you if you are able.

After our salvation, it is the "fruits" of Christ that God wants to share with us and produce in us for the benefit of not only ourselves but others as well. This fruit production is best encouraged and accomplished through our attendance at one of Christ's local congregations. Christ is returning not only to give you a new eternal body but also to harvest the fruit that you have allowed Him to produce in you. There is nothing like being lifted up and encouraged, not only by the pastor but also by your new brothers and sisters in Christ. There is also nothing like being able to encourage other members and even perhaps bring someone else in your life to salvation.

Governmental Types

I feel a need to briefly touch on the various types of Christian churches you have to choose from. I believe it is important to be aware of the type you might want to join or, as the case may be, the type you are associated with now. Some of you may not be aware that these various structures exist. As I have already said, I believe most people pay little attention to the governmental structure of the church that they join or are already a part of. If you are happy where you are, then this knowledge may simply confirm that you are in the right place. If you have not joined a Church yet, however, I think it is wise to consider the governmental structures available to you prior to committing yourself to any one church. The structure of a church does not define whether it is a part of the body of Christ. Neither does a governmental type define your salvation. However, you may feel more comfortable under one type of structure than another, and it is wise to consider all of the options.

Perhaps I can help narrow your search for a possible church by giving a brief synopsis of them. This may help to point you in the right direction in selecting one. In selecting a church, we can broadly categorize the existing churches into three recognized polities, or types of church governments; that of Episcopalian, Presbyterian, and Congregationalist.[1]

First we'll consider the Episcopalian model. "Episcopal polity is the predominant pattern in Catholic, Eastern Orthodox, Oriental Orthodox and Anglican Churches. It is also common in some Methodist and Lutheran Churches, as well as amongst some of the African American Pentecostal traditions in the United States such as the Church of God in Christ and the Full Gospel Baptist Church Fellowship."[2] Basically, you have a hierarchical structure with rule from the top down through a bishop who governs and is superior to other officers of the local churches under his authority. Many churches modeled after this type have "an archbishop which has authority over many (or all) other bishops."[3] For instance, the highest ecclesiastical office for the Roman Catholic Church is the Bishop of Rome, which is the Pope. A similar structure holds in the Orthodox Church. "The Patriarch of Alexandria is the archbishop of

Alexandria, and Cairo, Egypt. Historically, this office has included the designation pope (etymologically 'Father', like 'Abbot'). For the Coptic Christians it is the Bishop of Alexandria."[4]

It is interesting to note at this point that you really can't paint a major church, such as the Baptist, with one type of governmental brush by saying all Baptists are Congregationalist: "Although most Baptist groups are congregationalist in polity, some have different ecclesiastical organization and adopt an Episcopal polity governance. In those Churches the local congregation has less autonomy and the bishop oversees them, assigning pastors and distributing funds."[5] It can get even more confusing when you realize some nondenominational churches do some mixing of the types of governance. For instance, they may govern themselves with a mixing of Presbyterian and Congregationalist polity. This makes it difficult to label them as having a certain governmental type.

The second major type of church structure is the Presbyterian. Merriam-Webster defines this as: "characterized by a graded system of representative ecclesiastical bodies (as presbyteries) exercising legislative and judicial powers."[6] This type of church is basically ruled from the bottom up. The local congregations elect "elders" (often called a session) that govern the local church.[7] The pastor is considered one of the elders, with equal authority.[8] A presbytery is formed from members of the various sessions from the local churches in a geographical area, and generally has ruling authority over these churches.[9] From there, "some members of the presbytery are in turn members of the 'general assembly' which usually have authority over all the Churches in a region or nation."[10] The Presbyterian Church and many nondenominational churches utilize this type of government. For instance, the Seventh-day Adventist Church "is based on democratic representation, and therefore resembles the Presbyterian system of Church organization."[11] In some nondenominational churches there is a mixture of the Presbyterian and the Congregational model of governance.

The third major polity type is the "Congregational" model. Its beginnings date back to the sixteenth century in England.[12] This type of church government is probably the most popular type among "contemporary" churches.[13] This type is the most independent of all governmental structures, with each congregation as an "autonomous" law unto itself; hopefully as directed under Christ, of course. Each congregation is totally independent and self-ruling. There is a wide spectrum even within this type of church governance. Some of the tried and true, long-established churches who, for the most part, are Congregationalist are Baptists, the Quakers, Congregational churches, and many nondenominational churches.[14]

This type of church government can paradoxically produce some of the most exciting and fastest growing churches in the world, yet on the other hand, it is more subject to the possibility of heretical teachings, beliefs, and abuses. The more truly Christ-centered it and its leaders are, the less likely this problem is to exist. One fundamental strength and paradoxical weakness in the congregational form of governance is who finally decides the teachings, beliefs, and direction the Church will go. If power resides in a Christ-centered individual or in a few elders of a local board, the church is more nimble and able to move with projects that are deemed to further its gospel outreach to its members, its community, and even the nation. It is less entrenched and encumbered in the "pomp and circumstance" of church traditions that might be more difficult to change, when needed, in the other two types of church government. There are several types of government exercised by the Congregationalist churches. However, the two most prevalent popular types are the "single elder" and "plural local elders."[15]

Obviously, there is no perfect form of governmental rule that exists within the Body of Christ. All forms require faith on the part of their members. It is interesting that it is God who has allowed His ministers to set it up that way. The weakness here is that human nature tends to make it easier for us to look to a man than to Christ for spiritual answers and direction. To a certain extent this is good, but we must always keep our eyes on Jesus and His word for direction in our thoughts and actions. We should follow our pastor only as he follows our Savior. Perhaps God allows these different types of governance in order to teach us to respect and trust a man up to only a certain point, and to help us learn to recognize human frailties and look beyond men, resting our ultimate faith in Christ. We need to maintain a proper perspective of our ministers. We should respect their office, but we must be careful to look to them only as far as they follow Jesus Christ.

Be Careful Here

Of all the possible types of church government, the most vulnerable to corruption is that which resides in some of the Congregationalists. I call it the absolute "single elder" model, which is headed by a man who has total control of the local church. This single elder- or pastor-led model is:

> ...led by a single elder/pastor, [and] primary leadership in all decisions and doctrinal determinations is vested in a single leader.... Typically, this leader also performs the duties of a senior pastor/minister and provides the preaching and teaching ministries for the Church in addition to administrative leadership. Often, a congregational Church led by a single elder/ pastor was founded by that singular leader or by a previous singular leader who appointed the present leader.[16]

This is more troublesome, in my opinion, than all of the other Congregationalists models. I'm not saying, however, that you should not consider this model. It's sort of like a double-edged sword. On one hand, it could be deadly, and on the other it could be the most spiritually focused, joy-filled, exciting, gospel-preaching, and spiritually fruit-producing church on the face of the earth. I'm just saying, "Be careful!" Generally this "single elder" type starts "his own church" and controls every aspect of the church's activities. This type of "single elder" requires more faith of members to follow as an all-powerful leader who in effect has absolute control and rule of the local church. This type of rule is probably more difficult to detect than others. First of all, its governmental structure is most likely not made obvious to the church members. Its organizational structure and financial accountability most likely will be least open to scrutiny by the members. It is possible a "sham board" of elders could exist that, in essence, acts as a cover obfuscating the fact that the "single elder" actually maintains absolute control.

If there is a church board to which the single elder is "account-able," it becomes even more suspect and troublesome if no local church members sit on the "board of the church," or if they are a voting minori-ty. If the church does have a local board and the single elder has the ulti-mate authority to appoint and dismiss members of the board, this could be problematic. It certainly would be if the single elder has the power to countermand the voting majority of his board! Most troublesome of all would be if no one could fire the "single elder" for malfeasance! Would I ever belong to a church like this? Yes, if it is obvious the single elder is producing a great deal of spiritual fruit in his ministry, and if I had a great deal of faith in the spiritual integrity of that elder. With this being said, however, I'd sure be keeping a careful eye on the single elder, and I'd have my bags packed and be ready to move on to another church, if need be!

A Better Governing Model

I believe the best model might be that based on the "plural local elders" con-cept.[17] In short, the "plural local elders" governance model is comprised of a group of leaders selected by and from the local congregation who togeth-er have the same basic powers as does a "single elder" model.[18] This helps mollify the power of a single individual and inserts more accountability, balance, and protection for all members of the congregation.[19] No matter what form of government is set up in the church, I would recommend that ultimate power rest in the hands of at least a two-thirds majority of the voting members of the church. The senior pastor or pastors, as well as any boards, deacons, and elders, should ultimately be accountable to the vot-ing members of the church. To change or remove these individuals should probably require a three-fourths majority.

> History has shown that where authority is concentrated on a single person in top leadership level, it has resulted in a dis-proportionate high number of moral failures. The 'single elder' form suffers from a lack of mutual accountability. Many in this position can also suffer from excessive demands laid on them

by the Church. I believe it is this deficiency that has given rise to the plural local elder form of government. This form effectively preserves the pattern of plural elders while restricting authority to the local congregation.[20]

I suppose that the governmental structure of the WCG that I was a member of for three and a half decades was in actual practice that of the Episcopalian model. It exercises the most extreme of the authoritarian rule as described above by a "single elder." This is almost exactly like the dictatorial rule of Herbert W. Armstrong's church. In my opinion, the two are actually the same, which is Episcopal in polity and was actually more autocratic than the rule of the Pope in Rome. At least the Pope was elected to his position by the College of Cardinals. The single elder and Mr. Armstrong were not elected; they began their own church from scratch and maintained total control of it. It is interesting that even the Pope relies on advice concerning matters governing the Universal Church from eight cardinals selected from around the world.[21] The Pope can't be fired for any reason;[22] neither can the sovereign authoritarian Single Elder. I guess they both have that one thing in common. Of all the hundreds of WCG congregations that existed around the world, none of them were self-regulating and independent of the worldwide headquarters located in Pasadena, California. In effect, Herbert W. Armstrong was the "Pope" of the WCG. Absolute rule of all congregations around the world ultimately resided in the hands of this one man.

We must face it, until the return of Christ, this maze of differing and fighting churches will remain. And as I said, there is no perfect governmental type on earth. All of them contain born-again Christians belonging to the worldwide body of Christ. But some churches are much healthier than others for preaching of the gospel and caring for the well-being, and fruitful growth of their members. No matter the size of a church and how well it is established in a community, it could be cold and near spiritual death, with few fruits of God's love being produced in the Church and in the lives of its membership. Furthermore, in spite of all I've said so far, it is also possible that a church under authoritarian single-elder rule could be as healthy and nourishing as any church polity in the body of Christ. It just depends on how truly the single elder follows the lead of his only recognized head, Jesus Christ!

The elders are shepherds over the flock under Christ. As newly born children of God, we are to look to the body of Christ to nourish us with the sweet milk of God's Word to strengthen us and mature us as we grow into Christ's likeness. It is obvious from the many different congregations of Christ available to do that job that it is up to us to be in control of choosing which one we want to feed and nourish us. In the next chapter we will see why our church is so important to properly nourish us. For each of God's children on earth, He has given wonderful gifts which He wants them to enjoy and share with Him and others. The very purpose of the church is to proclaim the gospel and to feed and nourish its flock to encourage the growth and production of fruits to be enjoyed by others. That is the purpose of a Christian's fleshly journey on this earth as he or she waits for the coming resurrection to eternal glory. Let's discuss this next.

14

OUR EARTHLY JOURNEY WITH GOD

Although much of the story of my Christian walk features extreme legalism practiced in naive ignorance, who am I to decry the road on which God has seen fit to lead me in this life? I now see God's hand in my spiritual journey and understand its purpose. From beginning to end, I strove to seek after the truth of God as He revealed it to me along the way. As a result, though I ignorantly walked into the sludge pit of legalism, I eventually walked out of it, because with each step my heart continually yearned for and sought after the truths of God's mysteries.

We each have our own path to walk in this life in following Christ. Our spiritual journey was meant to be one of continually moving out of darkness into more of the light of Christ. As we see Him better, we are to be constantly adjusting our wrong perceptions of Christ and allowing Him to mold us more into who God wants us to be. We call this "the transformation process." Scripture describes it this way: "Now the Lord is the Spirit, and where the Spirit of the Lord is, there is freedom. And we, who with unveiled faces all reflect the glory of the Lord, are being transformed into His image with intensifying glory, which comes from the Lord, who is the Spirit." (2 Cor. 3:17-18, BSB).

Our Christian learning process is unending from the time we are saved to the time we die or are raised at Christ's return (see Philippians 1:6). Our entire spiritual journey is one of continually growing from spiritual infancy toward the maturity of Christ. This requires us to constantly be changing by allowing Christ to transform the old wrong satanic programming of our minds (our flesh) from the past and present with its exhibited sins, misunderstandings, vain imaginations, habits, and "self-righteous" concepts, which are contrary to Christ. As we allow Christ to eradicate the "old man" in us produced by Satan, we experience God's continual transformation process of molding us more and more into the very mental image of Jesus Christ. In our daily walking and talking with Christ, we are continually increasing in our ability to think, feel, and act just like Him.

Spiritual Blinders

Many years ago, when horses were used to pull a wagon or plow for a farmer, blinders were often put on the sides of the horse's eyes. This was done to keep his eyes on the road straight ahead and help prevent the horse from becoming distracted. As a result, the horse did not have a full view of the countryside in which he traveled. It is amazing how many of us wear spiritual blinders, either that we put on ourselves or that someone else put on us. We see only the narrow road ahead of us, although there is much more unobserved scenery on both sides of our narrow view of the road. Our blinders make it nearly impossible for our beliefs about reality to be challenged in any way. We can't or don't want to see anything contrary to our preconceived beliefs, whether right or wrong. It's like saying, "Don't confuse me with the facts, my mind is already made up! I have too much invested in my past and present reality, so I don't want to change!"

Growing in Christ is not always easy, because it sometimes means admitting that we have been wrong or ignorant about certain things and must change our way of thinking. We don't like to admit we are wrong. Change is difficult, and we often avoid it by our clinging to erroneous beliefs. It is an odd quirk of human nature that the more a person has invested in a certain way of living, thinking, and doing, the more difficult it is for him to admit the error of his ways and make a change—even when his ways create very miserable circumstances in his life.

A good example of the difficulty of removing blinders is when

God brought the Worldwide Church of God to a much deeper under-standing of His grace, and the church completely repudiated all of its ties to the Old Covenant legalism and its ensuing works. I was amazed that so many pastors and their congregations refused to acknowledge the new understanding of grace in the New Covenant. For me God had removed the blinders of legalism, and it seemed as plain as the proverbi-al "nose on your face" that we had been horribly wrong. I wondered why in the world so many of my fellow ministers and church members could not see the glorious new freedom in Christ being revealed. I believe a lot of it had to do with spiritual blinders.

As with the pharisaical priesthood of Jesus' day, whole lives had been invested into a righteousness produced by a legalistic system, think-ing that it was God's righteousness and therefore its followers would be granted eternal life someday. Over the decades, many had stacked up a lot of self-righteous works that would have to be thrown away as a bunch of garbage if they acknowledged the new truths. If they admitted they had been wrong, a great deal of "eating crow" would be in order, along with drastic changes in their lives. Yes, the whole process of being able to admit errors and change was not easy. The changes to be made were stunning and earth shattering to our old worldview of our faith, to say the least. No, it was not easy to admit we were wrong, and many did not! We had long prided ourselves in living by the revealed truth of God. We felt we had all truth already wrapped up in one neat little package. Admitting that this was wrong would require, in a sense, starting our walk with God all over again from scratch; which many were not willing to do.

I feel anyone who honestly studied the new understandings with an open mind and followed the truth should have been willing to make any change that God would want. I think for many who were not willing, it was simply due to their inability to admit that they had been wrong. Satan's previous programing of our fleshly minds remains hostile to God and, therefore, makes it hard for us to admit that we have been wrong. After all, when we have spent years and even decades building a house of righteousness cards composed of many human efforts and self-righ-teous works, it is not easy to simply admit we were wrong for the most part. Another big factor is simply that our human flesh wants to earn our salvation and righteousness our own way. We wanted to be in control of producing righteousness brick by brick by our actions. Relying on God to do that is a bit scarier. It is difficult to believe that God will write His laws, thoughts, and character into our hearts as He promised He would do in the New Covenant. It takes faith that God can and will do that in us by the many trials we face in our daily Christian lives. We simply can't take the love that Christ offers with no strings attached. It is just too much to believe eternal salvation in Christ could be so simple as to just change one's mind and embrace the forgiveness God has already given us in Christ.

Many in the WCG, like me, had spent decades working hard to keep the Sabbath, the Ten Commandments, and the Old Testament Holy Days; tithing; not eating "unclean" meats like pork and catfish; not keeping the "pagan holidays" of Christmas, Easter; and on and on I could go. We had built up a fairly large storehouse of what we felt were righteous works and had a lot invested in this way of living. Our righteousness was a double-edged sword. On the one hand, it was comforting that I could do things that made me "feel" righteous. On the other hand, checking things off the righteous "to-do list" was burdensome and exhausting and produced guilt when not all of it was accomplished. Additionally, it was easy to feel guilty because of the sins of omission, leaving me always feeling I could have done more or might not have done enough.

By nature humans have a very deeply ingrained basic trait: when we are given something, we feel we must give something back. Haven't you noticed how hard it is to receive a gift from anyone without feeling you should also give something in return? If someone buys you a meal, you feel you should buy his or hers next time. That person probably believes you should too! If someone slaps you, you naturally want to slap that person back. That's just the way it is when we walk after the flesh in this world; it is a "give in order to get," "this for that," "tit for tat" mentality.

Many people also try to earn salvation and righteousness that way. They simply can't take the love that Christ offers with no strings attached. It is just too much for them to believe that eternal salvation in Christ could be so simple as to just change one's mind and embrace His forgiveness. It seems strange, but there is some comfort contained in burdensome legalism. It gives you a list of "dos and don'ts," and all you have to do is obey them and *voilà*, you're righteous! This diminishes the need for faith. Just do your righteous steps (church, prayer, bible reading, offerings, etc.), and you're good to go for that day. Checking things off the list requires little, if any, faith. Do a few basic "righteous things" each day and very little else is required. In this way you can avoid the distasteful recognition of your remaining old sinful patterns that God is waiting on you to let Him transform and the need for such mundane things as serving and loving others as God does. These things are true Christianity and sometimes that is not easy.

In God's Good Time

Let's consider Peter's spiritual journey after the resurrection of Jesus Christ. He had walked with Christ for three and a half years. During this time, the Savior had personally instructed him and the other eleven apostles. Scripture seems to suggest that Peter was a leader or spokesman for the apostles after the resurrection of Jesus. If anyone understood the mysteries of the gospel, surely he did. After all, wasn't he taught by God in the flesh?

From Jesus, Peter learned about the gospel and understood that salvation was only for the Jews, not the Gentiles. Jesus' example was to keep the Law of Moses, which Peter also kept after Christ had ascended to heaven. What else was there to know after that event? Surely all the mysteries of God had been given to them by Jesus when he walked with His apostles on earth. Peter was sure and resolute that he had down pat the understanding of his mission for God concerning salvation and the mysteries of God. All that they learned face-to-face with Jesus was the totality of the apostles' understanding for a few years after His resurrection. Peter and the rest of the apostles were making great strides in preaching the "true gospel" and building the Jewish Church they thought Christ wanted.

Then one day God gave Peter new understanding in a vision. He was told to go to the house of a Gentile named Cornelius, a Roman

Centurion. Peter went and addressed Cornelius, his family, and friends. Peter said to them: "…You know how unlawful it is for a Jew to associate with a foreigner or visit him. But God has shown me that I should not call any man impure or unclean" (Acts 10:28b, BSB). When was this revealed to Peter? This was a new revelation to Peter that Jesus had not told him about. While Peter was preaching the gospel to the group, all of a sudden God poured out His Holy Spirit on all the Gentiles gathered there. Scripture says that, "All the circumcised believers [Jews] who had accompanied Peter were amazed that the gift of the Holy Spirit had been poured out even on the Gentiles" (Acts 10:45 BSB). Why were they astonished? It was because the Christian Jews thought salvation was only for the Jews!

God had just revealed a great deal more about His mystery of the gospel than Jesus had revealed to Peter when he was alive. Why didn't Jesus himself tell Peter that salvation would also be for the Gentiles? The simple answer is it was not yet God's time for it to be revealed. What if Peter had refused to go to Cornelius's home, saying, "We had all doctrine and truth of God's mysteries revealed to us by none other than Jesus Christ Himself! I refuse to make any additions, deletions, or changes to the teachings of Jesus! Not only that, but how about that new upstart Saul or Paul of Tarsus? He is claiming that he is the one called by God to unveil the fullness of the mysteries of God! On top of that, he is claiming to be an apostle of God. How can this be? He was not with us, the twelve apostles who were handpicked by Christ. Paul did not walk with us during the ministry of Jesus when the only real truths were delivered! Who does he think he is? Christ gave us all we need to know about the mysteries of God. Even if God were going to give us new understanding concerning them, He would have revealed it to me, or at least one of the other eleven who knew and walked with Christ."

Thankfully, Peter understood that Christ had not exclusively given him all the answers to the mysteries of God during Christ's physical ministry on earth. Peter was willing and ready to humble himself and follow new revelations from God whenever and wherever they came—even from Paul, who had, prior to his conversion, wreaked havoc on God's people.

Growing In The Likeness

We did not obtain spiritual maturity immediately when we were first saved. We were but babes in Christ. But just as babies grow into adults over time, we are to continually be growing in knowledge and understanding, and thus, becoming more like Christ in thoughts and actions, which brings us increasing liberty and joy. Hopefully, my story as told in this book will help you avoid what I had to learn the hard way. I pray that it may aid your spiritual walk with Christ, helping you to be fruitful and overflowing with the love, joy, and peace that God intends for you.

God has always revealed portions of His mysteries when the time was right for Him to reveal them. This has been so since the beginning of time. And so shall it be forever. God has an eternity of beautiful, wonderful mysteries He will reveal to us in their due time, bringing us new surprises, excitement, and great joy. We must learn to expect, welcome, and adjust to them. The transformation process is one of God's mysteries that Paul was entrusted with and taught us about in his inspired writings.

> Surely you heard of Him and were taught in Him in keeping with the truth that is in Jesus. You were taught to put off your former way of life, your old self, which is being corrupted by its deceitful desires; to be renewed in the spirit of your minds; and to put on the new self, created to be like God in true righteousness and holiness. ~ Ephesians 4:21-24, BSB

He said Christians are to put off those things remaining in us that are unlike Christ and allow God to clothe us with more of His truth, glory, and likeness.

Though many of the mysteries of God will not be understood during our lifetime on earth, God has permitted many of these mysteries to be revealed. This knowledge can aid us in our spiritual walk with God and enrich our understanding of Him and His character. You are blessed indeed if you are given correct understanding of the way to eternal life. Satan hates that preaching and understanding. We now live at the end of this age of Satan rule of the earth. It is his great desire to keep the correct knowledge of eternal salvation from those who remain in darkness to the truths of God we have been discussing in this book. The scriptures speak of these days and tell us that during this time there will be a renaissance in the preaching of the true gospel; however, at the same time Satan will foster a counterbalancing false gospel that will be preached in secular philosophies and false religions of the world; as well as infecting even Christian churches in an attempt to hide the wonderful true gospel message that brings eternal salvation. In order to be properly warned and aware of Satan's sinister efforts to pervert and prevent the salvation gospel, let's next turn our attention to that false gospel which is making great strides around the world.

15

INCLUSION IS NOT THE TRUE GOSPEL

The gospel of salvation and grace is sweeping the world. This gospel contains the essential central story of the good news brought by Christ. How Christ in you, which is the hope of glory, can be obtained is the crucial message that the gospel must deliver in order to fulfill in anyone the purpose of God's love mystery. This aspect of the good news is wonderful and exciting; but another sinister revolution is riding in on the coattails of salvation and grace. It is called "Inclusionism" and also known as "Universalism." It wraps itself in the mantel of grace, but crosses the line, becoming a perverted gospel, when it allows sin without repentance and salvation without accepting Jesus Christ's sacrifice. This false gospel is the mirror opposite of the ditch fallen into by the work-based legalistic gospel. It slides past the true grace gospel right into a cavernous ditch called "licentious grace," which is more dangerous and damaging than the error of legalism. At least the gospel of legalism correctly teaches that in order to receive salvation, each individual must heed God's call, repent, and accept Jesus Christ as their savior. Satan hated this gospel, but he took some solace in that it camouflaged how saints were to allow God to produce "righteous fruit" pleasing to Him. Still, those who did repent upon God's calling did receive the Spirit of God, which gave them an "eternal birth" as children of God. Contrarily, a licentious grace gospel slams the door shut to eternal life when it removes the need for individuals to repent and accept the sacrifice of Jesus. At its heart and core, unless it is repented of, this leads individuals to committing the unpardonable sin and blaspheming the Holy Spirit.

Satan loves this new licentious grace gospel much more than he did the gospel of legalism, for it effectively prevents the unsaved from becoming sons and daughters of God and entering into His eternal kingdom. What conclusions would you draw if you heard a preacher, as I did, make the following comments in his sermon concerning all those in the world who have not accepted Jesus Christ as their savior?

> *All [mankind] have been saved. The sad thing is they just don't know it!*

> *What a powerful message: you all are saved; you just don't know it!*

> *What I am saying is that a Buddhist is saved! Does he know who saved him? Does he know what he has in Christ? No! Is he going to live a life that is full of God and Christ? Probably not! Is he an evil person? I don't know; I can't judge him!*

In his closing prayer without a call to repentance, he stated:

> *This prayer isn't going to save you. You already are! When we pray as a group, our mind and spirit—helps with our awakening to grasp the reality of what we already have.*

This inclusion gospel teaches that repentance is not necessary by anyone because "all are already saved." As a matter of fact, no one needs to even know or hear of Jesus or the gospel to be saved because "all are already saved." So, I ask, what need is there to preach the gospel or ask anyone to repent? Inclusionists say it would be nice if all those ignorant did hear their version of the "good news," which is simply that they need to wake up to the fact they are "already saved." However, even this exercise of their "gospel" is not necessary, for they believe everybody is already saved, whether or not they ever hear the gospel. Paul clearly states that Satan inspires the perversion of the gospel, hiding its real truth about Jesus, and thus prevents eternal salvation, which comes from understanding, belief, and repentance: "The god [Satan] of this age has blinded the minds of unbelievers so they cannot see the light of the gospel of the glory of Christ, who is the image of God" (2 Cor. 4:4 BSB).

In this paragraph all emphasizes noted in the following scriptures were added. The apostle Paul clearly stated, "…I am not ashamed of the Good News of Christ, for it is the power of God for salvation *for everyone who believes* [action verb]…(Rom. 1:16a, WEB). According to Paul, it would logically follow that no one has salvation until they first hear the gospel and then believe. Jesus said himself, "Most certainly, I tell you, *he who believes in me has eternal life*" (John 6:47 WEB). And John said, "For God so loved the world, that he gave his one and only Son, that whoever believes in him should not perish, but have eternal life. For God didn't send his Son into the world to judge the world, but that the world should be saved through him. *He who believes* in him is not judged. *He who doesn't believe has been judged already,* because he has not believed in the name of the one and only Son of God" (John 3:16-18, WEB). From these Scriptures and many others it is quite obvious that only those individuals who believe and accept Jesus Christ as their Savior will be granted eternal life.

Licentious Grace

If the gospel is not preached or is obscured to the point that no one can understand and believe it, then there can be no real repentance. Just preaching stories about Christ without the requirement for each person to repent and believe in Him becomes more than just a broad-minded grace. It becomes a licentious grace. Merriam-Webster's Dictionary defines licentious as, "lacking legal or moral restraints." With no repentance there is no restraint of sins. Sin becomes whatever imaginary line the human mind cares to draw based on self-justification and human reasoning. Any "salvation gospel" that disallows the need of accepting the Savior's sacrifice and allows salvation without a restraint using God's definition of sin is a licentiousness gospel. Jude warned of this and said this false gospel would appear in the last days and he characterized it as being anti-Christ:

> For certain men have crept in among you unnoticed—ungod-
> ly ones who were designated long ago for condemnation. They
> turn the grace of our God into a license for immorality, and they
> deny our only Master and Lord, Jesus Christ. ~ Jude 1:4, BSB

These individuals Jude warned of denied Christ and are thus anti-Christ. They in effect taught doctrines that denied our Lord and Savior Jesus Christ. They probably said something like this, "You don't need
to repent of anything or accept Jesus Christ in order to receive eternal
salvation. God loves you so much He has already saved you without your
repentance. He loves you so much you don't even ever have to know
Him. It doesn't matter if you have God's code of conduct to live your life
by. Live life according to what you think is best; that's all that matters!
After all, you already have eternal life; all you need to do is recognize it."
This is the doctrine that most inclusionists believe in.

This message denies the very core reason the Messiah came into
this world, which was to reveal the only pathway to eternal life and to offer it as a gift; not to force it on anyone, but to allow us free choice to accept or reject it. Jesus' beliefs would be heretical to a universal inclusionist if He really meant these words: "I am the way and the truth and the
life. No one comes to the Father except through Me" (John 14:6, BSB). It
seems pretty clear that anyone calling upon Buddhism, Islamism, Shintoism, Hinduism, or Satanism is not calling on Jesus Christ. Many of the
apostle Paul's statements would be heretical to inclusionists because he
excludes all from being "saved" except as he states, "Everyone who calls
on the name of the Lord will be saved" (Rom. 10:13, BSB). I ask, how can
you call on Jesus if you've never heard of Him? It's interesting to note
that Paul asked the same question.

> How then can they call on the One they have not believed in?
> And how can they believe in the One of whom they have not
> heard? And how can they hear without someone to preach? And
> how can they preach unless they are sent? As it is written:
> "How beautiful are the feet of those who bring good news!"
> ~ Romans 10:14-15, BSB

Inclusionists would say, "How dare you believe you must go through any steps prior to being saved! That is requiring 'works' to be saved! You are excluding people from eternal life." I say that it is not I, but Jesus Himself, who does the excluding when He says that only those who repent and accept Him will gain eternal life. Those who deny the process that Jesus said one must follow in order to be saved are the ones who deny Christ and who therefore are anti-Christ. These days, Christians who believe the words of Christ and Paul are under attack and are being called exclusionist by those who preach inclusionism.

Vain Imaginations

Too many Christian churches today are accepting the values and philosophies of this world's secularist and political elites. They use human reasoning rather than God's to define concepts of good and evil. These elites of the world embrace the words at the heart of Christianity such as love, justice, equality, liberty, and truth, but they twist and pervert them to suit their own purposes and selfish advantage. They reject the true Godly meanings of these words, to conform to what seems reasonable to their human minds. Paul, in contending with a vain and ungodly teaching, warned Christians not be taken in by the vain ideas of ungodly people, no matter how wonderful they might sound. He asked, "If you have died with Christ to the spiritual forces of the world, why, as though you still belonged to the world, do you submit to its regulations [values, philosophies, and ideals]" (Col. 2:20, BSB)?

He continues, "These will all perish with use, because they are based on human commands and teachings. Such restrictions indeed have an appearance of wisdom, with their self-prescribed worship, their false humility, and their harsh treatment of the body; but they are of no value against the indulgence of the flesh" (Col. 2:22-23, BSB). Justification for sensual fleshly indulgence is their bottom-line motivation. Paul here gives the major underlying cause for mankind formulating their vain imaginations. Be they political, secular, or religious, these imaginations are formulated to justify people's lust to indulge in their own sinful desires. Scripture reveals an even more sinister unseen spiritual force prodding them when it warns, "Now the Spirit expressly states that in later times some will abandon the faith to follow deceitful spirits and the teachings of demons, influenced by the hypocrisy of liars, whose consciences are seared with a hot iron [dead to sin]" (1 Tim. 4:1-2, BSB).

Such a vain imagination is that which is expressed in inclusion doctrine. Inclusion doctrine teaches that the lost can be in a saved state without hearing about, much less repenting and accepting, Jesus Christ as their Savior. If you want to step into vain imaginations of demons and mankind, then step into the current world of inclusion doctrinal teaching. Things get rather wild and crazy very fast. Inclusion teachings open the floodgate to an attitude of anything goes. Sin is no longer defined by God but by man's philosophies, which, as you will see, can become quite flexible. Sin thus can become irrelevant or even nonexistent in inclusion circles.

"Christianity" Without Boundaries

Let's take a brief look at just how licentious inclusion doctrine can become. In an InfoWars article, author Michal Snyder gives us some insight into where inclusion thinking can lead once you cut loose from sin as defined in the Holy Bible. Mr. Snyder states:

> If you want as many people to attend your Church as possible, why limit yourself to just Christians? All over America, 'radically inclusive' Churches that embrace all religions and all lifestyles are starting to pop up. Church services that incorporate elements of Hinduism, Islam, native American religions and even Wicca [Satanists] are becoming increasingly common. And even if you don't believe anything at all, that is okay with these Churches too.[1]

Mr. Snyder continues to relate some of the comments of various ministers of different inclusionist churches that help show the liberality of their teachings. One such minister said there is "no hell except what one creates with one's own actions."[2] Another stated, "Someone quipped that my congregation is BYOG: Bring Your Own God. I use that and invite people to 'bring their own God'—or none at all…. While the symbol 'God' is part of our cultural tradition, you can take it or leave it or redefine it to your liking."[3] Mr. Snyder continues to tell about a church in San Francisco that now allows lesbians, gays, bisexuals, and transgender (LGBT) people to practice their sexual desires, not adhering to any celibate lifestyle as Christians. Their church pastor wrote, "Our pastoral practice of demanding life-long 'celibacy,' by which we meant that for the rest of your life you would not engage your sexual orientation in any way, was causing obvious harm and has not led to human flourishing."[4] So, instead of letting God's Word define what is good or evil, human observation and reasoning is used.

It is interesting to note that apparently many inclusionists who have departed from faith in God's inerrant Word primarily express that truth to them is defined by the "leading of the spirit" from day to day. This gives them wide leeway in deciding for themselves doctrinal teachings concerning salvation, heaven, hell, and what is good and evil in their own lives, yet they still claim be clothed in the "righteousness of Christ." Cut loose from the Word of God, these Christians become "seekers of truth." They put on an imaginary "coat of righteousness" but deny the biblical words of God, which describe true righteousness. This inevitably leads to a licentious grace.

It is human nature to avoid that which condemns you. Christians need to be careful not to try to use grace as a cloak for what God calls sin. One easy way around sin, as defined in the Bible, is just to "walk by the spirit" apart from God's Word. In doing so you can then be free to be a "seeker of truth" daily as "the spirit leads you." If the Spirit is not leading you daily on the immovable rails of God's Word, how then is this type of truth any better than that of a godless world filled with people who walk after the imaginations of their own hearts. The Scriptures are clear that, "All the ways of a man *are* clean [righteous] in his own eyes" (Prov. 16:2a, KJV). This is the self-righteousness of mankind, not God's righteousness. Only a true Christian can enjoy the righteousness of God. However, even Christians can, if they are not careful, end up walking again in the vanity of their own minds just as they did prior to accepting Jesus Christ. This will happen if they cut loose from the moorings of the

Holy Bible. When Christians allow only the "holy spirit" to guide them, they will inevitably use their "Savior" as justification for vain imaginations based on their own desires of the flesh.

Mr. Snyder asks an important question in his article:

> But if people can just "believe whatever they want," what makes these Churches "Christian" at all? We live in a society in which it has become very trendy to "choose your own path" and in which nobody wants to do anything that might "offend" someone else. For instance, consider the words that one CNN reporter used to describe her transition from "Christian" to "seeker." "After years of spiritual reflection and inquiry, I am at a place where I don't want to feel guilty, hypocritical, judgmental, closed-minded or arrogant. So, where do I stand now—30 years after 'finding God,' questioning my faith, committing sins, seeking hazardous adventure and trying to love life and people to the best of my ability? I am a 'seeker.' A constant seeker within this world, among people and, of course, for spiritual enlightenment of all kind. Because if I did possess the truth—the 'final answer'—I am convinced I would spend the rest of my years missing out on the enrichment and surprise of seeking it."[5]

This sounds to me like spiritual mumbo jumbo that allows "seekers" to avoid the mirror of God's Word and thereby formulate whatever "truth" sounds good to them so they can indulge their illicit desires and not feel guilty. "Seeking truth" is at times easier than having to deal with the real truth of God, which is the "final answer." Being a "seeker" can help you avoid any truth or theology that might be contrary to what you prefer it to be. Thus, you don't have to deal with guilt for not facing the real truths of God. As the CNN reporter just said, "I don't want to feel guilty, hypocritical, judgmental, closed-minded or arrogant." As a "seeker of truth" without biblical guidance, you will never be as free as you could be; for God's Word says that it is only God's truth that can set you truly free at last (see John 8:32).

The Only Door To Eternal Life

Inclusionists do not agree with God's Word that clearly shows that the pathway to eternal life is denied to the unsaved by negating the necessity of first God's call to repentance, and then acceptance of "Jesus Christ our only Sovereign and Lord," after which a new person is born again, receiving the Holy Spirit of God and eternal life. So, the importance of the true gospel being preached is essential. First one must hear the true gospel, then God must open your mind, which will enable you to repent (change your heart and mind), if you so choose (see John 6:44-45, 65; Acts 2:47). God the Father decides when the best time is to open each person's mind to an awareness of "good and evil," as He defines it in their lives. This moment in time is the most critical moment of that individual's entire life; for he or she will be choosing between eternal life and eternal damnation! Only God knows when that exact time will be in each individual's life and for how long the "moment" will last. It is at this "moment" in time that the person is then allowed for the first time in his or her life an opportunity to believe in and accept the One who will save him or her if they so choose.

The only process involved for the individual is for God to first call that person to repentance, which simply means changing his or her mind about the direction he or she has lived all of his or her life thus far. The ones who accept God's call and choose eternal life through Christ do nothing but simply accept Jesus as their Savior and follow after Him in faith the rest of their lives. How long the "moment" for the opportunity for salvation lasts for each individual, only God knows for sure. But that "moment" will come in each individual's life when he or she will most likely say "yes" when given an opportunity by God for eternal life with Him. God is a fair and just God and will make sure each one is called at the most opportune moment in their life. As Peter said, "...I now truly understand that God does not show favoritism, but welcomes those from every nation who fear Him and do what is right" (Acts 10:34-35 BSB). A just God will give every man, woman, and child their moment for entry into the Kingdom of God. That moment of time will last until God knows for sure that the individual will not now or ever accept eternal life with Him.

If you choose to repent, accepting Jesus Christ as your Savior, then you are born again through the Holy Spirit. All this can happen in a split second. It doesn't take a lot of time on the part of one coming to salvation. However, being given eternal life with Jesus is impossible without one experiencing these phases of the gospel message (see Ezekiel 36:26-27; John 3:3, 6-8; Romans 10:13-15).

There is nothing the unsaved individual can to do to become saved! God is the only One who can impart eternal life. There is nothing an individual can do to deserve it! It is a gift from God. All God requires of the individual is repentance and faith in Jesus Christ. The individual no longer believes in his self-righteousness, but rather now chooses God's righteousness by simply believing in Christ. When God sees the sincerity of the person's heart, eternal life is granted through the Holy Spirit. At that moment a newborn child of God is formed with all the Spiritual DNA of God the Father. The saint from then on is to strive for the rest of his or her physical life to walk by faith according to the revealed way of the Father. The walk expresses itself in true loving thoughts, feelings, and actions. However, these statements I have just made concerning salvation would be considered heretical by most of those who believe in the inclusion doctrine.

Why Do People Believe In Inclusion?

If people do not agree with God's Word concerning heaven, hell, and sin, then I can see where they might move into a state of denial and begin to formulate their own theology concerning the matters of doctrine. The Holy Bible is quite clear about the existence of heaven, hell, and sin. As I have just related, it is quite clear what steps are necessary to be granted eternal salvation and entry into God's kingdom.

Inclusionists say that all mankind is already saved without the need for the gospel, repenting, accepting Jesus, or receiving the Holy Spirit. Guess what? Inclusionists reject, not just one or two steps, but all of the required steps to eternal life with Jesus! In this sense the spirit of being against Christ's teachings, or anti-Christ, as Scripture defines it, is being clearly demonstrated and proclaimed. I am sure this tickles Satan, for indeed the minds of the unbelievers remain blinded to the only way one might gain eternal life which is through Jesus (see 2 Corinthians 4:4). A false gospel removes part or all of the prerequisites for eternal life to be imparted to the unsaved. The true gospel teaches that Jesus' sacrifice did indeed remove the sins of all mankind. This reconciled God to mankind. This is good news indeed. God took the first step in reconciling with mankind. However, mankind must respond by accepting the sacrifice of Jesus. Paul said:

> ...God was in Christ reconciling the world to himself, not reckoning to them their trespasses, and having committed to us the word of reconciliation. We are therefore ambassadors on behalf of Christ, as though God were entreating by us: we beg you on behalf of Christ, be reconciled to God. For him who knew no sin he made to be sin on our behalf; so that in him we might become the righteousness of God. ~ 2 Corinthians 5:19-20, WEB

When God invites us to receive His Holy Spirit and become an eternal born-again son or daughter, He will not force us to accept His offer. Notice the loving desire for sinful mankind in His plea, "I have blotted out, as a thick cloud, your transgressions, and, as a cloud, your sins. Return to me, for I have redeemed you" (Isa. 44:22, WEB). That price was the life of God's Son. Through Jesus' sacrifice He has removed all our sins that make it possible to be reconciled to Him. All we have to do is accept God's offer and turn to Christ in faith. Of all the several commentaries I have read on 2 Corinthians 5:20 concerning reconciliation to God, I like Meyer's NT Commentary the best: "...man cannot reconcile himself, but is able only to become by means of faith a partaker of the reconciliation which has been effected on the divine side; he [man] can only become reconciled, which on his side cannot take place without faith, but is experienced in faith."[6] God has done all the work necessary that reconciles Him to man. All that a man or woman has to do is to accept it in faith. The long and short of this matter is that in order for reconciliation to take place, there need to be at least two parties that agree to be reconciled. God initiated it by offering the sacrifice of His Son, removing the sin that separated God from mankind. Man must accept that offer in order to make the reconciliation complete. After this the New Covenant is agreed upon by both parties and is initiated. In inclusion doctrine both reconciliation and the New Covenant agreement being accepted by both God and mankind are excluded.

Which God Is More Loving?

Scripture states, "He [God] has made everything beautiful in its time. He has also set eternity in their hearts, yet so that man can't find out the work that God has done from the beginning even to the end" (Eccl. 3:11, WEB). Satan cannot extinguish man's desire to live eternally, so he strives to satisfy that desire by offering a counterfeit method for obtaining it. Satan's message is, "If God is a truly a loving God, then He would satisfy our desire for eternity by simply giving it to all mankind. A truly loving God would do that!" The teaching at the heart and core of inclusion doctrine is that the God of traditional Christianity is a less loving God than what inclusionism offers. Inclusionism is a stroke of delusional genius by Satan. By offering a "more loving" god to mankind than that of traditional Christianity, Satan tries to camouflage and diminish God's love as being inferior and selfish. Sadly, this appeal to human reasoning too often is accepted and thus excludes the eternity that the heart of the individual seeks.

By not preaching the true gospel, which requires repentance and accepting Jesus prior to salvation, a false gospel is proclaimed. Satan is glad to promote a partly errant "gospel" as long as it keeps the minds of unbelievers blinded to the correct gospel necessary for salvation. Satan accomplishes this blindness by disseminating a totally incorrect, or even a partially correct, gospel. Either gospel adds up to a false gospel, which Satan uses to prevent a lost soul from receiving the Spirit of God and thus access to eternal life. Remember Satan's encounter with Eve in the Garden of Eden. The lie he told Eve is the same one inclusionists believe in. Eve said to Satan:

> Of the fruit of the trees of the garden we may eat, but of the fruit of the tree which is in the middle of the garden, God has said, "You shall not eat of it, neither shall you touch it, lest you die." The serpent said to the woman, "You won't surely die, for God knows that in the day you eat it, your eyes will be opened, and you will be like God, knowing good and evil." ~ Genesis 3:2b-5, WEB

The inclusionists today, in effect, are saying, "You will not die if you don't repent and accept Jesus Christ as your Savior. God knows you are already saved. It would just make your life happier if you realized it!"

The Anti-Christ

Satan certainly likes the false gospel that all are already saved. That way, without the vital steps of God's call, repentance, and embracing Jesus, the unsaved remain blinded and unsaved. This false teaching is definitely in the spirit of being "anti-Christ." The apostle John makes this point very clear: "…many false prophets have gone out into the world. By this you know the Spirit of God: every spirit who confesses that Jesus Christ has come in the flesh is of God, and every spirit who doesn't confess that Jesus Christ has come in the flesh is not of God, and this is the spirit of the Antichrist, of whom you have heard that it comes. Now it is in the world already" (1 John 4:1b-3, WEB). Many believe Christ existed as a "good man." Others believe He was just a prophet. For instance, Islam acknowledges that Jesus came in the flesh as a prophet, but they do not believe He was and is the Son of God.[7] Not properly acknowledging the office, work, and message of the Messiah is the spirit of being against Christ. There is nothing worse than preaching a gospel that denies the very purpose of the gospel, which is eternal life to the hearer. It is in this spirit and fashion that Jesus Christ is being denied by those who teach this doctrine John warned of. This is so because it only partially displays the glory of Christ. If a minister is guilty of this, that minister has an attitude and philosophy aligned with that of the prophesied one world government and religion led by the Antichrist that is to come in the end of days. This does not necessarily mean this minister and his or her church are not Christian; they may simply have been deluded by Satan's teaching. That minister and that church simply need to recognize their error and begin to teach the true gospel again.

Some of the politically correct ideas of inclusionism are not necessarily a bad thing. Take for instance the matter of discrimination, nobody wants to be unfairly discriminated against and thereby excluded from what others in society enjoy. America's creation and rise to world power can be attributed to her faith in good inclusive statements shared in America's Declaration of Independence: "We hold these truths to be self-evident, that all men are created equal, that they are endowed by their Creator with certain unalienable Rights that among these are Life, Liberty and the pursuit of Happiness." God grants these rights, in all aspects of our political and religious lives, to us. The whole civil rights movement worldwide has been powered by this idea. However, when inclusiveness transgresses God's morality, it becomes abusive and licentious. Holding the banner of inclusion high in order to drive a human desire contrary to God's will is very wrong. It is definitely wrong when in the name of inclusion you begin to remove God's moral restraints concerning such sins as abortion, homosexuality, immorality, drunkenness, bestiality, pedophiles, thievery, and the like.

Satan's Drive To Unite The World

The philosophy of inclusion not only has become a religious drive but is also embraced politically by the nations of the world. It is assumed that for the righteous ideas of peace and happiness to exist around the world, there needs to be a removal of any barriers that divide religions and nations. It is believed that through such efforts world unity among nations and religions can be achieved. This is the driving force behind the formation of the United Nations organization. There is a dream of a "new world order" that will bring harmony and happiness to all nations of the world. The words "political correctness" are a guiding light that promises to deliver world peace. Many nations and spiritual leaders recognize that world unity cannot be achieved without removing the differences that separate the various great religions of the world. The easiest path to move forward on this front is to do what is "politically correct" by legitimizing all religions. Political correctness demands that all religions be recognized as valid and all peoples support each other's right to their faith. Legitimacy is to be given to all faiths by saying, "It matters not how or which god you serve. We respect and accept everyone's religion, for we all serve the same god." To not be exclusionist, all nations and faiths must agree to this inclusion theology. Those that don't will be considered bigoted and heretical.

The Scriptures prophesy that prior to the return of Christ, a political and religious new world order will be establish among nations on earth. This new world order will be a political and religious axis that will gain great worldwide power (see Revelation 13:11-17). From the religious perspective, this new alliance will be proclaimed and promoted by a fallen Christian religion, called in the Bible a "prostitute," headed by a "false prophet" (see Revelation 17). This whorish church is described as riding a "beast" that is comprised of ten nations. The governmental head of this powerhouse of ten nations is described in the Scriptures as simply "the man of sin." The false prophet, in an effort to achieve his religious desires, will work together with the Beast power in an attempt to bring about mankind's dream of peace and harmony. He will use his spiritual influence to aid the Beast power and force the worshiping of its leader, known in Scripture as the "man of sin" and the "Antichrist."

This head of the Beast power will unify his political dreams of bringing all nations under his political and religious power. The false prophet who assists him is referred to as a second beast and is described as one who "…caused the earth and those who dwell in it to worship the first beast…" (Rev. 13:12, BSB). This will be accomplished through removing any barrier to uniting the world under one worldwide government and faith. The Beast power will believe that their Utopian dream can be achieved only when all religions and political differences are eradicated. The tenets of inclusion will be enforced in the name of unity, love, social justice, liberty, and world peace. The false prophet will strive to bring unity among nations spiritually by proclaiming the new gospel of inclusion, which embraces all faiths as being acceptable to God. This new faith will effectively state, "It makes no difference what you believe. It matters not if you believe in Christ, Buddhism, Islamism, Shintoism, Hinduism, Wicca, or something else! We all serve the same God. God loves us all the same and does not exclude anyone. We are all now saved and are accepted by God!" Their unifying false message of inclusion is now at work, being introduced to the secularist and great religions of the world. These tenets of the gospel of inclusion are helping guide all governments and religions toward unification, a process that will ultimately come under the rule of the end-time prophesied Antichrist. Those who do not agree and refuse to worship this new Beast power will be persecuted. Sadly, many Christians will be deceived into believing the false prophet's vain theology, and they will yield to the power of the Beast and "worshiping" its leader, who is the Antichrist. However, a certain group of Christians "...who know their God shall be strong, and do [exploits]. Those who are wise [Christians] among the people shall instruct many; yet they shall fall by the sword and by flame, by captivity and by spoil, [many] days" (Dan. 11:32b-33, WEB). The leader of the Beast power will ultimately be revealed as the prophesied Antichrist. Then he will unleash great fury, persecution, and martyrdom for a three-and-a-half-year period of time upon those who resist him, Jews and Christians alike. This is the reign of terror called the great tribulation in the Scriptures. Jesus will return to rapture His saints and to stop the carnage that is taking place at the battle of Armageddon and to save the world from utter destruction. The Antichrist and his armies will unsuccessfully fight Jesus and His army of angels as they descend to earth. Christ will destroy all the world's armies who oppose Him and set up His eternal kingdom (see Revelation 17:14; 19:11-21).

So, in summary, the gospel of Inclusionism is being stealthy introduced into many churches and is gaining in popularity. Inclusion is not the true gospel God sent to earth. Inclusion teaches eternal salvation without the need for Jesus Christ as the savior of mankind. Inclusion is Satan's version of salvation which is a lie. The very purpose of God to produce His eternal children is thwarted by Satan's lie which is now being preached by the gospel of Inclusionism (AKA Universalism). Christians need to be aware of this insidious threat to them as well as to non-Christians. It is sad but true that many of those introducing these satanic teachings are so called "Christian" pastors of churches. All Christians need to be alert to any vain teachings advocating legalism or licentiousness. The worst of all these heresies is that which denies the need for salvation through Jesus Christ. This is the spirit of the Antichrist which prevents mankind from receiving the Spirit of God which He made mankind to need. Receiving the Spirit of God gives mankind eternal life and access to the very freedom, love, joy, and peace that he so desperately yearns for. Not receiving the Spirit of God means eternal damnation in Satan's kingdom. Inclusionism is inspired and driven by Satan for the purpose of preventing eternal salvation for mankind as children of God. It is also Satan's effort to destroy all human life on earth in a worldwide nuclear conflagration resulting from Satan uniting the nations to fight Jesus Christ at His second coming. This subject is so important we need to look into it more deeply so we can better arm ourselves against its seditious teachings. In the next chapter we will gain a deeper understanding of this insidious doctrine of Inclusionism now affecting many Christian churches so we and our loved ones will not be swap away with this satanic heresy.

16

WHAT IS INCLUSION DOCTRINE?

Inclusion teaching is an ungodly doctrine that is anti-Christ. God warned of ministers coming who would present vain imaginations. God said, "Don't listen to the words of the prophets who prophesy to you: they teach you vanity; they speak a vision of their own heart, and not out of the mouth of Yahweh" (Jer. 23:16, WEB). I do not judge if they are Christian or not. If they have repented and accepted God's call in faith concerning the sacrifice of Jesus, then they are Christian. They may just be diluted as to the truth concerning aspects of the gospel. Only God is our judge. Even though they may be Christian, they have created doctrines based on human selfish reasoning formulated from their own ideas, which directly contradict God's Word. Some of these imaginations are born from their disdain of some topics described in the Scriptures. For instance, one such subject the Bible speaks of is eternal punishment in hell for the unsaved. Some inclusionists can't imagine a loving God creating an eternal burning hell, so they must craft their gospel message so that it eliminates anyone going there, except for possibly Satan and his daemons (see Revelation 20:10). These ministers who deny the Scriptures speak of imaginations born of their own desires and attribute them to God. Are they sincere? I don't doubt that! However, even though they may be sincere, they are sincerely wrong.

This dangerous new gospel of inclusion wraps itself in the mantel of their perverted version of God's loving grace; but it is certainly not the true gospel of grace. There are basically two branches of inclusion doc-

trine. Both teach that everyone on earth is saved (historical reconciliation), or eventually will be saved (ultimate reconciliation), even though
they don't know it.[1] One branch, called "universalist inclusion," teaches
that there is no need for people to repent and accept Jesus as their Savior
because everyone, whether or not they know it, will eventually be eternally
saved. The other branch of inclusion doctrine goes under the banner of
"trinitarian inclusion."[2] They generally believe that in Jesus all mankind
has already been forgiven of all sins and saved, whether or not they know
it. Some of them believe, however, that those saved must come to realize
they are already saved and then come to repentance and accept Jesus.[3] One
added caveat to this teaching is that although you are saved, you can become unsaved if you don't eventually come to repentance. In other words,
it is the ultimate oxymoron, which in effect states: you are saved to begin
with, but can become unsaved and wind up in hell if you don't ultimately
repent and accept Jesus as your Savior. Yes, I know it sounds a bit convo-
luted, but it is what it is. I must say this doctrine is closer to the true gospel than other inclusion doctrines because at least they require ultimate
repentance and acceptance of Jesus Christ to be eternally saved, which is
correct.

For the world in general, universalism expressed in religious as
well as secular circles espouses similar beliefs. "A community that calls
itself *universalist* may emphasize the universal principles of most religions and accept other religions in an inclusive manner, believing in a
universal reconciliation between humanity and the divine. ... A belief
in one common truth is also another important tenet. The living truth
is seen as more far-reaching than national, cultural, or religious boundaries."[4] Universalism is the world's efforts to find common ground in all
faiths and be a uniting influence among them. I think that desire is fine,
as long as it does not transgress the will of the one true God, the Father
of Jesus Christ.

There are some Christians who embrace a Christian version of
universal reconciliation. Essentially, they hold, "the view that all human
beings will ultimately be restored to a right relationship with God in Heav-
en and the New Jerusalem."[5] They believe that it does not matter what god
(Buddha, Allah, etc.) one serves; all will eventually be saved. This would

mean that no human being will ever go to the eternal hellfire that the Bible speaks of. This would also mean that, although it is preferable to know Christ as your Savior, it is not necessary to hear the gospel of salvation requiring repentance for one's sins and acceptance of Jesus in order to receive eternal life.

In the nineteenth century, there were universalists who claimed that the early Church fathers taught that even the devil and the fallen angels would one day come to salvation.[6] I have no doubt some believe this today. If the fallen angels are to eventually become saved, then there really would be no eventual need for hell at all. I suppose some could argue that hell will only be needed for a period of time to teach fallen angels a lesson prior to their restoration in heaven. In this scenario hell would eventually be done away with. Yes, I know this sounds heretical to the biblically literate Christian, who would immediately start listing all of the Scriptures throughout the Old and New Testaments showing the existence of hell and the need for each individual to repent of their sins and receive Christ as their Savior; then and only then are they given immortality to live with Jesus for eternity. These false universalist doctrines should be a much smaller threat to people who know and believe in the inerrant Word of God, but they certainly are a major threat to the vast majority of the biblically ignorant or challenged masses around the world, be they Christian or not.

The two branches of inclusionism have spawned other hybrid beliefs that fall loosely inside the inclusion doctrinal camp. In short, as far as I can tell, they all share one belief that fallen mankind has already been or will ultimately be saved and united with God eternally. The only exception I know of is that of the Trinitarian stripe, which believes salvation can be lost. Author Paul Ellis gives an overall general perspective of inclusion doctrine: "Inclusionism teaches that Jesus died not as one of us but as all of us and that humanity was included in his resurrection and ascension. Since 'all are in Christ,' everyone is now reconciled, justified, sanctified, and filled with the Holy Spirit whether they believe it or not."[7]

This simplistic explanation becomes more complex when one tries to understand the variant offshoots that have been born from universalism and trinitarian inclusion doctrines. If you desire to delve more deeply into inclusion doctrines, then I suggest you go to Paul Ellis's web-site, where you can review several of his study-notes on the subject.[8]

Could You Be Deceived?

The following is related to you for the sole purpose that you might be ed-ucated and hopefully inoculated against falling prey to the various types of inclusion doctrines. Were you aware of inclusion doctrine before you read this book? Although I was a church minister for twenty-five years, I was totally unaware of inclusion doctrine until about six months ago. You need to be made aware that this hideous, satanically inspired doctrine is catching fire all across America and is spreading around the world. If one Sunday your pastor, after years of preaching the true gospel, all of a sudden began preaching an errant gospel on which Saint Paul put a double curse (see Galatians 1:8-9), would you be able to spot it? The following will be helpful to you in identifying an inclusion-laced sermon.

There are key words, phrases, and scriptures used that will tip you off to inclusion doctrinal teaching. The basic question that has in-spired inclusion teaching is, "What must one do in order to be saved?" It is only from God that we can derive the truth to this question. There are only two sources that Christians can follow in ascertaining spiritual truth. One is the Holy Bible and the other is the Spirit of God. To which must we look to recognize the truth? The answer is actually both! God's Spirit and His Word are indivisible. Like a beautiful puzzle, they fit per-fectly together. If any of the following words of Scripture are not true, then the very foundation of Christianity is destroyed! "All scripture *is* given by inspiration of God, and *is* profitable for doctrine, for reproof, for correction, for instruction in righteousness: That the man of God may be perfect, throughly furnished unto all good works" (2 Tim. 3:16-17, KJV). If you find yourself disagreeing with some Scriptures, there are only two reasons for that; either you are ignorant of God's true purpose and meaning, or you are defiant of their truth.

Why Would A Loving God Do That?

A major fallacy in some inclusion teaching is that they seem to think they better know how God should "save" mankind than the way God actually reveals that He will in Scripture! Apparently, some inclusionists believe they have a better idea that will save more people, than what God says. They ask, "How could a loving God allow the existence of an ever burning hellfire?" "How could a loving God be so vicious and judgmental as He was in the Old Testament?" Inclusionists think they can offer you a more loving God than the Old Testament reveals. This "more loving god" is introduced as one who would not only forgive mankind of all sin but also eternally save everyone on earth without them repenting of their sins. For that matter, people don't even have to know or believe God exists in order to be saved. This is a big selling point for inclusionists. How much more loving could a god get than this? This "more loving god" is appealing to human reasoning, and this leads many to buy into inclusion theology.

The one and only true God is love! That is His very essence. How dare any man stand up to God and say that he has devised a more loving god? That is tantamount to Lucifer standing up to God, as he did, and declaring his ways are more loving than God's. God has not and will not ever change. He is and always will be "the same yesterday and today and forever" (Heb. 13:8, BSB). The God of the Old Testament is as loving as the God of the New, because they are one and the same Being. Your different perceptions of the God of the Old Testament and the God of the New Testament are simply due to a lack of understanding of the purposes of the one and only true God of both Testaments. Ponder this one simple statement in the Scripture: "For God so loved the world that He gave His one and only Son, that everyone who believes in Him shall not perish but have eternal life" (John 3:16, BSB). This clearly shows that the love expressed in the New Testament was made possible because the same love existed in the Old Testament God. This most famous Scripture in the Bible connects and unites the love existing in both the Old and New Testaments.

This is the way it should work in dealing with our thoughts versus God's thoughts: "Let the wicked forsake his way, and the unrighteous man his thoughts: and let him return unto the LORD, and he will have mercy upon him; and to our God, for he will abundantly pardon" (Isa. 55:7, KJV). If your thoughts and words differ from God's, the only question is, will you allow Him to change your mind to conform to His? It is basic human fallibility that allows man to think he knows better than God what is right and wrong. It is from this perspective that inclusion beliefs have sprung forth. In short, for most who believe in inclusionism, it is a vain attempt to do away with hell. Know what? That's exactly what Satan would like us to believe too.

What Is True?

Just because a person can't understand why God did this or that, or because he can't agree, for instance, with the book of James or Revelation; that does not expose a failing of God. Quite to the contrary, it simply exposes the ignorance of the dissenting individual. The mind of God cannot to be fathomed or harshly judged by the mind of man. God does not need man to justify His actions. God invites mankind to ask questions, but the Word of God is truth as God defines it and does not have to fit within mankind's definition or understanding. Jesus emphatically states in a prayer to God, His Father, "Sanctify them by the truth; Your word is truth" (John 17:17, BSB). Every word placed in the Scriptures is put there out of love by God the Father. You or I, with only our human ability to reason, may not agree with or understand some of God's words as being loving, but that does not negate the fact that they are. It is not up to us to characterize God's actions as loving or unloving. Our disagreement with God only exposes our lack of understanding of the thinking of God. God said, "For my thoughts *are* not your thoughts, neither *are* your ways my ways, saith the LORD. For *as* the heavens are higher than the earth, so are my ways higher than your ways, and my thoughts than your thoughts" (Isa. 55: 8-9, KJV). The individual would be wise to realize that his or her differences with God only expose his or her lack of proper understanding of God's thoughts and reasoning.

Two Gods In The Bible

Some people question the love of God. They believe that the Bible contains, in effect, two Gods, the harsh God of the Old Testament and then the loving God of the New Testament. The God of the Old is often viewed as strictly legalistic, judgmental, cruel, and vengeful; a God who thought little of slaughtering entire nations of peoples, even mothers and babies along with all their livestock! This merciless, vindictive God was the one who destroyed the entire populations of the cities of Sodom and Gomorrah, save Lot and his family. This God once, with a flood, wiped out all life on earth, saving only eight people in Noah's ark.

We are told that a very different God is revealed in the New Testament. There, He is kind, loving, nonjudgmental, compassionate, and forgiving of sins. He is a God who loves us so much that He was willing to send His beloved Son to die for each of us. For many, it is difficult to see how the God of the Old Testament and that of the New Testament could be the same one and only God. Some believe that the God of the Old Testament is a demanding and self-glorifying God. They wonder how such a God, who requires that only He be worshiped, can be loving. They think God is selfish and vain for all the adulation He commands. Vanity or selfishness in God, whose very essence is love, is impossible! Every thought He thinks, every emotion He experiences, every action He takes is initiated from His essence, which is pure love.

There is only one God! He is the Supreme Creator, whose being is summed up in the Scriptures with three words: "God is love" (1 John 4:16, BSB). In this one word, *love,* is packed the totality of all that the Creator of all things is. Love undoubtedly is the most powerful word in the universe. Every bit of worship we give to God comes back in blessings to us. All the praise and love He has ever received or ever will receive will not go to His Head; therefore, only God can handle it. Does not the Creator of all things have a right to all praise and honor? As Creator of all things, only God is worthy of worship and praise; not angels or mankind, only God! Pure Love created all things for the express purpose of producing the desire of His heart, which is the soon coming manifestation of His superhuman eternal children. As the Scriptures succinctly state it, "Worthy are you, our Lord and God, the Holy One, to receive the glory, the honor, and the power, for you created all things, and because of your desire they existed, and were created" (Rev. 4:11, WEB). How dare anyone judge our Creator!

Is There An Eternal Hell?

There are several motivating factors that have inspired some to reject or reinterpret Scriptures, allowing justification for the creation of inclusion doctrines. If there is any one doctrine in the Scriptures that has inspired inclusionism, it is that of an ever-burning hell! It is in the natural mind of man that anything that is repugnant in the Scriptures (such as hell) needs to be improved or altered to fit one's sensitivities or else to be totally expunged all together. Hell has been the most basic inspiration to engender Christian universalism: "Universal salvation may be related to the perception of a problem of Hell, standing opposed to ideas such as endless conscious torment in Hell, but may also include a period of finite punishment similar to a state of purgatory. Believers in universal reconciliation may support the view that while there may be a real 'Hell' of some kind, it is neither a place of endless suffering nor a place where the spirits of human beings are ultimately 'annihilated' after enduring the just amount of divine retribution."[9] To a Christian universalist, the thought of an ever-burning hellfire into which anyone could be thrown by a loving God is repugnant and unacceptable. Inclusionism is, in essence, an attempt to make God conform to man's concepts of what he thinks heaven and hell should be like, rather than the other way around. That's exactly what Lucifer thought. He thought he had more wisdom and understanding than God. He thought he had a better plan than God's revealed way. It is from Satan that this type of thinking has inspired inclusionism. God will not change His plans of hell or His gospel of salvation to conform to the way the human mind and Satan think they should be.

Inclusion is in defiance of the reality of hell, which is clearly shown to exist in Scripture. Satan knows that if he can do away with hell in the minds of mankind, then he can get rid of the true gospel of salvation being preached. The first step toward this goal is to inspire mankind to reject God's plan for hell. Satan tempts human reasoning with the horror of such a reality as an eternal hellfire. Mankind reasons, "surely a loving God would not condemn the vast majority of mankind to hell!" So, the first step in doing away with hell is to do away with God's requirement for repentance and acceptance of Jesus Christ in order to receive salvation. The second step is to ignore or spiritualize away all Scriptures that clearly show hell exists and that every single person must repent of their sins and accept Jesus Christ in order to stay out of hell and receive eternal life with our Savior. Inclusion doctrine often pays only lip service to some Scriptures, tending instead to use only those Scriptures that can be easily twisted to seemingly support their "all are saved" theory. The third step is for inclusionists to become more led by the Spirit than by God's Word. To them, being "led by the Spirit" takes precedence when they feel the Scriptures do not line up with their ideas of what they should be saying. That way they can ignore the Scriptures that clearly deny their desired vain imaginations. I will have more to say on this in the next chapter.

Are You A Job?

God can do only what is in the best interest of all that He has created. He cannot and therefore will not do anything else. Just because we humans think that some of the actions God took in the Old Testament were un-loving doesn't mean that they were. It means we are a bit like Job. If we cannot understand why God has done or allowed what has been done as revealed in His Scriptures and dare to suggest that a loving God would not have done those things, then we run the risk of committing Job's folly of self-righteousness (see Job 32:1-2). Does your "righteousness" dare condemn the Creator of heaven and earth? Every action God has ever done is out of love, no matter whether you judge Him otherwise. It would be the better part of wisdom to assume you simply lack enough understanding concerning the matter. Just because we don't yet grasp how some of God's actions could be loving, condemning God would not be wise.

Our lesson lies in the story of Job. God allowed the devil to take Job's health and wealth from him. He even allowed Job's wife and children to die. Job thought that God had brought these horrendous disasters upon him. Job said, "...the LORD gave, and the LORD hath taken away; blessed be the name of the LORD" (Job 1:21b, KJV). Guess what? God did not do any of the evils that befell Job![10] But He did allow Satan to do them. God had a great purpose and lesson for Job to learn through his sufferings. When Job finally learned his lesson, God enlightened Job as to why He allowed his trials. It is interesting to note that God explained everything after Job's trials, not before. Job was in darkness beforehand about the details of the why of his trial or that God allowed it to create in Job more of God's maturity. Job's only solace was a few friends and his faith in God. It was only after the fact that Job got the point of it all. As a result, Job humbly repents to God. God had asked Job, "Who *is* he that hideth counsel without knowledge (Job 42:3a KJV)?" Job then fesses up that he was the guilty party who questioned God. Job admits his abject ignorance, saying, "I uttered that I understood not; things too wonderful for me, which I knew not" (Job 42:3b, KJV).

Those who condemn God for an eternal hellfire into which the unrepentant will be thrown need to learn this lesson from Job. Don't condemn what God clearly reveals in His Word. God may not have told you everything yet about events that surround the reality of hell. Yes, I agree that the vast majority of mankind will be condemned to this hell unless God has plans that He has not yet revealed to most of Christianity. Is that possible? Absolutely. The children of Israel journeyed in the wilderness and all died not crossing into the Promised Land, save for Caleb and Joshua. God knew in advance this would happen and didn't take the time to explain every event and detail of His plan concerning their journey to them, or even to Moses, for that matter. The sole purpose of their journey was to send a message to the body of Christ to come thousands of years later. Paul clearly states that this is the case: "Now all these things happened to them [Israel] by way of example, and they were written for our admonition, on whom the ends of the ages have come" (1 Cor. 10:11,

WEB). Wow! You mean God used the millions of those who lived and died in the story of Israel just to make invaluable spiritual points for us today? The answer is "yes!" Now, don't begin to judge the righteousness of God for doing this. Just accept the truth of it all and trust that our great God is loving, righteous, and just. Accept that in His great wisdom and plans that we have not yet fathomed, He will one day make it all plain to us all.

As far as the matter of an ever-burning eternal hell is concerned, there is a case to be made from the Scriptures that most of mankind who have ever lived will not go to hell, but will eventually be saved and enter into the kingdom of God. We know God is a fair God and is no respecter of persons. Years after Christ's resurrection, Peter was amazed to realize that God poured out His Holy Spirit on the gentile household of Cornelius giving them eternal salvation. This was the first time the gates of God's Kingdom were thrown open to the gentile world. God then revealed to Peter as he stated, "I now truly understand that God does not show favoritism, but welcomes those from every nation who fear Him and do what is right. He has sent this message to the people of Israel, proclaiming the gospel of peace through Jesus Christ, who is Lord of all (Acts 10:34b-36, BSB). My question is how can anyone who ever lived fear God and do what is right if they have never known name of Jesus Christ by which one must be saved? The vast majority of all who ever lived fall in this category. As Paul says, God is no respecter of persons. He is a fair and just God! This fair and just God will not send anyone to eternal hell fire who has not had a fair chance to hear and accept the gospel.

From Adam to the apostle Paul's day the Israelites were excluded from eternal salvation, except for as many as God called to repentance. Ancient Israel only understood God from a legalistic perspective. They lived in ignorance of the spiritual aspect of God and His purpose for their lives. If Israel was blinded in part to who God was, where did this put the rest of gentile nations of the world? Years after the resurrection of Jesus, the time had come to reveal from God's treasure chest a new astounding marvelous mystery. Of God's many mysteries, each one has been and will revealed at the precise time and place of God's choosing. God's time had come for Paul to say, "I do not want you to be ignorant of this mystery, brothers, so that you will not be conceited: A hardening in part has come to Israel, until the full number of the Gentiles has come in (Rom. 11:25, BSB). Notice Paul said Israel was hardened "in part." Why? An interesting account is given in scripture where John gives a reason as to why the Israelites did not believe in Jesus as their Messiah. John said:

> Although Jesus had performed so many signs in their presence, they still did not believe in Him. This was to fulfill the word of Isaiah the prophet: "Lord, who has believed our message? And to whom has the arm of the Lord been revealed?" For this reason, they were unable to believe. For again, Isaiah says: "He has blinded their eyes and hardened their hearts, so that they cannot see with their eyes, and understand with their hearts, and turn, and I would heal them John 12: 37-40, BSB)."

Who blinded their eyes and hardened their hearts? Paul answers this:

> What Israel was seeking, it failed to obtain, but the elect [Christians] did. The others were hardened, as it is written: "God gave them a spirit of stupor, eyes that could not see, and ears that could not hear, to this very day (Rom 11:7b-8, BSB)."

Israel knew only of the legalistic God of the Old Covenant; not that of the New Covenant. Their understanding of God was restricted to the legalistic letter of God's Word, not to a spiritual understanding of Jesus as our New Covenant. This "hardening" or "blinding" of Israel's mind is still ongoing because "the times of the Gentiles" will not end until just before the return of Christ. Since Israel was blinded to salvation, then where did that leave the rest of the gentile nations of the world? Most of Israel, and by far the vast majority of the world throughout history, have been and are blinded to the spiritual truths of God. Paul continues unveiling more about God's mystery concerning the blindness of mankind. He states clearly," For God has consigned all men [not just the Jews] to disobedience, ***so that He may have mercy on them all*** [emphasis added] (Ibid, vs. 32). Even Jesus said of Roman soldiers who were killing him, "Father, forgive them, for they do not know what they are doing (Luke 23:34b, BSB)." Why would He ask this unless they would someday have an opportunity to hear the gospel, repent, and experience God's mercy just as Paul said they would?

Exactly how all this mercy of God will be extended to the vast majority of mankind who never even knew the name of Jesus Christ is actually another story worthy of a book by itself. It is sufficient at this point to know that Satan will not win the war with God for the souls of mankind. Most of Christianity believes Satan has already won that battle by far. They believe that the vast majority of mankind are now roasting in hell like a pig on a stick for all eternity. I believe that God's scriptures pertaining to His Love Mysteries contain clear types, shadows, and statements not yet revealed to the vast majority of Christians. This mystery shows that God will yet shower His mercy on the vast majority of all mankind. Perhaps this task will be accomplished through a general resurrection yet to occur for all who never heard or understood God's offer of eternal salvation. Perhaps they will be given a period of time in a future resurrection to hear and accept or reject the gospel of salvation in Christ. If so, I believe most all of them will gratefully and joyously embrace it. I'm overjoyed at this thought and marvel at how endless and great is the mercy, depth, and breadth of God's love. I firmly believe that when God set out to redeem a fallen earth and mankind from the consequences of Adam's sin, His redemption will include the vast majority of all mankind. Satan will lose big time! Only the few who refuse God's offer to inter His Kingdom will suffer eternal damnation. This future resurrection is not the first time this mystery has been raised. I learned of it over fifty years ago in the Worldwide Church of God. I believe they were correct in this teaching based on the scriptures. I believe that this resurrection to life of all the billions upon billions who have never had a first chance to hear the gospel is still a mystery soon to be unveiled to the vast majority of Christianity.

God did not and does not give those He blinded an opportunity for salvation their lifetime because of their "free moral agency;" the ability to choose for themselves what they will or will not do. Our free moral agency is the only avenue by which God can create beings who truly love Him. However, "free moral agency" is the only thing in the universe that God cannot control which can stand in our way to eternity with Him. Paul said God "desires all men to be saved and to come to the knowledge of the truth (1 Tim 2:4, BSB)." Don't you believe since that is God's desire, He will do all within His great power to accomplish it? God desires above all things that every child He has created will join Him in eternity as His son or daughter. After all, He wanted it so much so that He sent His only beloved Son to die to make it possible for every impregnated egg He gave life to, born or aborted. God will move heaven and earth to make sure that the moment in time in which we are given to know about Him and His offer of eternal salvation, that we will most likely choose to accept it. God will not give anyone access to the gospel until he or she is at the point in their lives where they most likely exercise their free will by saying "Yes, yes, yes!" That is the mind set of our loving creator God. He is working the angles of history and our present lives to make sure when He finally opens our eyes and calls us to accept the gospel, that we will most likely embrace it and gain eternal life in His Kingdom.

Suffice it to say that the mystery of which I speak declares that God will win the war for most all the souls of mankind. In the end, our loving and just God will provide a way for all who never knew Him to have an opportunity to do so. It may even take a future resurrection to life for a long enough period of time for the unsaved to be able to come to know God and accept or reject the gospel. However, and whenever God gives them their first and only chance for salvation, I believe the overwhelming majority of all whoever lived will accept the gospel and enter into eternal glory in the Kingdom of God.

God Can Do Only Good To Us

What a wonderful glorious loving God we serve. It is God's desire that every single soul He has ever given life to will be in His Eternal Kingdom. This brings out a wonderful aspect of God's character that should be most comforting to each of us. It is this, God can only do what is good for us. He can never do evil toward us. Some of the bad things that happened in history and some of the bad things that happen to us quite frankly are blessings in disguise. If we blame God for them, then you and I someday might say to God, "I was talking about things I knew nothing about, things far too wonderful for me." I think at times we have been as guilty as Job in judging God concerning His actions or why He allows things to happen to us and to our loved ones. We may even blame God for these trials and difficulties. God allows trials to come upon us, but only for our eventual good. God promised his New Covenant Christians, "I will not turn away from them, to do them good" (Jer. 32:40, KJV). God promises His saints that He will do only good to them. He can never do evil to us. When Satan brings evil or disaster into our lives, Scripture tells us, "…we know that God works all things together for the good of those who love Him, who are called according to His purpose" (Rom 8:28, BSB). Furthermore, we are promised by God that, "No temptation has seized you except what is common to man. And God is faithful; He will not let you be tempted beyond what you can bear. But when you are tempted, He will also provide an escape, so that you can stand up under it." (1 Cor. 10:13, BSB). I know some of my most trying and difficult trials ultimately produced some of my greatest blessings. If God allows trials in your life, He can and ultimately will deliver you out of them. You, and possibly others as well, will learn wonderful invaluable lessons from what you have suffered. As a result, perhaps then we might be able to say, like Job, "I had heard of you [God] by the hearing of the ear, but now my eye sees you. Therefore I abhor myself, and repent in dust and ashes" (Job 42:5-6, WEB). As difficult as it might be to understand why God does something or allows certain things in our lives and the lives of others, we must understand in faith that it is indeed done out of love.

In order to accomplish God's grand plan, every thought and action He took in the Old Testament was done out of love. It may be difficult to humanly understand today, but the whys will be clearly revealed to all of us someday. Until then, just know that God did what had to be done in order to achieve the purpose of His mysterious master plan, the birth of His eternal children.

A Few Of Israel's Lessons

In God's master plan, for instance, as we have just discussed, God knew that the nation of Israel would exist and from them we would draw many valuable lessons to help guide us today. God knew He would make a covenant with them that they could not keep. Because sin had been in the world for nearly three thousand years by then, it was necessary to expose it and its destructive effects on mankind. God realized that, at that point in history, it was necessary to make with Israel a legalistic Old Testament Covenant that would outlaw and expose sin. There are many lessons in Israel's history written for the purpose of tutoring God's saints in order to guide us through the wilderness of this world into the promised coming kingdom of God. One of the main purposes of the story of Israel is to expose the need for Jesus. It teaches Christians how to walk in faith (wherein ancient Israel did not) with God into the Promised Land. Another major lesson is that it teaches us to recognize the need for the New Testament Covenant of grace, which was to come. The Old Testament exposed the problem that arose after God granted free will to the angels and then also to Adam and Eve. As a result, sin was introduced, which dictated the need for the solution given in the New Testament. The Old and New Testaments fit hand in glove.

Every word in both Testaments is God breathed and exuding with His love. For God's grand purpose the ends justify the means, even though some humans can't in their ignorance understand this. For God only, the ends do justify the means He uses to complete His grand mysterious love mystery. God can only use loving means to achieve it, even if that means allowing suffering and even death of sinners and saints. God allowed the great suffering of many of the Old Testament saints for a special purpose. The purpose of all of our trials is to allow God to build His faith and mind in us; and to allow us to be a witness for others. As Peter clearly states:

> … now for a little while you may have had to suffer various trials, so that the authenticity of your faith—more precious than gold, which perishes even though refined by fire—may result in praise, glory, and honor at the revelation of Jesus Christ. Though you have not seen Him, you love Him; and though you do not see Him now, you believe in Him and rejoice with an inexpressible and glorious joy, now that you are receiving the goal of your faith, the salvation of your souls. ~ 1 Peter 1:6b-9, BSB

God allows our trials and suffering for a special opportunity to build His faith. God does not bring these trials on us. Satan does! But God allows them and purposes to turn all our trials to work out for our good.

Paul did not blame God for the suffering and even death of the saints. He did not question the love of God when he spoke of their sufferings. The saints of old did many mighty deeds through faith and were great conquers. Paul said of them that they:

> … were tortured and refused their release, so that they might gain a better resurrection. Still others endured mocking and flogging, and even chains and imprisonment. They were stoned, they were sawed in two, they were put to death by the sword. They went around in sheepskins and goatskins, destitute, oppressed, and mistreated. The world was not worthy of them. They wandered in deserts and mountains, and hid in caves and holes in the ground. These were all commended for their faith, yet they did not receive what was promised. God had planned something better for us, so that together with us they would be made perfect. ~ Hebrews 11:35b-40, BSB

I think we do well as Christians in all of our trials and sufferings to remember that God didn't promise us a rose garden. He did, however, promise us eternal life with Him in the kingdom of God. Both the Old and New Testaments were and are necessary to provide us a road map to our eventual eternal deliverance from all trials into a coming new universe free of sin, suffering, and death. The Old Testament made it possible that the New Testament through Christ could deliver us into our coming new existence where only love, joy, peace, and eternal blessing will flow.

In this chapter we have seen how human reasoning, inspired by none other than Satan himself, has been used to justify a departure from the clear statements in the Bible concerning our need for Jesus Christ to receive eternal salvation. The basis for their theology is simply a loving God would not send anyone to hell cutting them off from access to heaven eternally. They throw in a virtuous sounding statement that their contrived god is therefore a more loving god than the one the bible describes. The only problem is that the God of the bible simply does not agree with them. God warns His people about those who fabricate their own vain imaginations contrary to His word:

> The Lord said, "Because this people draws near with their mouth and with their lips to honor me, but they have removed their heart far from me, and their fear of me is a commandment of men which has been taught; therefore, behold, I will proceed to do a marvelous work among this people, even a marvelous work and a wonder; and the wisdom of their wise men will perish, and the understanding of their prudent men will be hidden." ~ Isaiah 29:13-14 WEB

Again it is important to heed the scriptures warnings: "…'In the last times there will be scoffers who will follow after their own ungodly desires.' These are the ones who cause divisions [in the church], who are worldly and devoid of the Spirit" (Jude 1:18b-19 BSB). The result of these teachings invading the Christian church will cause divisions. The scriptures also warn about the results of these divisions: "Now the Spirit expressly states that in later times some will abandon the faith to follow deceitful spirits and the teachings of demons" (1 Tim. 4:1 BSB). Notice what one of their main heresies will teach: "…there were also false prophets among the people, just as there will be false teachers among you. They will secretly introduce destructive heresies that even deny the Master who bought them, bringing swift destruction on themselves" (2 Pet. 2:1 BSB). Yes, this teaching follows a Universalist doctrine that even denies the need for Jesus Christ!

Consider this fact, it makes inclusion doctrines extremely dangerous and deadly. To warn and protect the Church we must expound more on this important subject in the next chapter. We will take a closer look to see how these insidious doctrines of demons might be preached to seduce a gullible and unsuspecting church congregation.

17

WHAT AN INCLUSIONIST MIGHT PREACH

Another major fallacy of human reasoning by inclusionists is thinking that following after the Spirit when it contradicts the Scriptures is the will of God. If one touts that he or she is being led by "the Spirit," which is contrary to God's Scriptures, that is a red flashing light warning you that either that Christian is deluded or he or she is motivated by selfish desires. Inclusion preachers might state something to the effect that they "now walk more by the Spirit or God than by theology (meaning understanding of Scripture)." Beware of this kind of talk! God's Word and His Spirit are one and cannot contradict each other. I maintain that you must not exclude or diminish either one. If the Spirit of God is leading you, your faith in the Spirit and your actions must rest comfortably on the rails of God's Word as revealed in His Holy Bible. If not, then the spirit you follow is not that of God; it is the spirit of the god of this world that you knowingly or unknowing follow (see 2 Corinthians 4:4).

God and His scriptures are in perfect agreement with each other. Wherein you think they disagree, that is due only to your own rebellion against or misunderstanding of one or both. People can and often do misunderstand or knowingly pervert the Scriptures to justify their desired actions. They often justify their actions by giving more weight to "being led by the Spirit" than to what the Word of God says. It is a human tendency to believe our knowledge, wisdom, common sense, and understanding as being equivalent to that of God's. Guess what? Without God, none of what we think or believe is equivalent to that of God's. We cannot understand, think, or believe even one righteous thought unless God gives it to us. Without God, all that we naturally think God should think can only be based on our self-righteous thoughts and beliefs. Only God is infallible; humans are not. We should approach God's Word with an understanding of our own fallibility versus the immutability of God's Spirit and His Word. Our approach should be prepositioned with a consecrated desire to let Him change our pre-conceived thoughts, feelings, ideas, and imaginations to His when they are in conflict. When we do this, we allow God to do to us as He promised in the New Covenant agreement with us: "I will put My Laws in their hearts and inscribe them on their minds " (Heb. 10:16b, BSB).

Beware if your pastor begins to denigrate the necessity for every person to repent and believe the gospel in order to be saved. Our traditional gospel that each person must first hear God's call and then accept Jesus as their Savior to receive eternal life is the one taught for the last two thousand years. Inclusion preachers teach a different gospel. Their gospel is that not only is all mankind forgiven, he is also saved! Forgiven? Yes! Saved? NO! In order to try and prove all have been saved, inclusionists will use a Scripture like this: "For as in Adam all die, so in Christ all will be made alive" (1 Cor. 15:22, BSB). Inclusionists emphasize the "all will be made alive," meaning that all humanity who know or don't know Jesus Christ will receive eternal life. Their point is that "all" means "all humanity," not just those who hear the gospel about Jesus and "repent." That would be true, unless the scriptures did not further qualify that the "all" must also accept Jesus Christ as their savior (Rom 10:12-15, Acts 2:21, John 10:9, 11:25, 14:6, 14:23-24, 1 Corinthians 1:2).

Inclusionalist believe that all mankind is already saved. They believe this is what the apostles taught in their ministry. They teach that it was later that the Church descended into legalism limiting salvation only to those who repent of their sins, and accept Jesus; condemning the rest of mankind to eternal hell fire. The fact of the matter is the inclusionists are correct in that the sins of mankind have been forgiven, whether they know Jesus or not. But the Scriptures time and again clearly show that Jesus did not give all of mankind eternal salvation in His sacrifice without them knowing Him and repenting. Jesus will impart eternal life only to those who "all" come to know Him at God's calling; then repent and accept Jesus as their savior. Then and only then is eternal life imparted to them "all." So keep in your mind that salvation and entry into God's Kingdom is a three-step process. First an individual must hear the gospel. As scripture asks:

> How then can they call on the One they have not believed in? And how can they believe in the One of whom they have not heard? And how can they hear without someone to preach? And how can they preach unless they are sent? As it is written: "How beautiful are the feet of those who bring good news [the gospel of salvation]!" ~ Romans 10:14-15 BSB

Secondly, just as Jesus said: "…No one can come to Me unless the Father who sent Me draws him…. Everyone who has heard the Father and learned from Him comes to Me…." (John 6:44a-45b BSB). Third, as Paul said concerning the gospel:

> …that if you confess with your mouth, "Jesus is Lord," and believe in your heart that God raised Him from the dead, you will be saved. For with your heart you believe and are justified, and with your mouth you confess and are saved. Romans 10:9-10 BSB

Only those who God calls to hear the gospel and accept the sacrifice of Jesus as their savior are saved.

Vain Inclusion Examples

On a blackboard a small circle inside of a much larger circle was drawn by the minister declaring that the small circle represents those who know they are saved and the large circle represents the rest of mankind. Both are saved it was declared and the only difference between the two circles is that the large circle of people just do not know they are already saved. A proof scripture was given stating, "Therefore, just as one trespass brought condemnation for all men, so also one act of righteousness brought justification and life for all men" (Rom. 5:18, BSB). For inclusionists the emphasis is upon "life for all men," meaning all mankind. "All" means "all," he may point out, ignoring the many scriptures qualifying that salvation will come only to those who come to know and believe in Christ (Acts 2:38, Acts 3:19, Acts 4:12, Acts 5:31, Acts 10:43, Acts 20:21, Acts 26:18, John 20:31, Rom 10:8-15, Acts 13:38-39, Mark 1:15, Mark 16:15-16, John 1:12, John 3:16-18, John 5:24, John 6:47, John 17:3, Isaiah 59:20, etc.).

Would the circles above and one Rom 5:18 scripture concerning "all men" nullify the gospel of salvation and destroy the many other Scriptures clearly proving that salvation can come only through Jesus Christ and only after repenting and accepting Jesus as your Savior? Would it convince you that all of mankind who have ever been born are destined to be in heaven even if they never heard the name of Jesus? Not me!

Drawing two circles proves nothing. At best it illustrates a belief, but does not prove it. Proof of the inclusion doctrine does not get much deeper than this. You are given a superficial and grandiose claim with a weak illustration, perverting one or two Scriptures for support. Here is a point to ponder. If all mankind has been saved, whether or not he wants to be, and will be blissfully united with God for all eternity, then who goes to hell? The pastor may not ask this question at this point, but the obvious answer is none of mankind will. Some might say that hell is for the devil and his demons. Good point! What about the inclusionists who believe that the devil and his demons will eventually be in heaven too? Who goes to hell then? Another point to ponder is that if every person and angel who has ever been born or created is going to heaven, whether or not they want to, then why didn't God just stick us all there to begin with?

Did Paul Preach Inclusion?

Not to belabor the point, but in order to irrefutably establish this "all are saved" main theme of inclusion sermons, I will give a few other examples you might expect from a pastor going rogue with inclusive doctrinal beliefs. What if an inclusion preacher gave you these Scriptures, as one gave me, concerning the apostle Paul's imprisonment to prove a major point in his inclusionist beliefs?

> The jailer got a torch and ran inside. Badly shaken, he collapsed in front of Paul and Silas. He led them out of the jail and asked, "Sirs, what do I have to do to be saved, to really live?" They said, "Put your entire trust in the Master Jesus. Then you'll live as you were meant to live—and everyone in your house included." ~ Acts 16:29-31, *The Message*
>
> On the Sabbath, we left the city and went down along the river where we had heard there was to be a prayer meeting. We took our place with the women who had gathered there and talked with them. One woman, Lydia, was from Thyatira and a dealer in expensive textiles, known to be a God-fearing woman. As she listened with intensity to what was being said, the Master gave her a trusting heart—and she believed. ~ Acts 16: 13-14, *The Message*

The pastor used these scriptures to show that all you need do to be saved is simply to trust Jesus and put your trust in the fact that you were already forgiven and saved before the minister preached the gospel to you. Wow! Where in any of these Scriptures does it say that you were already forgiven and saved prior to hearing the gospel? The pastor preached this, and for me to believe it, I would have had to twist my head around 360 degrees in one direction a couple of times and then take a giant leap of faith. If you carefully reread these scriptures, there is no way you could conclude what the pastor did. If I have already been saved before even hearing the gospel, why would I need to put my trust in Jesus and have any faith? It looks to me as if this interpretation of Scripture got a bit corrupted in its translation.

The inclusion sermon I have been relating to you used only a total of five scriptures to prove the inclusion gospel. They are 1 Corinthians 15:22, Romans 5:18; and three Scriptures from Acts 16. Have these Scriptures that Inclusionists use convinced you yet of their new gospel? I hope not; for they are vague, at best, in proving inclusionism's new earth-shaking gospel. These Scriptures do not prove our traditional gospel of salvation is wrong. Using a few Scriptures like these hardly wipes away two thousand years of our understanding of the salvation gospel. Yet inclusion preachers stand up with such feeble Scriptures as these and loudly program a new and totally different gospel, stating that all of mankind have already been saved, whether or not they know it. As a result they now proudly proclaim that our mission as a church is to simply make all of those who are un-aware that they are saved, aware of it.

Was Jonah's Story One Of Inclusionism?

Let's now look at another inclusionist argument. How about the story of Jonah? Jonah was called by God to go to the great city of Nineveh, capital of the Assyrian empire. It just so happened to be the enemy and greatest threat to Jonah's nation of Israel. Jonah was commanded by God to tell Nineveh that He was going to destroy them because of their wick-edness. Jonah thought that the destruction of Nineveh was the good part of God's command. The part he objected to was he having to go and warn them of their demise. Jonah undoubtedly thought, "I can't believe God would tell me to go to Israel's mortal enemy and warn them of their destruction. I can't and won't do that!" He, like inclusionist, thought he had a better idea than God on this issue. It took a bit of convincing by God to get Jonah to obey Him. However, after Jonah spent three days and nights in the belly of the great fish God had prepared for him, Jonah decided that preaching in Nineveh was not that bad of an idea after all. Jonah marched into Nineveh and began telling them that they had forty days left before God destroyed them all. The story of Jonah teaches us of the great mercy of God being extended to even a wicked Gentile nation.

How would you suspect that a preacher might handle the story of Jonah to prove inclusion doctrine? He might do this. He might refer to Jonah's story in general without referencing a particular scripture to make his point that we should not be judgmental like Jonah was of God for wanting to save the lives of the wicked people of Nineveh. I heard a minister use this very point to say we should not be angry about God giving salvation to whom He wills, meaning every soul that ever existed. Would you be upset, he asked, if even Hitler were allowed into heaven? The pastor claimed that Jonah's story is about how loving and forgiving God is and how it shows God's grace. An Inclusionist might use Jonah's story as an example that we should be forgiving and accepting like God who saved a nation totally ignorant of Him. Apparently he was unaware of the fact the people of Nineveh had to repent before they were saved. The preacher concluded that Jonah's story adds a lot of weight to his theology that all the world is now saved without repentance. Yes, you could draw that conclusion if you too were unaware or ignored the fact of the necessity to repent. I clearly drew from Jonah's story that before salvation comes, there needs to be repentance. After all, Nineveh was saved only after all of its people recognized their grievous sins and bitterly repented before God. Then and only then were they saved.

Who Does The Saving?

Next let's look at another reason why inclusion ministers love to preach that everyone is already saved, whether or not they know it. It is because their inclusionist message lets these ministers off the hook of having to try to "save" anybody. After all, hasn't their main job for the past two thousand years been to try and save sinners from hell? Many ministers feel a great burden when they feel it is their responsibility to get people to repent and accept Jesus in order to be saved. They feel pressure to say exactly the right words that will cause the sinner to repent. If they are not constantly saving people, they feel responsible for not saving some who will surely go to hell. Also, it is kind of an embarrassing situation when, after having preached one of your most inspired sermons to hundreds, no one responds to your alter call.

An inclusionist preacher is set free from this burden of guilt for not doing a good recruiting job for Christ. If everybody is already saved, the pastor avoids the embarrassment of people not repenting and coming to Jesus. If everybody is already saved, this takes the pressure off of him, since his job is no longer to save sinners. He simply changes his gospel commission from calling people to repentance from sin to just telling them that they are already saved and that he wants them to know it! All these pastors have to do is deliver this "good news" to those who are ignorant of the fact that they are already righteous. They add the fact that God loves them so much that they are now and always have been saved and are going to heaven. They assure the ignorant that they are already loved and accepted by God and that they have been included in the body of Christ all their lives but they just haven't known it. They add that the people don't have to do anything. All they have to do is wake up to that fact and smell the roses that they are saved and going to heaven.

The inclusion preacher does not have to tell a Buddhist that "your religion is in vain, for you do not worship the one true God." Nor does he have to tell a Buddhist that unless he or she repents, he or she is going to hell. He can say to that Buddhist, "You are saved and always have been. God has always loved you. You're on your way to heaven; you just haven't known it." As a matter of fact, according to inclusionists, they have no choice about going to heaven. The inclusionist preacher soothes his mind, thinking this new gospel message is so much easier to preach than the old salvation gospel of hellfire and damnation. He comforts himself and his congregation that this new gospel is so much more loving and powerful than the old.

How Are You To Spread Inclusionism?

An inclusion preacher may encourage his congregation to be ready for persecution if they begin to share this new understanding of the gospel message. He will mostly likely tell his congregation that old-time religious preachers, friends, and family will try to argue with them by presenting a long list of Scriptures about the need to repent of sins and accept Jesus as Savior. Those who argue will claim there are many Scriptures that prove the existence of hell. However, the inclusion preacher may say, "Don't be fooled by what they tell you. Actually there probably won't be that many repent or burn-in-hell Scriptures; and the ones given will likely be rather vague." I heard two preachers tell their members to simply not argue with people who disagreed with them. It is interesting to note from the samples of inclusion teaching given above that they did not use a long list of Scriptures to prove their inclusion theology. As a matter of fact, in one inclusion sermon I heard, there were only five Scriptures used in the entire sermon, all of which were extremely vague at best.

The Greatest Tragedy

You may now be asking, "At this point and time, what difference does it make?" You may think that as long as Jesus is being preached, that is all that counts. What counts is given in this question: "…what must I do to inherit eternal life" (Luke 10:25 BSB)? Just learning about Jesus does not save anyone. As we have clearly seen, a person must not only hear the Word of God about Jesus but they must also be called by God, repent, and accept Jesus as their Savior. A sure sign that you are dealing with an inclusion doctrine pastor is if he no longer offers the unsaved in your congregation an opportunity to accept Jesus Christ as their Savior. The greatest tragedy of this service is that the pastor talks about Jesus and His love and then denies those unsaved attending his service the opportunity to repent, accept Jesus, and thereby receive eternal life in His kingdom.

Denying eternal life to these people is an act tantamount to being in the spirit of the Antichrist. The pastor would be denying Christ when it was for this very reason that He came to this earth to live, die, and be resurrected. If the pastor does not offer eternal life through the gospel message of repentance and salvation, then he is failing his main calling by God. In an attempt to camouflage this failure, he may instead offer a prayer that somehow "we are to spread the word of God's great love to all who are already saved. They desperately need to know this, so they can rest in what they already have in Christ." Although he denies the need for accepting Christ as their Savior to gain eternal life, he may still offer the giving of the Lord's Supper with the bread and juice for all attending that Sunday. This ceremony may seem sweet, but is actually a profane exercise when one observes it and does not believe in the need for the sacrifice it represents. He may give some type of prayer that sounds warm and lovey dovey, but in effect is spiritual pabulum. This is just double talk that avoids the whole point of why Christ came to earth, which was to offer eternal salvation for the unsaved through repentance and accepting Jesus as their Savior.

Would You Be Shocked?

I would hope that if you heard such a sermon that you would be shocked. You probably would want to visit with the pastor to make sure you heard what you thought you heard. And if so, you'd want to try and convince him of his error in order to protect the church members and those unsaved who might attend in the future. What if you did visit with him for a couple of hours, during which it became obvious that he did indeed believe in an errant inclusion doctrine? Let's say you tried to reason with him from the Scriptures, but to no avail. And in a final attempt to persuade him, you brought up the story of the two thieves nailed to a cross on each side of Jesus. You pointed out to the pastor that one of them repented and accepted Jesus. Jesus told the repentant thief that he would be with Him in Paradise that day. You ask the pastor, "What happened to the other unrepentant thief that mocked Jesus?" What if the pastor replied, "He is in Paradise too!" Shocked, you reply, "The Scriptures do not say that." He responds, "They do not say he wasn't there!" At this point you'd probably realize the pointlessness of continuing the conversation.

So, the sum of this chapter is that the word of God in the Scriptures and Christians being led by the Spirit of God should synchronize with one another. They are not mutually exclusive of each other. They are in perfect agreement. There is no perfect church, minister, or member, but my suggestion would be that when you realize that a church or minister disassociates the equivalency of Scripture and God's Spirit, then it's time to find yourself another church and or minister for spiritual guidance and nourishment. The proper church and ministers are critical to a Christian's spiritual growth. The very purpose for both is to feed

God's Children so they can mature in the likeness of Jesus Christ. You therefore want to wisely choose those who feed you your spiritual food. Legalism or licentiousness tends to elevate either the Scriptures or Spirit one over the other and thus diminishes the saints' ability to properly worship Christ. Either extreme is not a balanced nourishing spiritual diet for God's Children.

The height of futility is if a minister tries to feed you the heresy that eternal salvation can be gained in any other way than through Jesus Christ. This heresy at best delays or withholds true salvation knowledge to the individual and at worst attributes to their eternal damnation. Just because one may attend a so called "Christian Church," does not mean that it really is one. Have a critical ear to what is preached there. Don't accept everything you hear. Legalism or licentiousness being taught are both horrible to the spiritual health of the saint, but even worse than that is the big red flashing light warning you that the church or minister you are following does not proclaim that eternal salvation can only be obtained through accepting Jesus Christ as their personal Savior. That is the proper time to walk out their door. Inclusionism is a strategy devised by none other than Satan himself to destroy mankind and God's plans to give birth to His children into His eternal Kingdom. Let's next look more deeply into this plan of Satan and how he will try to use it to destroy God's plans and all of mankind in the next few years.

18

WILL INCLUSION DELIVER PARADISE?

God has placed within the heart of mankind an innate desire to return to the paradise that Adam and Eve lost. Countless attempts have been made by mankind to recapture this Utopian existence since the dawn of humankind. Man has dreamed of a world in which spiritual and political peace, happiness, justice, and material blessings for all reign supreme. Most of our lives are spent pursuing this Shangri-La. History is strewn with vain attempts to achieve this dream by unifying the world politically and religiously. Each of these attempts have promised utopia, but all of them have failed. The major problem has been that none of these entities have been able to agree on exactly how to achieve paradise. Due to quarrels among nations over what should constitute paradise and what the best pathway to it is, warfare between them has been the primary method used to try and impose one nation's ideology over another.

There is now another drive to unify the world politically and religiously. The present-day religious attempt in this direction is that of the inclusion doctrine. What is known as "political correctness" is a tool being utilized to force us all ultimately into the elite's ideal of a unified utopian political and religious state. The truth, however, is that mankind, limited to just his physical world and carnal desires, is incapable of creating paradise. Man's desires, without God, limit him to seeking happiness solely through the gratification of his fleshly imaginations and desires. The real reason mankind's dream is not achieved is because there is only one Being in the entire universe that can bring about a return to paradise. That's right, only God can do this! This fact is a major lesson that God is using history and the fast-approaching end-time events to teach mankind. It is only through Christ that the desire of paradise can be achieved on earth. This is exactly why Christ is returning. He will give to mankind the paradise our hearts yearn for. This truth, however, has not dissuaded men and nations from attempting to achieve paradise without God. Hope seems to spring eternal in the heart of man to achieve a heaven without God. However, this is impossible. Only God can unify all nations and achieve harmony, peace, and prosperity.

Satan's Attempts To Unite The Nations

Satan has tried to manipulate this desire in mankind for paradise in order to achieve his purpose of destroying all life on earth. Satan's intent has been to avoid his fatal demise in hellfire, which will happen at the hands of the promised coming Messiah. After the sin of Adam and Eve, God told Satan that from their seed would come the Savior of the world that would deliver him a fatal blow, crushing his head. From that moment on, Satan's obsession was to kill the seed of Adam and Eve so that Jesus Christ would not be born. Satan probably thought that Adam's son Able would be the Messiah, or at least the one who carried the seed from which Jesus would come. Satan thought that if he could kill Able, he could nip God's prophecy in the bud and God's plans would be spoiled. Without God's permission, He did not give Satan the power to destroy any individual or nation on earth. Satan is only allowed to influence peoples and nations to do his killing through his evil selfish spirit which infects them. Undoubtedly Satan believes that as long as mankind exist, they pose a threat to his kingdom on earth. Satan knows God intends mankind to join Jesus Christ, their elder brother, in replacing his tyrannical rule of the earth.

Satan did kill Able, not by his own hand, but through that of Cain, his brother. Adam and Eve had many other children after that. And as they began multiplying on the earth, it soon became impossible for Satan to know for sure from which man's seed the Savior would come. At that point I believe Satan decided he had to bring about the destruction of all mankind to remove any possibility that the Savior would be born. Satan probably had high hopes that if he could somehow cause all life on earth to be destroyed, this would accomplish his purpose. He probably was very excited and thrilled to hear God tell Noah that He was going to destroy all life on earth by a flood. At least the flood narrowed down the fact that the promised seed could come only from Noah or one of his three sons on the ark. I'm sure Satan thought he could sabotage the ark's construction during the next 120 years it took Noah to build it. That failing, he undoubtedly tried to figure out some way to sink the boat, once floated, killing everybody. However, God miraculously saved Noah's family through the flood to repopulate the earth.

The Tower Of Babel

The flood came and billions died, save only the eight of Noah's family. Satan's hopes were dashed that all would die. Eventually a renewed hope may have sprung up in Satan's perverted mind. Perhaps he could harness man's drive to achieve paradise by convincing him that peace and happiness could be achieved by unifying into a single ruling political and religious force. Soon after the flood, approximately 4,364 years ago,[1] we see the first recorded effort of mankind under Nimrod to unite the world in the story of the Tower of Babel. "The Bible states that he [Nimrod] was 'a mighty hunter before the Lord [and]... began to be mighty in the earth.' Extra-biblical traditions associating him with the Tower of Babel led to his reputation as a king who was rebellious against God."[2] If this is so, then Nimrod was the first biblically recorded world-ruling Antichrist. His selfish attitude was expressed by his people as Scripture describes:

> And the whole earth was of one language, and of one speech. And it came to pass, as they journeyed from the east, that they found a plain in the land of Shinar; and they dwelt there. And they said one to another, Go to, let us make brick, and burn them throughly. And they had brick for stone, and slime had

227

they for morter. And they said, Go to, let us build us a city and a tower, whose top *may reach* unto heaven; and let us make us a name, lest we be scattered abroad upon the face of the whole earth. And the LORD came down to see the city and the tower, which the children of men builded. And the LORD said, Behold, the people *is* one, and they have all one language; and this they begin to do: and now nothing will be restrained from them, which they have imagined to do. Go to, let us go down, and there confound their language, that they may not understand one another's speech. So the LORD scattered them abroad from thence upon the face of all the earth: and they left off to build the city. ~ Genesis 11:1-8, KJV

God has not sanctioned or allowed mankind since Babel to have just one shared language, nor has He allowed one government politically and religiously to rule all peoples of the world. God gave only one reason for confusing the language and scattering the people. God said that if He did not do so, "then nothing they plan to do will be impossible for them." One might ask, "What would be so bad about that?" For one thing, it is probable that unless God confused and scattered the people, God's time-line for the future of mankind would have been shortened drastically. God knew that if He allowed mankind to unite under one government, the people would have developed scientifically very fast and have been capable of bringing the world to the edge of nuclear destruction within a couple thousand years. God also knew that if He allowed them to remain united as one nation with one language then they would never have achieved the political or religious the utopia they sought. They would have eventually divided into various warring factions, politically and re-ligiously. By then, with nuclear capability, they could have destroyed the world, preventing the birth of the Messiah.

The timeline of history was not granted to mankind to deter-mine. History's sole purpose and timeline has been determined by God to maximize, as much as possible, the number of births of His sons and daughters into His eternal kingdom. If God did not control history's timeline, Armageddon could have occurred a few thousand years be-fore now, bringing the destruction of the world and end of all life for mankind. Satan would have loved that scenario and has sought to bring that to reality time and again throughout history. For whatever reason, we know that what God did at the Tower of Babel was best for mankind and God's future plans. This scattering of peoples into various nations around the world definitely did slow down the scientific progress of mankind. However, God did not quench the desire He placed in the human heart for paradise. Satan throughout history has tried to manipulate this God-given desire to serve his purpose in destroying all life on earth, thus preventing the Messiah from replacing him as the god of this world.

Since the Tower of Babel, nation after nation with various competing Utopian ideas have vied to unite the world politically and religiously in order to forge their ideals of unity and peace. The rallying cry and banner under which they all have marched has been freedom and happiness to be delivered through world conquest in the name of their various gods. Undoubtedly Satan has had a hand in these attempts to unify the world, not to bring the peace that man seeks but to bring war, devastation, and utter destruction.

When Satan's efforts failed to destroy all mankind during the Flood, he thought that if he could just destroy Israel or at least the tribe of Judah, then surely the prophesied coming God King who was to replace him as ruler of this earth could not come. Satan's goal has never been to return paradise to the people; rather it has been to use this desire in mankind to ultimately destroy every last one of them. Satan's influence over the people at the Towel of Babel is noted when their purpose for building it was stated. They said they wanted to build a tower to heaven so, "we may make a name for ourselves," not to praise God. Their purpose was not to glorify their Creator; quite to the contrary, it was to glorify themselves and defy God's will.

Try And Try Again

Since God did not grant Satan the ability to destroy all human life, his only hope of a worldwide massacre was either for God to do it or for mankind to do it to themselves. Noah's flood showed it was not God's intent to destroy all of mankind. At Babel, to prevent mankind from eventually destroying himself, God confused their languages and scattered them around the world. Since Babel, history has been filled with countless stories of man's attempts to reunify the world as it was at the Tower of Babel. In every attempt since, Satan's desire was to use the attempt at unification to bring about mankind's total annihilation. It is the same song and same verses over and under the guise to "bring world peace" through war. Satan has been the catalyst for all of the major wars throughout history, using nations to try to impose universally a particular religion and governmental structure. The most notable examples of this would be that of Babylon, Persia, Greece, Rome, Napoleon's France, and more recently Hitler's Nazi Germany. Some of the bloodiest and fiercest wars fought for world domination have been between different religions, including the wars between the Christian Crusaders and the Muslims in the twelfth and thirteenth centuries.

Satan's Last Attempt

Satan is once again influencing the nations to try and unite to achieve paradise. However, Satan intends that this unification will produce his desired Armageddon and the end of the world. The groundwork for prophesied end-time events is now being laid in attempts to achieve peace and a New World Order (man's idealized brand of paradise) through political correctness, progressivism, and military means. We see it today in a revival of an attempt to impose the Muslim faith not only on the nations of the Middle East but around the world. This is being done by two major Islamic faiths. One is that of the radical Sunni brand of Islam known more commonly now known as Daesh, ISIS, and ISIL. In 2014 they established the Islamic State of Iraq and the Levant. The other faith attempting to impose their religious and political views is the radical Shia brand championed by Iran. Both are religious extremists and their armies are now fighting with one another in Iraq and Syria. Although these two Islamic faiths are united in their worship of Allah, they are divided doctrinally in how Allah wants to be served. Each wants the other and the rest of the world to convert to their particular brand of Islamic doctrine. Each is vying to usurp the other and usher in their apocalyptic end-time's eschatology. Author Joel C. Rosenberg, describing each, said:

> The Islamic Republic of Iran today is ruled by an apocalyptic, genocidal death cult. So is the Islamic State, also known as ISIS or ISIL. The former are Shia. The latter are Sunni. Both believe the End of days has come. Both believe their messiah—known as the 'Mahdi' — is coming at any moment. Both are trying to hasten the coming of the 'Mahdi' is ruled by an apocalyptic, genocidal death cult. Yet each has entirely different strategies. ISIS wants to build a caliphate. Iran wants to build The Bomb. ISIS is committing genocide now. Iran is preparing to commit genocide later.[3]

ISIS's stated goal is to expand by conquest their caliphate state to engulf, physically and spiritually, not only the Muslim world but all nations on earth. All of this is being done, they believe, in the name of and at the bidding of their god, Allah. Preferring one Islamic terrorist state over the other demands a difficult choice. ISIS is now engaged in killing as many infidels as they can, whereas the other (Shiites, aka Iran) will much more effectively kill far more of them at a later time after they acquire nuclear weapons. "Longer term, Iran is the most dangerous, especially if the President approves this nuclear deal that is emerging. Why? Because the apocalyptic leaders of Iran are biding their time to build a nuclear arsenal capable of killing millions of people in a matter of minutes."[4]

Where Are We Now?

Where does all of this position us at this point in time? It is in one sense a return to the desire Satan had for the Tower of Babel and Noah's flood. Satan failed to use them to destroy all mankind as he had hoped. Satan will once again try by gathering together the nations of the world under the false banner of peace and freedom. However, his real purpose is not to restore the paradise he promises but to utterly destroy all life on earth. Satan realizes that the world now has the scientific capability to deliver his dream, which is the destruction of all life on earth through the use of nuclear weapons. At this very moment, as I write, Iran is close to producing nuclear weapons. The United States is now in serious negotiations with Iran, striving to agree on a treaty to limit Iran's nuclear capability. On March 17, 2015, the following exchange took place between John Bolton, former U.S. Ambassador to the United Nations, and reporter Bill Hemmer in a Fox news report:

John Bolton said, "I think the negotiations [between the United States and Iran] themselves have already provoked a nuclear arms race in the Middle East. Saudis, Egyptians, Turks and others are not waiting for Iran to demonstrate it has a bomb; but [are] going ahead now and [developing] their own nuclear capability." Bill Hemmer then questioned, "Within those countries, there's a process now underway [in] Saudi Arabia, Turkey, and Egypt?" Mr. Bolton answered his question by expanding on it: "And maybe more [countries], cause they see [the] United States isn't going to stop Iran. They [Saudi Arabia, etc.] have to look to their own defenses and get nuclear capability. I think the Saudis could purchase it [nuclear bomb] from the Pakistan very quickly. Others may have to, through the process of building nuclear reactors and gaining control over the nuclear fuel cycle. But, there's no doubt nobody in the Middle East wants Iran to have nuclear weapons. They see this deal as do American critics of the deal as an open highway for Iran to get it done." Mr. Hemmer responds with, "Well, that's a steep charge! That race is already underway you believe?" Mr. Bolton answers, "I think these negotiations have accelerated what would have happened on the day we would know Iran had a nuclear weapon. I think the Saudis and others now foresee it now as essentially inevitable and they're not going to wait. They are going to act now while there's still time in their view."[5]

Conservative Prime Minister Benjamin Netanyahu of Israel was re-elected to his office on March 17, 2015, after a very hard-fought election campaign. In order to elicit more votes from the conservative base in Israel, he changed his stance, which called for the possibility of a Palestinian State. He stated that he would not allow a two-state solution to the Palestinian crisis. And, not only that, he said that would allow increasing Jewish settlements in the West Bank. Netanyahu's seemingly recalcitrant stance against a two-state solution infuriated many Palestinians and elicited a United Nations condemnation. The day after Netanyahu's stunning reelection win, he tried to modify his statement by saying that until the removal of the terrorist organization of Hamas from the peace equation and the recognition Israel's right to exist by the Palestinians, there cannot be a two-state solution. This elaboration of Netanyahu's stance did little to pacify President Obama. "The White House, unmoved by Netanyahu's effort to backtrack, delivered a fresh rebuke against him... and signaled that Washington may reconsider its decades-old policy of shielding close ally Israel from international pressure at the United Nations."[6] This threat would possibly allow a UN resolution establishing a Palestinian State without Israel's consent. It is becoming obvious that there definitely is a gathering storm among all nations against Israel. Even Netanyahu's modified statement allowing the possibility of a Palestinian State has done little to assuage the anger of President Obama and has increased international isolation. Yahoo news wrote:

> Speaking anonymously to the *New York Times,* several unnamed officials said the Obama administration might agree to a UN Security Council resolution enshrining a two-state solution in a move which would be anathema to Netanyahu. "The premise of our position internationally has been to support direct negotiations between the Israelis and the Palestinians," a senior White House official said.[7]

The West Bank is occupied and is controlled by Israel. If the United Nations did declare that the West Bank is a new Palestinian State without Israel's consent, war could easily erupt. I believe *New York Times* bestselling author of *The Islamic Antichrist,* Joel Richardson, has made an important statement that injects some understanding into the current Middle East dilemma. He said, "People need to understand that the main way Satan affects the world is through empires and armies. And his rallying cry at this time in history is for war against Israel."[8]

Prophecy from now forward solely revolves around the nation of Israel. Satan has tried many times to annihilate all Jews from the face of the earth. He will make one more final attempt to completely destroy not only Israel but all of mankind by stirring up the nations against Israel and gathering them to battle against her. The prophecies reveal this will happen just prior to the return of Jesus to earth. Satan's overt rallying cry will be that Israel is the pariah of the world and that only by destroying Israel will it be possible to bring peace to the earth. The current angst worldwide against Israel is the beginning of hostilities that will crescendo into this world's end-time events prophesied in Scriptures. Satan probably thinks that if he can destroy all life on earth, this will prevent not only the return of Jesus but also the resurrection of God's sons and daughters, who under Christ are to replace the devil's reign on earth. If Satan can destroy mankind, he makes a liar out of God, who clearly states He will save Israel and usher in the Utopian paradise for which all mankind yearns. Pretty weird thinking, right? Well, Satan's a pretty weird fellow. Whoever said he was rational after his first attempt to overthrow God?

It is now time to turn our attention to what happens between now and the Battle of Armageddon at the return of Jesus Christ at which time God's love mystery will be manifested to all the world to see. At first in this next chapter we will look into when the next stage of God's plan will occur. This will be the sixth stage which is the resurrection and glorification of the children of God. It is at this stage that sons and daughters will be gloriously manifested for all the world to see. Christians today refer to it as the Rapture. There is much division among Christian circles as to exactly when this will occur. Let's now take a close look at this question.

19

WHEN IS THE RAPTURE?

It is obvious that there is a lack of unity in understanding from Scriptures exactly when Christ will return to give His saints who are dead and alive their new eternal bodies. The point I want to make here is that exactly when He will return is not as important as the fact that we all should be ready now, for none of us know for sure if we will see tomorrow. It is obvious that correct knowledge of when the Rapture will occur is not necessary for salvation. For some reason, Christ is allowing our lack of unanimity on this subject. With this being said, I can safely say that the Second Coming of Christ will follow one of the following interpretations. Trying to understand the various beliefs regarding the return of Jesus to Rapture His saints can be daunting. I will try to keep it as simple as I can.

First of all, let's get a general understanding of the terminology concerning what many call the "tribulation period." This time period is seven years. It is believed this tribulation period to be the same as the last week of Daniel's seventy weeks prophecy (Dan. 9:20-27).[1] Let's note concerning Daniel's seventy weeks prophecy that his last week (the seventieth) would last seven years (a year for each day of the week), immediately followed by the return of Christ to establish His kingdom on earth. Although this last seven years of time is generally recognized as "the tribulation period", the first three and a half years of tribulation will be mild compared to the last three and a half years. The last three and half years is referred to as the "great tribulation" because of the persecution and martyrdom of Jews and

Christians. The first three and a half years are seen as just "the beginning of sorrows" (see Matthew 24:8), after which the Antichrist will unleash his satanic terror on Jews and Christians.

There are six basic Rapture views. I believe these six that can be further divided into two basic groups: those who believe that the Rapture occurs prior to the revealing of the Antichrist and those who believe it will be after this time. Let's take a brief look at each of these Rapture beliefs, beginning with the *pre-tribulation Rapture view*. It champions the belief that the Rapture will come prior to what is known as the "seven year tribulation period."[2] They believe that Christ will rapture the saints just prior to this time, thus shielding them from the seven vials of God's wrath which many believe will be unleashed on the world during the tribulation period. After the tribulation period, Christ will return to vanquish the devil and rebellious mankind at the Battle of Armageddon.

There are those who believe in a *mid-tribulation Rapture,* which will occur just prior to the beginning of the of the last three and one half years of the great tribulation.[3] There is a *partial Rapture* view, which teaches that the Rapture could occur anytime in or after the last seven years.[4] This Rapture or series of Raptures could vary in time for each Christian, depending on when they were converted. It could also depend on their faith and walk with God during this time.[5] There are also those who believe in a *Pre-wrath Rapture.*[6] They are not sure when, but they believe that the Rapture will occur sometime during the last three and one half years. They believe that the three and one half years[7] will be cut short based on what Christ said: "If those days [great tribulation] had not been cut short, nobody would be saved. But for the sake of the elect, those days will be shortened" (Matt. 24:22 BSB).[8] Christ will then Rapture His saints and then unleash His seven vials of wrath on the earth. Now let's consider those who believe in a *post-tribulation Rapture.*[9] They believe Christians will have to endure great tribulation occurring during the last three and a half years after the Antichrist is revealed.[10] They believe the Rapture occurs immediately after the great tribulation at the sounding of the seventh and last trumpet.[11]

Lastly there are those who believe in a *Post-Millennialism Rapture* which, "...is essentially the position held as well by amillennialists, who view the millennial rule of Christ as allegorical to Christ's rule in the believer through sanctification (II Pet. 3:8) thus precluding literal interpretation of a thousand-year period.[12] Amillennialists commonly view the rapture of the Church as one and the same event with the second coming of Christ."[13]

Of all the Rapture theories available, personally, I would love to believe in the pre-tribulation Rapture. I know of no Christian who looks forward to the idea of having to endure the persecution and possible martyrdom during the great tribulation. It would be quite natural to desire a way of escaping this prophesied horrific end time holocaust. However, as much as I desire to believe in escaping this through a pre-tribulation Rapture, I'm sorry to say I believe the scriptures teach a Post-tribulation Rapture. It would be a pleasant surprise if I am wrong and the Rapture occurs prior to the great tribulation. However, I find it difficult to believe in the pre-tribulation Rapture when a post-tribulation Rapture seems to be made clear by the apostles and even Jesus Himself.

It would be quite natural, if you are a Pre-tribulationalist, for you to close up this book and not want to hear any opposing views. I recently heard Brian Kilmeade on the Fox & Friends morning show say that people do not like to think about what they don't believe. I think that simple statement is quite true and profound. I would like to add to it that people also don't even want to hear what they don't believe. Human nature tends to believe what it wants to believe in face of any headwinds to the contrary. It's like saying "please don't confuse me with the truth. My mind is already made up!" This truism has led many down an errant pathway to many problems when truth and reality are ignored and subjugated to personal desires. It is far better for us to believe the truth rather than what we would like to believe is true. In the same vain we need to strive to know and believe what God means in His word rather than what we would like for it to mean. When saints hold two different doctrinal views concerning the same scriptures, it is wise to hear opposing arguments to make sure no adjustments of our beliefs need to be made. We should not square off and argue with one another. Scripture says, "… avoid quarreling over words; this is in no way profitable, and leads its listeners to ruin. Make every effort to present yourself approved to God, an unashamed workman who accurately handles the word of truth" (2 Tim. 2:14b-15, BSB). Both parties should be respectfully listen to each other allowing for the possibility of being wrong in the name of seeking God's real truth concerning an issue, even if it differs with what we or our favorite preacher would like to believe.

It would be wise to verify our biblical beliefs based on what the scriptures say rather than just what someone tells us they think it says. God gives us the method we should follow in formulating any religious belief. The apostle Paul preached a sermon to the people who lived in Berea. Rather than just swallowing hook, line, and sinker what Paul said scripture reports, "Now the Bereans were more noble-minded than the Thessalonians [Church], for they received the message with great eagerness and *examined the Scriptures every day* [emphasis added] to see if these teachings were true. As a result, many of them believed [what Paul said]…" (Acts 17:11-12a, BSB). I will present to you what I believe concerning the scriptures and why. You can study it and of course make up your own mind. Then one day we can visit in God's Kingdom and one of us can laughingly say, "I told you so!"

Concerning The Rapture

Now, concerning the Rapture, there are only two possible narratives; the Rapture is going to be either before the appearing of the Antichrist or after it. Other than the Holy Bible, there is no other authoritative ultimate source that one can subscribe to in discerning the truth of this matter. All other writings or speculations concerning the Rapture by individuals throughout history may be interesting and helpful but unless they are verified by the inspired writings of the bible, they are useless. Now all those who fall into either a pre- or post-Antichrist Rapture camp claim to use the bible to justify their stances. However, obviously only one of these groups can be correct. The only thing standing in the way of the truth is the misunderstanding and/or misinterpretation of the scriptures that are often unintentionally motivated by personal desires.

It is asserted by Post-tribulationalists that none of the early

Church fathers promoted any pre-tribulation doctrine. They maintain this doctrine did not appear in any Church writings until approximately 1,800 years after the resurrection of Christ.[14] The challenge made to the pre-tribulationalists is that their Rapture doctrine did not exist before John Darby invented it in 1830. It is asserted that, "before it [the pre-tribulation Rapture theory] 'popped into John Darby's head' no one had ever heard of a secret rapture doctrine."[15] This is a very bold and most unlikely true statement made by a post-tribulationalist. I believe there were some prior to 1830 who thought a secret rapture might occur before the holocaust of the great tribulation. Knowing human nature and sometimes its unintentional tendency to color interpretations of scripture based on personal desires, my contention is why wouldn't there be some Christians during the first eighteen hundred years of the Church who would chose to believe in a rapture which would spare their lives from possible martyrdom in the great tribulation? After all Jesus did say that Christians should, "…watch at all times, and pray that you may have the strength to escape all that is about to happen [the great tribulation] and to stand before the Son of Man (Luke 21:36b, BSB)." What better way could there be to escape the great tribulation than having Christ come to Rapture us before it occurs?

Post-tribulationalists have declared that there was no one believing or writing about a pre-tribulation Rapture prior to 1830. This is a weak and shaky argument at best. The implication in this argument is, since there are no written records to the contrary, a pre-tribulation doctrine must therefore be fictitious! So, a pre-tribulation belief must be wrong! Right? No, Wrong! Just because there is no historical records of such a doctrine does not necessarily mean a pre-tribulation Rapture doctrine is wrong. Theoretically it is possible that the Apostles taught the pre-tribulation Rapture from the scriptures, but that doctrine became corrupted and eventually lost over the next three or four hundred years as it was replaced by a post-tribulation belief. Likewise, on the other hand, if there was an early "Church Father" (or several Fathers) who wrote about a pre-tribulation Rapture in the fourth century, that does not prove the pre-tribulation Rapture doctrine is true! My contention is why wouldn't there be at least a few throughout the last two thousand years who believed in and perhaps even wrote about a pre-tribulation Rapture? If during the apostle Paul's life time there were some preaching an errant premature Rapture, surely there would be some who would preach it after his death! We will discuss more on this shortly.

Since the post-tribulation proponents have charged there are no historical records promoting a Rapture before the great tribulation, pre-tribulationalist have not let this challenge go unheeded. They have made a concerted effort to prove the existence of historical documents about a pre-tribulation Rapture! They have been diligently searching the archives to try and find support for their Rapture doctrine. What do you think their chances are in finding just such a record? I would be surprised if they didn't find something! Well guess what? They have indeed found a champion for their doctrine. His name is Ephrem the Syrian. He was a fourth century major Christian theologian of the early Byzantine Eastern Church.[16] The following is from a Syriac text known as the "Pseudo-Ephraem."[17] Concerning the coming great tribulation, it states that Christians would be spared by being "taken to the Lord lest they see the confusion that is to overwhelm the world because of our [the world's] sins."[18] If the text was referring to a Rapture here, this would indeed dispute the post-tribulationalist claims that no one prior to 1830 knew of or wrote about a pre-tribulation Rapture. Post-tribulation proponents say the document is a forgery not written in the fourth century in which Ephraem lived, but written by some unknown author in the 8th century or later.[19] Post-tribulationalist also claim that other text in the "Pseudo-Epraem," rather than prove a pre-tribulation Rapture, actually prove that Christians will be martyred in the great tribulation.[20] Who knows? Back and forth it goes! If you wish to read the Syriac-text version of the "Pseudo-Ephraem," for yourself then check the website in my End Notes.[21]

Only The Scriptures Hold The Truth

To me, it makes no difference who is right. It doesn't change one word in the God's Holy Bible. Even if it can be proven that there were several fourth century Church Fathers who believed in and wrote about a pre-tribulation Rapture, unless they agree with the bible, they are all wrong! Consider the gospel I have proclaimed in this book. Much of it has not been proclaimed in writings or preaching for the last 2,000 years. Does that make it heretical? The answer is no; unless it disagrees with the scriptures. Take for instance the gospel of grace. There is no history I am aware of, apart from the bible, showing that it has ever been proclaimed like it is today in the ministries of Joseph Prince, Creflo Dollar, Paul Ellis, Butch Bruton, Joel Olsteen, and many others. Is it possible that this grace gospel was what the Apostles taught during the first hundred years of the church and then as soon as they all died, it morphed over the next three hundred years into a legalistic gospel which became the predominately accepted "gospel" for the next fifteen hundred years? Absolutely! That is exactly what happened! And how does one justify the gospel of grace preached today; not by the writings of any early Church Fathers, but simply by the word of God in the scriptures and nothing else! How else do you think Martin Luther in the 16th century could justify his journey out of works by faith and defy the legalism of the Roman Catholic Church? It was his recognition of the true meaning of grace and faith that he saw in the scriptures which spurred his march to walk in faith out of smothering Church legalism. His "new" understanding was guided only by the pure light of God's word. Thus, I believe he was the genesis of the Churches' march out of legalism toward the true gospel Paul preached, which has not been completely restored until our present day. We now enjoy the gospel of abundant grace totally free of legalism which is now being championed around the world!

I do not relish the idea of having to go through the great tribulation where Christians will be slaughtered under the direction of the Antichrist. I must say that preaching an avoidance of the great tribulation by accepting Jesus Christ is very alluring to many today. It seems as if fears and desires sometimes drive our theology rather than sound interpretation of the Scriptures. I am afraid this may be true in the case of the pre-tribulation Rapture doctrine. Sadly, some preachers use this doctrine as a threat that if you don't repent and accept Jesus, you will have to go through the great tribulation. In this case it unfortunately is an attempt to scare people into salvation. I don't think this tactic is necessary. God is the One who opens the minds of those whom He invites to eternal salvation, not the minister preaching. God does not need to coerce anyone into His kingdom under threat of hell or the great tribulation. As much as I don't want to be martyred, I have had to settle for that possibility as a Christian, based on the Scriptures as I see them. There is no scripture in the Bible that states that the Rapture occurs prior to the great tribulation.[22] For a simple, clear, and unambiguous scriptural account of when the Rapture will occur, I would direct you to this website listed in my End Notes.[23]

Pre-Tribulation Rapture Proof?

Actually there is a record of a pre-tribulation Rapture being taught in the Thessalonian church during the ministry of the apostle Paul. It became such an issue that Paul had to dispute and correct it. Notice how Paul characterized this Rapture theory which he warned the church about:

> Now concerning the coming of our Lord Jesus Christ and our gathering [rapture] together to Him, we ask you, brothers, not to be easily disconcerted or alarmed by any spirit or message or letter presuming to be from us and alleging that the *day of the Lord* has already come. Let no one deceive you in any way, for it will not come until the rebellion occurs and the man of lawlessness [the Antichrist] (the son of destruction) is revealed. ~ 2 Thessalonians 2:1-3 BSB, emphasis added

Apparently there was a false teaching circulating among the Thessalonian saints that the Rapture of the Church was imminent because they believed the day of the Lord was at hand; so the Rapture could take place at any moment. It caused enough alarm and turmoil among the members that the apostle Paul had to set the record straight by explaining that two events had to occur prior to the Rapture. First, there would be a falling away from the faith by many in the Church; which then would lead to the coming of the Antichrist. Paul assures the Church the Rapture would not take place until these two events happened. If one does not like the obvious meaning of these scriptures, then a not so obvious interpretation must be conjured up.

Many pre-tribulationalists wrongly misinterpret the "day of the Lord" as being the great tribulation period in which God pours out His wrath upon mankind. They believe the saints will be Raptured before this occurs, thus they are termed pre-tribulationalist. Their interpretation concerning the "day of the Lord" is incorrect! Understanding whose wrath is expressed during the great tribulation is a major key in understanding when the Rapture will occur. Let's now explore this question. First we will see the wrath poured out through the martyrdom of saints during the great tribulation is not God's wrath. We later will look at when the day of the Lord occurs where He then unleashes His wrath on mankind.

Satan's Wrath

Many pre-tribulationalists believe the great tribulation is the day of the Lord. Surely God has nothing to do with the martyrdom of the millions of saints during this horrendous time. How could this time period be the day of the Lord? Scripture is quite clear that the wrath expressed on the saints during the great tribulation is not that of God, but that of Satan the devil (Rev. 12:17).[24] Just prior to the great tribulation period and the revealing of the Antichrist, Satan and his angels will once again battle God in a vain attempt to overthrow Him as ruler of the universe. Satan rather is vanquished by God's army of angels and is permanently cast back down to earth. As a result the scripture gives this warning: "Woe to the earth and to the sea, because the devil has gone down to you, having *great wrath* [emphasis added], knowing that he has but a short time" (Rev. 12:12b WEB).

Satan's time left as ruler of this earth is just three and one half years during the "great tribulation." It is during this period that Satan's wrath is unleashed on the saints; not on the people of earth. Notice after Satan loses his effort to dethrone God, he is cast down to the earth. The scriptures then immediately launch into the next event which is the execution of Satan's great wrath on the saints. "The dragon [Satan] *grew an-*

gry [emphasis added] with the woman [Israel], and went away to make war with the rest of her seed [Christian's], who keep God's command- ments and hold Jesus' testimony" (Rev. 12:17 WEB). Notice how Satan executes his anger and wrath on the earth, "It was given [by Satan] to him [Antichrist] to make war with the saints, and to overcome them" (Rev. 13:7 WEB). And a bit later the scriptures tell us that all peoples on earth will be made to worship the Antichrist and "as many as wouldn't worship the image of the beast to be killed" (Rev. 13:15b WEB). Those killed will be the Christians who refuse to renounce their love and wor- ship of Christ as their one and only Savior.

So we see that the great tribulation is the time period in which Satan pours out his "wrath" upon God's people, not on the whole world. Revelation 3:10 tells the saints that, "Because you kept my command to endure, I also will keep you from the hour of testing, which *is to come on the whole world, to test those who dwell on the earth* [emphasis added]" (WEB). Many pre-tribulationalists believe this verse proves a rapturing of the saints. They say this "hour of testing" is the great tribulation and that the saints will be Raptured and therefore not have to endure "the hour of testing." The problem is the "hour of testing" here in not speak- ing of the great tribulation or the martyrdom of saints. The "hour of testing' is God's wrath poured out in His seven vials which comes on rebellious mankind after the great tribulation. The hour of testing "is to come on the whole world," full of rebellious and wicked mankind; not the people of God.

More Proofs For A Pre-Tribulation Rapture?

If there were those incorrectly preaching the time of the Rapture during ministry of the apostle Paul, surely there would come after his death some who would sooner or later preach it in the next eighteen hundred years! Paul plainly stated that the Rapture will not come prior to a falling away of Christians from the Church and marked by the appearing of the Antichrist. Remember Paul said in 2 Thessalonians 2:3b that the Rap- ture, "will not come until the rebellion [an apostasy from the church] occurs and the man of lawlessness [the Antichrist] (the son of destruction) is revealed" (BSB). Paul clearly says the Rapture will not occur before the revealing of the Antichrist. However, in spite of this clear statement, today's pre-tribulationalist believe that the Rapture occurs before the revealing of the Antichrist. In an effort to squeeze in a verse from the bible that supports a pre-tribulation Rapture, some use the word "rebellion" in verse three (which is translated from the Greek word "*apostasia*")[25] and interpret another possible meaning for it rather than that of apostasy. According to Strong's Concordance the prime meanings of the word *apostasia* are "defection, apostasy, revolt," I believe the Holy Spirit of God inspired this word for the precise meaning it gives. Any other interpretation of it is incorrect. This apostasy refers to the prophesied "Christians," who defect, apostatize, revolt, and fall away from the faith before and after the coming of the Antichrist. Rather than embracing the obvious, the suggestion is made that this "*apostasia*" could be construed to mean "to depart." Pre-tribulationalist say that if this is so, then this translation could in effect being saying that the Church will depart from the earth by being raptured to meet Christ in the air escaping the coming "wrath of God during the great tribulation". I heard yesterday a noted theologian state that if this *apostasia* word does refer to a Rapture, then this single verse teaches pre-tribulationalism. I, for one, believe that the Holy Spirit would have inspired Paul to use the Greek word for depart which is "*aphistémi*"[26] rather than the word "*apostasia*" which he did use. To me this seems like trying to pound a square peg in a round hole. It seems like there is a lot of desperate "chicken scratching" to find something in the scriptures to feed pre-tribulation proponents. As a matter of fact, Pre-tribulationalist believe the Rapture of the saints occur three and a half years prior to the Antichrist's appearing.

He That Restraineth

Prior to the revealing of who the Antichrist is, Paul speaks of an entity that has been restraining the spirit of the Antichrist in the world and his eventual unveiling, after which comes the great tribulation slaughter.

Paul speaks of a certain "restrainer" who has been suppressing the activities of the Antichrist until the appointed time for the Antichrist to be revealed. Paul states:

> And you know what is now restraining him [the Antichrist], so that he will be revealed at the proper time. For the mystery of lawlessness is already at work, but the one who now restrains it will continue until *he is taken out of the way* [emphasis added]. And then the lawless one [the Antichrist] will be revealed, whom the Lord Jesus will slay with the breath of His mouth and abolish by the majesty of His arrival. ~ 2 Thessalonians 2:6-8, BSB

There are wide differences of opinion among many biblical scholars as to what exactly Paul's "mysterious words" might actually mean. In order, I suspect, to prove a pre-tribulation theory, a big question arose about who the "he" is who was "taken out of the way" in these verses. The fact of the matter is that no one knows for certain who "he" is. Any conclusion beyond what these verses clearly state, however, is only speculation. Pre-tribulationists say that the "he" spoken of here is none other than the Holy Spirit of God and when He is taken out of the way, the saints are raptured to the heavens. The key point to note here is that these Scriptures do not say that the "He" is the Holy Spirit. The Pulpit Commentary gives this rendering of these verses:

> The whole clause ought to be rendered, "The mystery of lawlessness is already working, only until he who restraineth is removed"; when that takes place, when the restraining influence is removed, the mystery of lawlessness will no longer work secretly, but will openly manifested....[27]

The pre-tribulationist and post-tribulationist both agree that there is a "restrainer" who has been limiting the unrighteous evil deeds of the Antichrist. They agree that the unveiling of the Antichrist cannot occur until the "restrainer" removes his hand that has been "restraining" the Antichrist. There are those in both camps who even agree that the "restrainer" is most likely the Holy Spirit. However, it is important to note that only circumstantial evidence is used to conclude that it is the Holy Spirit spoken of here. It may be the Holy Spirit or it could just be a powerful angel of God doing the restraining. These Scriptures do not say exactly who "He" is.

There are other instances in the Bible where spirit beings "restrained" other spirit beings for and against God's purposes. For instance, God sent an angel to give Daniel a message. This holy angel was restrained by a powerful fallen angel from delivering God's message to Daniel for a period of three weeks. It was only with the help of the archangel Michael in fighting the "Prince of Persia" (his restrainer) that the angel was able to finally break through to Daniel and deliver God's message (see Daniel 10:12-14).

Now let's look at another example where four angels have been restrained from doing their appointed duties. In this case their mission is yet to occur. It is their job to see to it that one-third of mankind on earth is killed just prior to the return of Christ to earth. Scripture states that this will occur after this command is given: "'Release the four angels who are bound at the great river Euphrates.' So the four angels who had been prepared for this hour and day and month and year were released to kill a third of mankind" (Rev. 9:14-15, BSB). Obviously, they are being restrained from performing their assigned duties for a period of time. The Bible does not say if these four angels are good or bad angels. Most likely they are demonic, however, because they have been bound up in area around the Euphrates River.

The point here is simply that the "restrainer" of the Antichrist could be another powerful angel and not the Holy Spirit at all. Believing that it is the Holy Spirit doing the restraining fits nicely into the imagination of a pre-tribulationalist Rapture narrative, as one describes here:

> Even as the servant of Abraham brought home to Isaac a bride, chosen of God, so will the Spirit lead home the Bride of Christ. When the Spirit is removed, then the Church must also be snatched away. To say otherwise is to make void the promise of Christ: "And I will pray the Father, and he shall give you another Comforter, *that he may abide with you for ever*: Even the Spirit of truth..." (John 14:16). The removal of the Spirit

takes place before the Wicked One shall be revealed, and this removal sets the time for the rapture of the Church.[28]

Another pre-tribulationist explaining these verses adds this perspective:

> Before the Antichrist can be revealed, Paul said a certain "He" must be taken out of the way. According to 2 Thessalonians 2:7, the "He" that must be removed is widely thought to be the Holy Spirit. It has been promised that the Holy Spirit would never leave the Church, and without the working of the Holy Spirit remaining on earth, no one could be saved during the tribulation. The removal of the Church, which is indwelt by the Holy Ghost, would seem the best explanation for this dilemma. The working of the Holy Spirit could go on during the tribulation, but His influence would be diminished because of the missing Church.[29]

As I have stated earlier, I will be thrilled if this is the correct meaning of these Scriptures. I have my doubts, however. I am not so convinced that just because the Holy Spirit is removed the Church must also be snatched away! Why does the Church have to be raptured here? Second Thessalonians does not say that the "he" (the Holy Spirit) that did the restraining went to heaven. These Scriptures do not even say that "he who restraineth" is the Holy Spirit. They also do not say that the "He" raptures anybody. Basically, all the Scripture says is that he (whoever the he is) no longer restrained the revealing of the Antichrist. That's it!

Let Us Reason Together

God, in His wisdom, has obviously allowed his saints to disagree on various doctrinal points. None of these disagreements define their righteousness before Him. The only thing that defines our righteousness is if we have been given new birth in Christ. Of course, all Christians should agree that this new birth is obtained only by each sinner hearing the gospel, heeding God's call by repenting (change of mind), and accepting the sacrifice of God's Son as their Savior. Christians need to be careful not to condemn one another over any other doctrinal disagreements. One reason why Christ is returning to earth is to settle these disputed theological issues and bring us all into perfect understanding and unity.

I shall not make a big deal of this, but I feel for the sake of those who believe in a post-tribulation Rapture that I should present a case for it in this chapter. As Christians, I believe we should be able to agree that we can disagree on non-salvation issues such as when the Rapture will be. We should be able to respectfully present our case without fear of judgment and recrimination. Then each of us should make up our own mind based on what we draw from the discussion. Please allow me to present my case for when the Rapture will be. After hearing this argument, you may of course decide for yourself if it has any value. We should be able to present and defend on scriptural grounds for the beliefs we hold dear. As scripture says, "Always be prepared to articulate a defense to everyone who asks you to give the reason for the hope that you have. But respond with gentleness and respect, keeping a clear conscience..." (1 Pet. 3:15b-16a, BSB).

Any Rapture theory is not a salvation issue one way or the other. However, a pre-tribulation stance presents to its believers a most precarious position if it is wrong. If Christians are anxiously awaiting a pre-tribulation Rapture that does not occur, they will be left in various stages of shock, fear, and loss of faith, and will have to face the prospect of possible martyrdom. I have interjected the possibility of the Rapture at this point in our sequence of prophetic events out of respect for my many Christian brothers and sisters who believe that it will occur prior to the revealing of the Antichrist. All I can say is that I pray that they are right and I am wrong. If so, then I will be one of the first to rejoice as I am raptured up to the clouds to meet our Savior prior to the great tribulation. I'd much rather be expecting the rapturing of the saints to occur during or after the great tribulation and be greatly shocked and overjoyed at being raptured prior to it. Let's just say I certainly will not be disappointed if that is the case. However, on the other hand, if I have been taught to believe the Rapture will occur prior to the great tribulation and that does not occur, there is a high probability that my faith will be greatly shaken. I might even wonder: "Well, if there is no Rapture now, how can I be sure there will be one later?" To say the least, I will be bewildered and terrified at the possibility that the Rapture has occurred without me and therefore ill prepared for the prospect of facing the great tribulation lying before me. Even worse, I might be more prone to apostatize, falling away from the faith temporarily due to the great deception of the Antichrist and False Prophet. I'm sure that Satan will be delighted at my new predicament if this indeed proves to be the case.

The Day Of God's Wrath

When is the day of the Lord and God's wrath? There is a lot of speculation on this question. No one knows for sure exactly when it begins, but we know that it will be sometime after the persecution and martyrdom of the saints in the great tribulation. Some believe the end time is cut short by God and the day of the Lord will begin near the end of the great tribulation. It is possible that it begins at the latter part of the great tribulation period and as Isiah 34:8 and 63:4 indicate it will extend over a period of one year.[30]

Because of the horrible atrocities committed in the great tribulation, God says His wrath will be filled to the brim and He will be ready to wreak His revenge on Satan and a wicked rebellious mankind. Note, speaking of the great tribulation, scripture says, "If anyone worships the beast and his image, and receives a mark on his forehead, or on his hand, he also will drink of the wine of the *wrath of God* [emphasis added], which is prepared unmixed in the cup of his anger" (Rev. 14:9b-10 WEB). God says of the wicked that, "… according to your hardness and unrepentant heart you are treasuring up for yourself wrath *in the day of wrath* [emphasis added], revelation, and of the righteous judgment of God; who 'will pay back to everyone according to their works'" (Rom 2:5-6, WEB).

The great tribulation sets the stage for the wrath of God to be unleashed upon sinful mankind. Notice:

Then I saw another great and marvelous sign in heaven: seven angels with the seven final plagues, with which *the wrath of God* [emphasis added] will be completed. ... Out of the temple came the seven angels with the seven plagues. They were dressed in clean, shining linen and wore golden sashes around their chests. Then one of the four living creatures gave to the seven angels seven golden bowls *filled with the wrath of God* [emphasis added], who lives for ever and ever. And the temple was filled with smoke from the glory of God and from his power, and no one could enter the temple until the seven plagues of the seven angels were completed. ....Then I heard a loud voice from the temple saying to the seven angels, "Go, pour out on the earth *the seven bowls of God's wrath* [emphasis added]. ...And I heard the angel of the waters say: "Righteous are You, O Holy One, who is and who was, because You have brought these judgments. For they have spilled the blood of saints and prophets, and You have given them blood to drink as they deserve." ~ Revelation 15:1, 6-8; 16:1, 5-6, BSB.

Let's establish a brief overall perspective of the end times prophesied events. The book of Revelation unveils coming end time prophetic events by the opening of seven seals; the blowing of seven trumpets, and the pouring out of God's wrath contained in seven vials (also referred to as bowls and plagues) ending with the return of Jesus Christ to Rapture the saints, and the establishment of His Kingdom on earth. Erwin Baxter's End Time Ministries give us an overall perspective:

The Seven Seals described in Revelation is the longest story of the end times – a series of disastrous events occurring with major impact on the world stage. The text also helps to understand when the opening of the seals will happen in our time, with the Great Tribulation happening between the opening of the sixth and seventh seals. The Seven Trumpets are sounded well into when the seals have been opened – but what many people do not realize is that five of the seven trumpets have already sounded. This is one of the biggest signs that the end time is upon us, especially with the Sixth Trumpet War (Revelation 9:13-21) that will soon take place in the Middle East where there is currently so much turmoil. The Seven Vials take place over the shortest period of time, and cover a series of specific disasters that will befall the world. The opening of the seventh vial coincides with the breaking of the sixth seal and the sounding of the seventh trumpet – the Second Coming of Jesus Christ. ~ Revelation 11:15.[31]

The seven vials of God's wrath begin to be unleashed near the end of the great tribulation period. The saints remaining alive during this rain of plagues on the Antichrist and his followers will be protected by God just as He did for the children of Israel during the plagues of Egypt.[32] The people of God are supernaturally protected from the plagues that descend from God on our rebellious world (Rev. 7:3, 1 Thess. 1:10, and 5:9). He said through Micah:[33]

> Let us see miracles like the time you [Israel] came out of Egypt. Nations will see this and be ashamed in spite of all their strength. They will put their hands over their mouths. Their ears will become deaf. They will lick dust like snakes, like animals that crawl on the ground. They will come out of their hiding places trembling. They will turn away from your presence in fear, O LORD our God. They will be afraid of you. ~ Micah 7: 15-17, GW

The seven vials of God's wrath are remarkably similar to the plagues poured out on Egypt that resulted in Israel being set free from bondage and slavery.[34] God will again set forth in His fury plagues as a prequel to setting mankind and the earth free from bondage and slavery to Satan's tyrannical earthly rule. Satan's demise will come at the end of God's wrath being poured out culminating in the return of Christ at the Battle of Armageddon.

The day of the Lord contains the seven vials of God's wrath. It will be the time of testing for the whole word, but not for the saints of God who were not martyred and able to live through the great tribulation. These saints will supernaturally be protected as was ancient Israel as the first six plagues of God's wrath are unleashed upon mankind. One of the main reasons God is returning is to avenge the blood of martyred saint. Revelation describes the carnage that follows as each bowl of God's wrath is poured out on the world. In these vials of wrath are festering sores; rivers, springs, and the seas turned to blood killing every living thing in them. The sun's fires will scorch people. Then the earth will be plunged into darkness and horrible sores. Unbelievable displays of lightings, rumblings, and thunder will occur. Then the worst earthquake mankind has ever experienced will level cities around the world. As the scripture says:

> And God remembered Babylon the great and gave her the *cup of the wine of the fury of His wrath* [Emphasis added]. Then every island fled, and no mountain could be found. And huge hailstones, about a hundred pounds each, rained down on them from above. And men cursed God for the plague of hail, because it was so horrendous. ~ Revelation 16:19b-20, BSB

The sixth and seventh seal and the blowing of the seventh trumpet all describe the time period of the second coming of Jesus.[35] Just prior to this period of time there are several things that occur. "At the very end of the Great Tribulation, the seven vials (plagues) of the Wrath of God [Day of the Lord] will be poured out (Revelation 16:1-21). The first vial is poured out on those who have received the Mark of the Beast during the tribulation period. When the sixth vial is poured out, the Great River Euphrates will be dried up in preparation for the Kings of the East to make their way down toward Israel for the Battle of Armageddon."[36] It is after this event near the end of this war waged against Israel, that the Seventh and Last Trumpet will sound while the armies battle Israel.[37] Jesus Christ will at this time rapture His righteous elect from their graves and those remaining alive on the earth (Matthew 24:29-31). The Marriage Supper of the Lamb will then occur, after which the saints will accompany Christ as He goes to fight on behalf of Israel at the Battle of Armageddon (Revelation 19). During the Battle of Armageddon, the Seventh Vial will be poured out upon the earth. This will result in great hailstones being rained upon those armies that have come down to fight against Israel at Armageddon."[38]

Revealing The Glory Given The Saints

The scriptures foretell about the wrath of God that will descend upon wicked mankind for the evil deeds he has done to God's people. One of the major reasons God's wrath is unleashed on the whole world at His return is because of the horrendous persecutions and martyrdom of the saints by rebellious mankind throughout history. The pouring out of God's wrath on those guilty will most certainly be the time of testing for "those who dwell on the earth." Paul speaks to the Church about the purpose for our present day trials and when God will avenge the Church for them. He encourages the saints to be patient and faithful in the face of persecutions saying:

> That is why we boast among God's churches about your perseverance and faith in the face of all the persecution and affliction you are enduring. All this is clear evidence of God's righteous judgment. And so you will be counted worthy of the kingdom of God, for which you are suffering. After all, it is only right for God to repay with affliction those who afflict you, and to grant relief to you who are oppressed, and to us as well, when the Lord *Jesus is revealed from heaven* [emphasis added] with His mighty angels in blazing fire. He will inflict vengeance on those who do not know God and do not obey the gospel of our Lord Jesus. They will suffer the penalty of eternal destruction, separated from the presence of the Lord and the glory of His might, *on the day He comes to be glorified in His saints*[emphasis added] and regarded with wonder by all who have believed, including you who have believed our testimony." ~ 2 Thess. 1:4-10 BSB

Did you catch that Paul said that it would be on the day Christ returns and punishes rebellious mankind, that His glory in the Rapture would be manifested in and admired among His saints. Therefore the Rapture of the saints will occur on the day that "the Lord Jesus is revealed from heaven." This event marks end Satan's rule on earth and the beginning of the first day of the eternal reign of Christ.

At the sound of the seventh angel's trumpet blast four spectacular events occur. The first event is as scripture states, "The kingdom of the world is now the kingdom of our Lord and of His Christ, and He will reign forever and ever" (Rev. 11:15b, BSB)." The second astounding event is described by Paul concerning the saints:

> We will not all sleep, but we will all be changed— in an instant, in the twinkling of an eye, *at the last trumpet* [emphasis added]. For the trumpet will sound, the dead will be raised imperishable, and we will be changed. For the perishable must be clothed with the imperishable, and the mortal with immortality." ~ 1 Corinthians 15:51b-53, BSB

The saint's new immortal body is described in scripture, "We know that when Christ appears, we will be like Him, for we will see Him as He is" (1 John 3:2b BSB). It is clear from the scriptures above that Christ pinpoints the day and time for the first resurrection in which the dead and living saints are given their new bodies reflecting His glory. Once raptured, all the saints will see and marvel at the new astounding glory of Christ displayed in themselves and their brothers and sisters! The very purpose of Christ's coming at this day is to glorify His saints, to punish and vanquish the rebellious, and establish His eternal Kingdom on earth. Pulpits commentary describes these events quite well:

> Christ will be glorified in his saints, inasmuch as their glory was the result of his sufferings and death, and their holiness is the reflection of his holiness; 'They will reflect as in a mirror the glory of the Lord.' And to be admired; wondered at, praised. In all them that believe; or, believed. The work of faith is past; the result of faith, the state of sight and glory, has commenced. The glorification of believers will thus become the glorification of Christ. The glory of Christ does not arise from the punishment of the wicked, but from the glorification of believers. Christ will indeed be glorified in the punishment of the wicked. His justice will be manifested and vindicated; but his glory will be especially seen in the manifestation of his mercy toward believers.[39]

It seems quite logical to me that the wonderful glory of the saints described above would not be manifested prior to the great tribulation, before the wrath of God's anger is filled to the brim during the great tribulation martyrdom. It is the result of the great tribulation that God says His wrath has been made complete and He is ready to wreak His revenge on Satan and his children. Note, speaking of the great tribulation, scripture says, "If anyone worships the beast and his image, and receives a mark on his forehead, or on his hand, he also will drink of the wine of the wrath of God, which is prepared unmixed in the cup of his anger" (Rev. 14:9b-10 WEB). God says of the wicked that, "... according to your hardness and unrepentant heart you are treasuring up for yourself wrath *in the day of wrath* [emphasis added], revelation, and of the righteous judgment of God; who 'will pay back to everyone according to their works'" (Rom 2:5-6, WEB).

The third great event that occurs after the seven trumpet blasts, and the saints are glorified, is described this way:

> Then the seventh angel poured out his bowl into the air, and a loud voice came from the throne in the temple, saying, "It is done!" And there were flashes of lightning, and rumblings, and rolls of thunder, and a great earthquake, the likes of which had not occurred since men were upon the earth—so mighty was the great quake. The great city was split into three parts, and the cities of the nations collapsed. And God remembered Babylon the great and gave her the cup of the wine of the fury of His wrath. Then every island fled, and no mountain could be found. And huge hailstones, about a hundred pounds each, rained down on them from above. And men cursed God for the plague of hail, because it was so horrendous. ~ Revelation 16:17-21 BSB

The fourth and last momentous event then occurs. At this very moment the rebellious armies of the world will have gathered for the Battle of Armageddon. They will be crushed by the angelic armies of God like grapes in a wine vat. Notice the scriptures description of this event. An angel is commanded to:

> 'Swing your sharp sickle and gather the clusters of grapes [armies] from the vine [nations] of the earth, because its grapes

are ripe.' So the angel swung his sickle over the earth and gathered the grapes of the earth, and he threw them into the great winepress of God's wrath. And the winepress was trodden outside the city [Jerusalem], and the blood that flowed from it rose as high as the bridles of the horses, for a distance of one thousand six hundred stadia. ~ Revelation 14:18b-20, BSB

A great slaughter is depicted here with the resulting blood to flow like wine from a winepress that will be outside of the cities gates of Jerusalem with a lake of blood some 160 miles in length.[40]

The Witness Of Jesus?

Paul warned us, "Let no man deceive you by any means: for *that day* [the coming of Jesus and the Rapture] *shall not come,* except there come a falling away first, and that man of sin be revealed…" (1 Thess. 2:3a, KJV). That obviously pushes the coming of Christ to sometime after the revealing of the Antichrist, which begins the great tribulation. Now as to the evidence for a post-tribulation Rapture, I can think of no higher human authority than the statements of God's Son, Jesus Christ. As we just saw above, Jesus Himself in Mathew 24 answered his disciple's question concerning when He would return to establish His kingdom on earth. Jesus spoke of the sequence of events to watch for that would immediately precede His return. These events included false prophets, wars, famines, earthquakes, martyrdom of saints, and preaching of the gospel. All these things have been going on since He spoke these words. However, Jesus next referred to an event that has not happened since the Roman legions destroyed the temple in Jerusalem in AD 70. In doing so the Romans set up what God considered was an "abomination" in the temple, which God had prophesied would happen through the prophet Daniel nearly five hundred years earlier. These actions by the Roman legions were just an anti-type of the final fulfillment Daniel referred to that would happen immediately prior to Christ's return at the end of this age. Jesus then introduced what will happen immediately after the great tribulation. He said:

Immediately after the tribulation [the great tribulation] of those days: 'The sun will be darkened, and the moon will not give its light; the stars will fall from the sky, and the powers of the heavens will be shaken.' At that time the sign of the Son of Man will appear in heaven, and all the tribes of the earth will mourn. They will see the Son of Man coming on the clouds of heaven, with power and great glory. And He will send out His angels with a *loud trumpet call* [emphasis added] and they will gather His elect from the four winds, from one end of the heavens to the other. ~ Matthew 24:29-31, BSB

Notice Jesus said that two things would happen at the end of the great tribulation (lasting three and a half years). First to happen would be startling heavenly signs involving the sun, moon, stars, and heavenly bodies. Next Jesus will appear, coming on the clouds of heaven, and He will immediately send his angels "with a loud trumpet call" to gather his saints from every corner of the earth. Saint Paul describes it this way:

Listen, I tell you a mystery: We will not all sleep, but we will all be changed— in an instant, in the twinkling of an eye, *at the last trumpet* [emphasis added]. For the trumpet will sound, the dead will be raised imperishable, and we will be changed. For the perishable must be clothed with the imperishable, and the mortal with immortality. ~ 1 Corinthians 15:51-53, BSB

This is the resurrection of the dead saints and the rapturing of Christians still alive on earth. Notice this intriguing statement made by Jesus concerning the Rapture: "And this is the will of Him who sent Me, that I shall lose none of all those He has given Me, but raise them up at the last day. For it is My Father's will that everyone who looks to the Son and believes in Him shall have eternal life, and I will raise him up at the last day" (John 6: 39-40 BSB). Jesus specifically said the resurrection of His saints would be at the last day. When is "the last day" that Jesus said the Rapture will occur?[41] I believe that the timing of the "last day" is clearly revealed in the following events: "Then the seventh angel sounded his trumpet, and loud voices called out in heaven: 'The kingdom of the world is now the kingdom of our Lord and of His Christ, and He will reign forever and ever'" (Rev. 11:15 BSB). It is then explained that "…. The time has come to judge the dead, and *to reward Your servants* [emphasis added], the prophets and saints…. (Ibid. vs. 18). It is at this precise moment that the Rapture occurs. This seventh trumpet is the last trumpet spoken of in the bible. Paul pinpointed the timing of the Rapture stating, "…we will all be changed in an instant, in the twinkling of an eye, at the last trumpet" (1 Cor. 15:51b-52, BSB).

This description of events that occur at the time these verses speak of do not occur seven years earlier prior to the great tribulation. They obviously occur during the Day of the Lord. The Day of the Lord is the time period in which God reigns down His seven plagues or vials of wrath on rebellious world. By the time the seventh trumpet sounds, six plagues have been unleashed, with one more to come. The day in which the trumpet is sounded is the last day of Satan's authority to rule the earth. It is the day in which Christ commences His reign upon the world. This day is obviously the "last day" of which Christ spoke of in John 6. This last day could be the last day of the Day of the Lord. It certainly is the beginning of the first day of Christ's reign on earth.

Notice the following event that is also described to occur after the sounding of the seventh trumpet. As we have just read, first the saints are rewarded and also "The time has come to destroy those who destroy the earth." God destroys those who destroy the earth at the Battle of Armageddon. I believe the rewarding of God's saints comes in their resurrection to glory by receiving their eternal new bodies. This occurs at the sounding of the seventh and last trumpet which is immediately followed by the pouring out of the seventh vial or plague of God. Notice, "The nations were enraged, and Your wrath has come" (Ibid. vs 18). God's wrath is horrendous and is described this way: "Then the temple of God in heaven was opened, and the ark of His covenant appeared in His temple. And there were flashes of lightning, and rumblings, and rolls of thunder, and an earthquake, and a great hailstorm" (Ibid. vs 19). This last vial is poured out at the last day of the time period known as The Day of the Lord. I believe it seems obvious from the context of these events that the Rapture occurs at this time; as Jesus said: are the fulfillment of what Christ said would occur: "…everyone who looks to the Son and believes in Him shall have eternal life, and I will raise him up at the last day" (John 6:40b, BSB).[42] "There is no scripture stating that the Resurrection happens seven years before the end of the age. The timing of the Rapture is linked to the timing of the Resurrection, and the Resurrection takes place at the last day, not seven years before."[43] Jesus stated:

> And this is the will of Him who sent Me, that I shall lose none of all those He has given Me, but raise them up at the last day. For it is My Father's will that everyone who looks to the Son and believes in Him shall have eternal life, and I will raise him up at the last day. ~ John 6:39-40 BSB

Jesus said the resurrection of the dead will be on the "last day."[44] The last day of this age does not occur seven years prior to the end of the great tribulation. Those martyred during the great tribulation by the Antichrist are also a part of the last day resurrection Jesus spoke of. Notice that John affirms this:

> And I saw the souls of those who had been beheaded for their testimony of Jesus and for the word of God, and those who had not worshiped the beast or its image, and had not received its mark on their foreheads or hands. And they came to life and reigned with Christ for a thousand years. The rest of the dead did not come back to life until the thousand years were complete. *This is the first resurrection* [emphasis added]. Blessed and holy are those who share in the first resurrection! The second death has no power over them, but they will be priests of God and of Christ, and will reign with Him for a thousand years. ~ Revelation 20:4b-6, BSB

There is a major point we can clearly draw from this which answers the question of when the first resurrection will be. The general resurrection or rapture described here is called the first resurrection. If the first resurrection, as the pre-tribulationist claim, must occur prior to the revealing of the Antichrist and the great tribulation; how is it then possible that the saints martyred during the great tribulation will be able to take part in the first resurrection which the pre-tribulationalists claim occurred before the great tribulation several years earlier? The obvious answer is that the first resurrection has to occur sometime after the appearing of the Antichrist and after the great tribulation![45] The verses above clearly show those martyred during the great tribulation will take part in the first resurrection and will reign with Christ for the next one thousand years after which the rest of the dead will take part the second resurrection.

The general resurrection of the dead that the apostle Paul spoke of is the first resurrection, and he pinpointed when it will occur, "...we will all be changed— in an instant, in the twinkling of an eye, *at the last trumpet* [emphasis added]. For the trumpet will sound, the dead will be raised imperishable, and we will be changed" (1 Cor. 15:51-52 BSB). Jesus spoke of the first resurrection as when He would resurrect the dead saints, His words concerning this resurrection is very encouraging to all saints. Notice:

> And this is the will of Him who sent Me, that I shall lose none of all those He has given Me, but *raise them up at the last day* [emphasis added]. For it is My Father's will that everyone who looks to the Son and believes in Him shall have eternal life, and *I will raise him up at the last day* [emphasis added]. ~ John 6:39-40 BSB

It is interesting to note at this point that the "last day" of this present age may be only a type of another "last day" at the end of the thousand-year rule of Christ just prior to Satan being bound eternally in hell. This second "last day" may also see the second resurrection in which all those left in their graves will be brought to life to face God's judgment.

Now, I think all pre-tribulationist and post-tribulationist would agree that the resurrection will occur at the last trumpet that Paul spoke of; so another point can be made to settle the issue of when exactly will this last trumpet will sound. For one thing, it obviously will be "at the last day." Does Scripture give us any clues as to when in the sequence of prophetic events the last trumpet will sound on the last day? Yes, it thankfully does. Paul again describes the coming resurrection. Notice:

> For the Lord Himself will descend from heaven with a loud command, with the voice of an archangel, and with the *trumpet of God* [emphasis added], and the dead in Christ will be the first to rise. After that, we who are alive and remain will be caught up together with them in the clouds to meet the Lord in the air. And so we will always be with the Lord. ~ 1 Thessalonians 4:16-17, BSB

Here again Paul speaks of a trumpet that will sound to signal the first resurrection. Is this the same as the "as the last trumpet" he spoke of in 1 Corinthians 15:52? Of course it is! Remember Jesus himself referred to this same trumpet, saying it would happen after the great tribulation:

> They will see the Son of Man coming on the clouds of heaven, with power and great glory. And He will send out His angels with a *loud trumpet call* [emphasis added], and they will gather His *elect* [emphasis added] from the four winds, from one end of the heavens to the other. ~ Matthew 24:30b-31, BSB

Jesus clearly states that it is after the great tribulation that the resurrection of the saints will occur. Some claim that the "elect" that the angels gather is the physical Israelites scattered around the world to bring them home to Israel. This is not the case at all. Israel was God's elect in the Old Testament, however, in the New Testament Covenant, whenever the "elect" is mentioned, it always refers to Christians, never unsaved Israelites.[46]

When we look at the sequence of events spoken of by the apostle John in the book of Revelation, we are given seven significant earth-shaking events, each of which is introduced by an angel of God sounding a trumpet. This is what happens at the sound of the seventh and last trumpet spoken of in that book: "But in the days of the voice of the seventh angel, when he is about to sound his trumpet, *the mystery of God will be fulfilled* [emphasis added] just as He proclaimed to His servants, the prophets" (Rev. 10:7, BSB). Here Paul clearly pinpoints when the Rapture will be. He says the resurrection will occur at the "last trumpet." The sounding of this seventh trumpet is the last trumpet mentioned in the Bible and as we just read, the fulfilment of God's mystery will occur during the days when the angel sounds the seventh trumpet.

As we have seen from previous chapters, the purpose of God's mysterious plan since before the beginning of time was to give birth to His glorified eternal children. Remember, speaking of the resurrection, Paul said, "Listen, I tell you a mystery [God's mystery]: We will not all sleep, but we will all be changed— in an instant, in the twinkling of an eye, *at the last trumpet* [emphasis added]" (1 Cor. 15:51-52, BSB). This scripture and Revelation's (Rev. 10:7) statement that the mystery of God is fulfilled at the time of the last trumpet absolutely pinpoints when the Rapture will occur. The Rapture and the fulfillment of the mystery of God is synonymous. They both occur during the "days of the voice of the seventh angel," which is approximately three and one half years after the revealing of the Antichrist and the beginning of the great tribulation. Obviously then there can be no pre-tribulation Rapture. God's mysterious plans center on the manifestation of His children in the Rapture at the sounding of the last trumpet. Paul describes the achievement of God's mystery this way:

> The creation waits in eager expectation for the revelation of the sons of God. For the creation was subjected to futility, not by its own will, but because of the One who subjected it, in hope that the creation itself will be set free from its bondage to decay and brought into the glorious freedom of the children of God. ~ Romans 8:19-21, BSB

Not only will God's love mystery be revealed culminating in the rapturing of His new sons and daughters, but also the liberation and healing from corruption, abuse, and decay of all plants and animals, along with the planet will begin to take place at the return of Christ. John describes what will happen at Christ's return:

> Then the *seventh angel sounded his trumpet* [emphasis added], and loud voices called out in heaven: "The kingdom of the world is now the kingdom of our Lord and of His Christ, and He will reign forever and ever." ~ Revelation 11:15, BSB

The next event is described this way:

> The nations were enraged, and Your wrath has come. The

time has come to judge the dead, and to reward Your servants, the prophets and saints, and those who fear Your name, both small and great, and to destroy those who destroy the earth. ~ Revelation 11:18, BSB

Those of us who believe in a post-tribulation Rapture believe that the sounding of this last trumpet will awaken and quicken the dead with a new eternal body. Immediately thereafter, those Christians remaining alive will join them. As Paul said, "...We will not all sleep, but we will all be changed— in an instant, in the twinkling of an eye, at the last trumpet." (1 Cor. 15:51b-52, BSB). We will join Christ as He returns to unleash His fury on the nations of the world amassed to destroy Israel in the battle of Armageddon.

The Important Thing

I have presented my case for a post-tribulation Rapture. God has not unified His Body of believers on this as well as many other doctrinal issues. The Rapture is an important doctrine, but its occurrence (post or pre-tribulation) does not determine our salvation. Although there is one true answer concerning when the Rapture will be, God allows each of us to believe as we wish concerning this matter. The major point of discussing the pre- or post-tribulation debate is that neither side needs to make this a divisive matter. We should give each other breathing space to believe in the doctrine as we see it in Scripture. Rather than allowing our differing beliefs to divide us, we should join hands as brothers and sisters celebrating Christ who unites us. That is the more important thing we should make of all our divisions. In spite of them we should do as Paul admonished:

> ...clothe yourselves with compassion, kindness, humility, gentleness, and patience. Bear with each other and forgive any complaint you may have against one another. Forgive as the Lord forgave you. And over all these virtues put on love, which is the bond of perfect unity. Let the peace of Christ rule in your hearts, for to this you were called as members of one body. ~ Colossians 3:12b-15, BSB

Notice, Paul said the most important thing we can do is to "put on love, which is the bond of perfect unity." We can rise above all our doctrinal differences if we look to and put on love. We can then dwell with each other in peace.

We should understand that our interpretation may be wrong on exactly when the Rapture will occur. So we should be prepared not to let such a possible error cause us division or to lose faith and fall away. We should be ready to be raptured whenever God has determined we should be. If the Rapture is before the great tribulation, that would surely be a blessing; if it is after the great tribulation, we should trust Him to see us through those coming turbulent years of suffering and even possible martyrdom, if that is the case. My hope and prayer is that you will be prepared for either one and that you will trust that, "…God is faithful; He will not let you be tempted beyond what you can bear. But when you are tempted, He will also provide an escape, so that you can stand up under it." (1 Cor. 10:13, BSB). Certainly the most important event to be aware of for any Christian is what we all agree on and that is that Jesus Christ, the Son of God, is coming to give each of us a new eternal body, to save remaining mankind from destruction, and to establish His eternal kingdom on earth.

Now in the next two closing chapters let's look into God's prophetic word more deeply to see what we can expect to happen between now and the setting up of God's Kingdom on earth. It is strange that a lot of Christians don't know or even want to know what God has to say about what is coming. The question should be asked, "Why did God put prophecies in the Bible? Consider this. Nearly one third of the Bible contains prophecies! Are they there to remind God what He is supposed to do next?" The answer is, of course not; God put them there for us. In the next chapter we will delve into these questions and see the wonderful reason for God revealing to Christians what is now about to happen to mankind and this earth in the near future.

20

OUR PROPHETIC FUTURE

Through prophecies God has given us a general outline of His future plans, though some may look like a slightly out-of-focus picture for now. As we draw nearer to their fulfillment, the fuzzy pictures will become more in focus and detailed. In one sense we are like several Christians working at putting together the pieces of a puzzle. We begin working around the edges because it is easier to find pieces that fit. All the pieces of the puzzle are there, and we can put many of them in their proper place. We just aren't sure about exactly where some fit together. It's rather exciting when we, under God's guidance, can see what were questionable pieces begin to fit together giving us more details of the picture. We don't yet have all the pieces of God's mystery figured out, but we know God will help us put them together in due time. I am a bit dubious of any ministry that purports to have already put all the pieces together.

Jesus gave a brief account concerning several events immediately preceding His return, stating:

> So also, when you see these things taking place, you will know that the kingdom of God is near. Truly I tell you, this generation will not pass away until all these things have happened. Heaven and earth will pass away, but My words will never pass away. But watch yourselves, or your hearts will be weighed down by dissipation, drunkenness, and the worries of life—and that day will spring upon you suddenly like a snare. For it will come upon all who dwell on the face of the whole earth. So keep watch at all times, and pray that you may have the strength to escape all that is about to happen and to

stand before the Son of Man. ~ Luke 21:31-36, BSB

It is obvious that the prophetic words of God are for His children for specific purposes. We would do well to read and be open to understanding them as God's reveals them. He gave prophecies to alert Christians about what is coming so we can be prepared and strengthened to faithfully walk through what God says will happen. Christ gave another key reason for prophecies when he told us, "I am telling you now before it happens, so that when it comes to pass, you will believe that I am He." (John 13:19, BSB). If you don't know what He says will happen, how can you benefit from His prophecies? We don't have to know every detail now, but we can be aware of a general outline of events to watch for.

Prophetic Signposts

It is rather difficult to be "always on the watch" when we don't even look, much less know what to watch for. At least if we have an awareness of possible events that will come to pass, then when these events happen it will validate and strengthen our faith. In this chapter I will provide an outline of specific events—or perhaps we should call them signposts—that God wants us to watch for. I will simply list them here in non-chronological order; however latter I will explore each signpost in greater depth and in the possible chronological order in which they will occur. I am not listing all the prophetic events to occur, only the major ones. These signposts are: the Rapture, the wars between the King of the North and the King of the South, World War III, the revived Holy Roman Empire, Israel's seven-year peace agreement, the rebuilding of the Temple, the temple sacrifices, the revealing of the Antichrist, the abomination of desolation, the Great Tribulation, the two witnesses, the martyrdom of Christians, Satan's war in heaven, the Gog and Magog war, the battle of Armageddon, the bowls of God's wrath, the seventh trumpet, and the return of Christ. These events form the outline of our puzzle and are major signposts that I will address in the remainder of this and the last chapter. We will first look at what is to happen between now and the

Great Tribulation. In the last chapter we will look at the Great Tribulation immediately preceding the return of Jesus to earth.

Most Christians agree that all of these signposts will occur. In spite of a general agreement about these various events occurring, however, there is considerable difference among theologians, biblical scholars, and prophecy students as to exactly who the participants will be and when and in what order they will occur. This confusion makes some people want to ignore prophecy and in essence "throw the baby out with the bath water." As I have said, God gave these signposts to Christians for our benefit. We need to keep the prophetic baby and throw out the dirty cloudy water. We need to be patient and let God sort out any confusion when He so desires. For instance, there are differences of opinion as to what nations will make up the revived Roman Empire, also known as the Beast power. The major point I want to make here is that it is not as important to know exactly when these events will occur or which nations will be involved as it is to be aware of the events that are to occur and leave it up to God to fill in the details when it becomes necessary. Prophetic events act as God's signposts for Christians. When these events are about to occur or have occurred, we should be able to recognize them as fulfilment of God's word and proof of what is yet to come. This can encourage us, give us faith to endure, and perhaps even give us an opportunity to avoid some of the fallout from these events that may affect our lives.

A Close Look At Our Signposts

In the remainder of this chapter I will give a detailed overview of what I believe lies before us leading up to the Great Tribulation. You are welcome to study these events and arrive at your own conclusion. It is clear that the Bible speaks of a coming war that will be the most devastating by far in all of history. I believe this war is now on the horizon and it will be World War III. I believe the major players in this war now exist and are positioning themselves to soon launch this most horrible war of all time. I believe Daniel's prophecies concerning warfare between the

King of the North and the King of the South speak of this war, which will occur eight or nine years before the final battle of Armageddon. The devastating aftermath of World War III will be the major justifying factor in unifying most nations of the world religiously and politically behind a revived Holy Roman Empire. This world power will be so corrupt and ferocious that Scriptures call this empire a beast. At its head a powerful man will ascend to take ccontrol of a combine of ten nations. I have heard many different scenarios of the end time sequence of events from various ministries, but I believe the Reverend Irvin Baxter's understanding concerning them is fairly accurate. Therefore, if I am to write about the prophecies to come, my sequence of events will essentially harmonize with Reverend Baxter's. There are a few things about the events concerning first five Trumpets as explained by Reverend Baxter that I am not sure of, however I do agree with him that World War III looms very soon on horizon. It is from this point I will start our journey into the future end time events. In this and the next chapter, I discuss the coming prophesied events with the rise of the Antichrist and the Beast power that supports him until the return of Christ and the setting up of His eternal Kingdom on earth. I will attempt to footnote each idea giving proper credit to the new understanding I gained from the teachings of Reverend Baxter.

Irvin Baxter is the founder and president of Endtimes Ministries. He hosts a television show entitled "End of the Age." He is an author, publisher, radio host, and international prophecy teacher.[1] Although I generally agree with much of Reverend Baxter's teachings, I am not as sure as he is about the exact makeup of the ten nations that constitute the Beast power. Although I believe he is probably correct on this matter, I am not quite as dogmatic as he is that the Antichrist will be from Europe and that the false prophet will be the final Roman Catholic Pope.[2] By the way, don't get excited if you're a Catholic. I believe most Catholics are just as Christian as most Protestants are!

Reverend Baxter may be right about who the false prophet is. He may also be wrong. One thing for certain is that God will make it plain to all of us in due time. However, Reverend Baxter's insights have greatly assisted me in describing what I now generally believe will happen just before and during the final seven years before the coming of Christ.[3] We know from Revelation that there are seven trumpet plagues (see Revelation 9:20) from God that sequentially sound one after another announcing major climatic events affecting the entire world. Reverend Baxter believes the first five trumpet plagues have been sounded. I believe he may be indeed be correct. I invite you to view his explanation concerning this matter on YouTube.[4] Whether or not Reverend Baxter is correct, I believe World War III will soon begin.

World War III

An angel of God will sound the sixth trumpet, which will signal the beginning of World War III. This war will be started in an area bound by the Euphrates River. This land comprises primarily the countries of Turkey, Syria, and Iraq. Exactly which nations are involved in this war is not stated here; nor is it revealed how widely this war will spread to other nations. Since this war will be centered on the Euphrates region, it most likely will involve Arab nations. I personally believe that the participants that could be involved here might be those of the battles between the King of the North and the King of the South (see Daniel 11:40-45). The King of the North is thought by some to be the revived Roman Empire, while the King of the South might be a confederation of Arab Muslim nations. This is a definite possibility.

It is interesting to note that just moments ago (on December 15, 2015) I read an article about an announcement of a newly formed Islamic military alliance to fight terrorism.[5] This new alliance consists of thirty-four members and is led by Saudi Arabia. This military alliance includes Turkey and several African and Asian nations. This, interestingly enough, could be the nations that make up the "King of the South." These nations are primarily Sunni Muslims led by Saudi Arabia. This thirty-four-member Islamic alliance "against terrorism" does not include the Shia Muslim–led nations of Iran, Iraq, and Syria. The Sunnis and Shiites have been fighting each other for over a thousand years, and continue to do so today. The major struggle in the Middle East today concerns who is going to be the preeminent Muslim power there. The primary objective of this "34-member Islamic alliance against terrorism" may actually not be so much countering "terrorism" as it is combating the fear of a nuclear-armed axis of nations headed by Iran. Is Saudi Arabia's new alliance of nations primarily formed to counter the growing influence of Iran and its nuclear threat?

Some believe that Iran, Iraq, and Syria could be the foundation upon which the King of the North will finally arise. Some believe that the King of the North will be Russia, Syria, Iran, Iraq, and possibly other Muslim nations. Possibly even China, India, and Japan could be involved. Who knows, even North Korea may be involved. When you look at the alignments rapidly developing today, it is quite interesting that Russia, Syria, and Iran have allied themselves against anti-Bashar al-Asaud Isis forces. Furthermore, recent reports, which may or may not be true, "state that Chinese troops are currently being ferried to Syria, to join with the Russian forces in the Latakia region before teaming up with the Syrian regime forces—all in an apparent effort to allow President Bashar al-Assad to stay in power. Other reports indicate that Chinese J-15 fighter bombers would shortly join the Russian air campaign that was launched last week and take off from the Chinese Liaoning-CV-16 aircraft carrier, which recently reached Syrian shores."[6] It is interesting to note that presidential candidate Ben Carson stated in one of his presidential debates concerning Syria that, "You know, the Chinese are there, as well as the Russians, and you have all kinds of factions there."[7] Did Ben Carson have access to inside knowledge not generally reported to the rest of us? Whether or not the Chinese join in the fight, it is obvious that Russia and China are cozying up to one another. Throw all these characters together into the mix and it may be possible that the main participants allied against Western interests in World War III are emerging.

The growing divide between Sunni and Shiite Muslim factions became starkly evident when Sunni Saudi Arabia announced on January 3, 2016, that it had executed forty-seven who were charged with terrorism. Among these was a prominent Shiite religious leader, Nimr al-Nimr. This invoked riots in Shiite Iran and the burning of the Saudi Embassy. Saudi Arabia retaliated by severing all diplomatic relations with Iran. This action was quickly denounced by Iran. A leading cleric in Iran, Ayatollah Ahmad Khatami, said that these actions would bring down the family that rules Saudi Arabia.[8] He said, "I have no doubt that this pure blood will stain the collar of the House of Saud and wipe them from the pages of history. The crime of executing Sheikh Nimr is part of a criminal pattern by this treacherous family … the Islamic world is expected to cry out and denounce this infamous regime as much as it can."[9] These events have created a seemingly unbridgeable chasm between these two warring Muslim faiths. The fallout has been immediate, with various nations now aligning themselves behind the two factions. Some major players are involved in this great divide. CNN reports: "The fallout of Saudi Arabia's execution of a Shiite cleric is spreading beyond a spat between the Saudis and Iranians, as other Middle East nations chose sides Monday and world powers Russia and China weighed in."[10]

Most major powers are calling for restraint between the two feuding Muslim nations. However, this current war of words is a very volatile situation, which possibly could lead to World War III. "KT" McFarland, who held national security posts in the Nixon, Ford, and Reagan administrations[11] and is now Fox News' national security analyst, in regard to a question on how she thinks this conflict between Saudi Arabia and Iran will play out, said:

> I think they are already at war. They are already at economic war. They are already at diplomatic war. They are already going after each other…. They are in a proxy war already. They're fighting a proxy war in Yemen. They are fighting a proxy war, each on the other side, in Syria. Do they start shooting at each other? Who knows…? I see this only escalating…. Here is what I think happens in the Middle East…. This is going to be a Shiite Sunni battle and everybody takes sides. It won't matter which country you are in because the borders are irrelevant now. It's going to be Shiite vs Sunni. Any moderate in the middle is going to get pushed to the side. And there are two groups who feel that they are preordained to usher in the Endtimes and they are going to be successful."[12]

I heard a reporter once ask what would happen if Iran lobs a missile into a Saudi oil field? If this happens, that could be the catalyst causing nations of the world to take sides. This could escalate ultimately into World War III.

It is unclear at this point exactly who will make up the opposing armies of World War III. However, whoever the participants are, an army of two hundred million soldiers is prophesied to participate. With such numbers one would have to consider the possibility of participation by China, Russia, Muslim nations, or even India. There now exist over a billion people in China, over a billion in India, and over a billion Muslims. Each one could field an army of two hundred million men. The result of the clash of armies between whichever powers constitute the opposing armies will be the killing of one-third of the world's population. The number prophesied to die is so unbelievable that most ignore it, while others spiritualize it away or say it is allegorical. Sadly, however, the truth is that it is real and that a terrible war that will literally kill one-third of mankind on earth (see Revelation 9:18). The current population of the world stands at slightly more than 7.2 billion.[13] This means that the staggering death count from this war will total more than 2.4 billion people. Estimates vary widely as to the number of civilian and battlefield deaths in World War II; but a conservative estimate is about sixty million worldwide died. As terrible as this death count was, it is small by comparison to the 2.4 billion yet to die in World War III.

Aftermath Of World War III

There are no adequate words to describe the psychological horror and carnage this war will wreak upon mankind. This will be by far the most gruesome and destructive war in the history of mankind. To wreak this kind of mass slaughter, nuclear weapons undoubtedly will be used. I personally believe that a nuclear arms race among Arab nations of the Middle East is now at full speed ahead in the wake of the recent so-called nuclear nonproliferation deal between the P5+1 nations (headed by the United States) and the Islamic Republic of Iran. This deal ensures that

Iran will soon obtain nuclear weapons. I believe this is the major event laying the foundation for the nuclear holocaust soon to engulf the Middle East. World War III will begin in the Middle East, and among the billions killed will undoubtedly be residents of many Arab nations in that region. This war will shake the earth to its core, both figuratively and literally. However, the reaction of mankind to this horror will not be to repent and seek God. You'd think that if anything would bring mankind to his knees before God, the massacre of 2.4 billion of the world's population, as will happen in WWIII, would! Rather than repent, however, mankind will be defiant toward God. Scripture says,

> The remaining men and women who weren't killed by these weapons went on their merry way—didn't change their way of life, didn't quit worshiping demons, didn't quit centering their lives around lumps of gold and silver and brass, hunks of stone and wood that couldn't see or hear or move. There wasn't a sign of a change of heart. They plunged right on in their murderous, occult, promiscuous, and thieving ways. ~ Revelation 9:20-21, *The Message*

This reaction will be in keeping with what Paul said about the utterly depraved state of mankind's character in the last days:

> In the last days terrible times will come. For men will be lovers of themselves, lovers of money, boastful, arrogant, abusive, disobedient to their parents, ungrateful, unholy, unloving, unforgiving, slanderous, without self-control, brutal, without love of good, traitorous, reckless, conceited, lovers of pleasure rather than lovers of God, having a form of godliness but denying its power. ~ 2 Timothy 3:2-5a, BSB

This is true to the words of Jesus, who said that just prior to his return, mankind would be just like those living before Noah's flood (see Matthew 24:37). Prior to the flood, mankind was wickedly self-absorbed, as the Scriptures have described: "And GOD saw that the wickedness of man *was* great in the earth, and *that* every imagination of the thoughts of his heart *was* only evil continually." (Gen. 6:5, KJV).

Gog And Magog War?

Several Christian theologians believe that the war that occurs prior to the Tribulation period will be the battle of Gog and Magog spoken of in Ezekiel 38.[14] Scriptures say that at the battle of Gog and Magog Russia and her allies (comprised of Middle Eastern nations) will descend on Israel to pillage and destroy the nation. I have my doubts that the battle described in the sixth trumpet is the battle of Gog and Magog spoken of in Revelation 20. However, the sixth trumpet battle may involve the same allied forces described in Revelation 20. The Scriptures show that the battle involving Gog and Magog and spoken of in Revelation 20 will occur one thousand years after Christ establishes His kingdom on earth. Notice:

> When the thousand years [after the Battle of Armageddon] are complete, Satan will be released from his prison, and will go out to deceive the nations in the four corners of the earth, Gog and Magog, to assemble them for battle. Their number is like the sand of the seashore. And they marched across the broad expanse of the earth and surrounded the camp of the saints and the beloved city. But fire came down from heaven and consumed them. And the devil who had deceived them was thrown into the lake of fire and sulfur, into which the beast and the false prophet had already been thrown. There they will be tormented day and night forever and ever. ~ Revelation 20:7-10, BSB

The details of this horrendous battle are given in Ezekiel 38 and 39. Could it be that the battle of the sixth trumpet is an anti-type of the final battle to be fought one thousand years later? The answer is yes! It is most likely that this horrible battle described after the blowing of the sixth trumpet is indeed a type of the final battle to come one thousand years later.

The Roman Empire Revived

In the wake of the billions killed in World War III, I agree with Irvin Baster that this horrible conflagration will drive the nations into further attempts to unify themselves in order to bring about world peace without God. This may well be the driving force that will bring together a reunion of the old Holy Roman Empire of Western and Eastern Europe. This could include a union of several Muslim nations as a part of the Eastern leg of the new Roman Empire. Sovereign nations will at last be willing to give up their independence and freedom to join a unified worldwide effort to obtain peace. It seems World War III will be the major impetus in driving the nations to unite under a powerful charismatic dictator the Scriptures call the "beast," the man of lawlessness (see Revelation 13:5; 2 Thessalonians 2:3). His true nature and identity will ultimately be revealed as Satan's man who opposes the God of heaven and His Son, Jesus Christ. As a result of this the Scriptures call him the "Antichrist." I will refer to him as such in the rest of this chapter. It is interesting that the character of this Antichrist is described as being lawless. I believe this will be a psychopathic individual who is totally self-absorbed and without conscience or allegiance to anyone other than his self and his master the devil, who probably possesses him and gives him his power (see Revelation 13:2). This Antichrist will ascend to head a group of nations that will be a final rebirth of the Roman Empire. He will forge with the help of his co-conspirator, the "false prophet," a powerful combine of ten nations. He will gain power by treachery and deceit (see Daniel 11:23). He, like Hitler, will promise the nations that if they unite under him he will end all wars and deliver them their Utopian world. In the name of peace, equality, justice, and freedom, the various nations will overlook their differences and unite under a political and religious banner.

This Antichrist despot will at first be seen as a wonderful savior of mankind. Once he has a complete lock on his power and authority, he ultimately will be unveiled as the "Beast" or "Antichrist" only to Christians. This Antichrist will maintain power ultimately to fight Jesus at His return. At first the world will look at him with awe and respect. Scripture tells us: "...all the world wondered after the beast. ...and they worshiped the beast..." (Rev. 13:3b-4b, KJV). Little will the people know that the one leading and inspiring their new dictator is none other than Satan, who is also known as the dragon (see Revelation 13:2). This new dictator will be seen as self-confident and invincible by the nations following him. He will claim that God gave him a mandate to lead the world to peace and prosperity. The god the Antichrist leads the nations to serve, however, is Satan and not the God whose Son must be accepted as Savior of the world in order to be granted eternal life! The Scriptures declare that Satan is "...the god of this world..." (2 Cor. 4:4a, WEB). Satan has been the god of this world since the fall of Adam and Eve. Since then, as we have seen, Satan has tried time and again to unify the world against the coming kingdom of Christ that will soon replace his reign on earth. Satan is the original Antichrist. He again is the force behind this final attempt to unite the world to fight Christ at His return. Satan hopes this final battle will destroy all life on earth. Jesus said himself, "For then shall be great tribulation.... And except those days should be shortened, there should no flesh be saved" (Matt. 24:21a-22a, KJV).

The Ten Toes

Traditionally, most of Christianity has thought that the revival of the Roman Empire would be comprised of ten European nations, from which the Antichrist and false prophet would come. It is believed that the "false prophet" will be the last Pope of the Roman Catholic Church. This is what I was taught and believed to be the case for the last fifty years. However, I now believe that the ten nations to be headed by the Antichrist will be comprised of a combination of five European nations and five nations (some or all of which are Islamist) now residing primarily in the confines of the territories of the ancient Eastern Roman Empire. What changed my mind? An interesting article I recently read has given me pause for thought concerning the final makeup of the beast power.[15] Exactly how this interesting mixture of Middle Eastern and European nations might evolve makes for some interesting speculation. It is believed that the end-time Beast power that will oppose Jesus Christ at Armageddon is described both in Daniel 7 and Revelation 13. Daniel 7 speaks of four beasts that are also referred to in Revelation 13. Daniel in detail describes a lion, a leopard, a bear, and a fourth beast with ten horns. Revelation 13 also uses the mouth of the lion, a resemblance of a leopard, and the feet of a bear in its description of the end-time Beast power. Obviously these animals used to describe the Beast are nations that at least support the Beast power, if not actually are part of the ten-nation union that will oppose Christ. It has been speculated that the lion represents Great Britain. The bear represents Russia and the leopard represents Germany.[16] If this is the case, then Great Britain, Germany, and Russia could also be a vital part of the one world governmental system that ends up supporting the Beast power.

A relatively new idea as to who will constitute the end-time Beast power has been presented by Joel Richardson in his books "The Islamic Antichrist" and "Mideast Beast." He believes that the Beast power will be a revived Islamic Ottoman Empire ridden by the whore of Revelation 17-18. He believes this harlot will be the present-day Kingdom of Saudi Arabia.[17] In exactly what way and to what extent Islamic nations will play a part in the formation of the last of the ten nations who oppose Jesus Christ at His return, no one can say for sure. However, there has been increasing interest in and support for the idea that they may play a very important part. Such notable researchers as "Chuck Missler, Joel Richardson, Walid Shoebat, Perry Stone, Joe Van Koevering and others … are championing the belief that we need to be closely looking at the Byzantine revival of Arab nations much more than previous generations."[18] The most popular belief has been that the revived Roman Empire of ten nations, along with its Antichrist head and partner in crime, the false prophet, would be born out of European nations. Recently I have become aware of scriptural indications that it might be possible that the beast power, the Antichrist, and false prophet could possibly come from a combination of European and Islamic nations.[19]

The major point here is that no one knows for sure what the final makeup of the allied Beast power will be. I maintain that it is not necessary for us to know exactly its final makeup for now. Yes, it is interesting to think about the possibilities, but the important matter is just that we understand there is coming a final ten nations, an Antichrist, and a false prophet that will be organized and inspired by Satan to rule the post–World War III world. The Scriptures call our attention to these basic facts and warn us of a mass slaughter of Jews and Christians during what is called the Great Tribulation lasting for three and a half years leading up to the last climactic Battle of Armageddon, where allied Antichrist forces will war against Jesus Christ at His return. Scripture says, "the kings of the East" (possibly Russia and mostly likely China and other Eastern powers) will join forces in this last great battle. God will make obvious the exact makeup of these nations and the identity of the false prophet and Antichrist in due time.

Nebuchadnezzar's Dream

The book of Daniel gives an interesting description of the ten kings ruling the earth at the time Jesus Christ returns to set up His kingdom. Daniel interpreted for the Babylonian King Nebuchadnezzar the meaning of a dream the king had concerning a huge dazzling statue made of gold, silver, bronze, and iron formed into the image of a man. Daniel revealed that this statue represented the succession of major world ruling empires from the time of Daniel to the establishment of God's kingdom on earth. The first empire was that of Nebuchadnezzar's Babylon, represented by a head of gold; next was the empire of Media-Persia represented by the arms and chest made of silver. The next empire to rise was that of Greece, represented by a bronze belly and thighs. The next great empire to arise was that of Rome, represented by two legs of iron. The two legs of the image revealed that the Roman Empire's power would be separated into two geographical areas, that of the Western Empire centered in Rome and that of the Eastern Empire (or "Byzantine Empire") centered in Constantinople.

Though separated, the Romans did not consider their two empires as divided; they considered themselves to be one state, though each ruled their own respective areas by having two separate imperial courts of administration.[20] An additional description of the image was added, stating simply, "...its feet [were] part of iron, and part of clay" (Dan. 2:33b, WEB). Now let's focus our attention on Daniel's description and interpretation of the two feet and ten toes of this statue:

> Whereas you saw the feet and toes, part of potters' clay, and part of iron, it shall be a divided kingdom; but there shall be in it of the strength of the iron, because you saw the iron mixed with miry clay. As the toes of the feet were part of iron, and part of clay, so the kingdom shall be partly strong, and partly broken. Whereas you saw the iron mixed with miry clay, they shall mingle themselves with the seed of men; but they shall not cling to one another, even as iron does not mingle with clay. In the days of those kings shall the God of heaven set up a kingdom which shall never be destroyed, nor shall its sovereignty be left to another people; but it shall break in pieces and consume all these kingdoms, and it shall stand forever. ~ Daniel 2:41-44, WEB

How interesting it is to see that the most detailed description of this image centers around the feet and toes. This is so because these feet and toes represent the last kingdom of man's rule on earth, which will be destroyed and replaced by God's kingdom. This union of the ten nations into one kingdom will be a weakly forged union, as Daniel describes it: "As the toes of the feet were part of iron, and part of clay, so the kingdom shall be partly strong, and partly broken. Whereas you saw the iron mixed with miry clay, they shall mingle themselves with the seed of men; but they shall not cling to one another, even as iron does not mingle with clay." (Dan. 2:42-43, WEB). One could draw from this that the union could be made of nations not necessarily traditionally friendly to each other. Perhaps some may once have been enemies. But, for the sake of a common cause like world peace, they are willing to unite not only politically but also religiously. It would be an unnatural alliance if, for instance, five eastern Islamic nations united with five European "Christian" nations. As Daniel described the union; "so the people will be a mixture [possibly European and Arab nations] and will not remain united." This is where the doctrine of inclusion, also known as universalism, would be required to forge such an unlikely union of Christianity and Islamism.

Spirit Of The Antichrist Unites The Nations

Scripture warns that, "...every spirit that does not confess Jesus is not from God. *This is the spirit of the Antichrist,* which you have heard is coming, and *is already in the world at this time* [emphasis' added]" (1 John 4:3 BSB). The spirit of the Antichrist existed not only during the first century of the Church; its beginning was when Lucifer led the first rebellion against God. Since that time that spirit of anti-God (also known as Antichrist) has been alive and is now careening to a showdown with Christ at His soon return. Satan is the original Antichrist. He is one of the most powerful spirit beings that God ever created. Satan is alive and well on present-day planet earth. He is the god of this present world and has been so since the time Adam and Eve vacated themselves from that position due to their fall. Satan has laid claim to every soul (excluding Christ) of mankind born from that time to the present. That is except for those that Christ has redeemed through His blood. It is the spirit of Satan that permeates all of mankind that lives in ignorance or contrary to the gospel. The Spirit of God and the spirit of Satan are the only two entities that can influence and drive the minds of those who exist. Satan is the Antichrist, "...spirit who now works in the children of disobedience" (Eph 2:2b WEB).

The enemy of all Christians is none other than Satan and his spirit that permeates every other living being on the planet. Saints are warned of their enemy: "For our struggle is not against flesh and blood, but against the rulers, against the authorities, against the powers of this world's darkness, and against the spiritual forces of evil in the heavenly realms." (Eph. 6:12, BSB). Satan has been the reason mankind has lived in darkness to the truth of the gospel. "The god of this age has blinded the minds of unbelievers so they cannot see the light of the gospel of the glory of Christ, who is the image of God." (2 Cor. 4:4, BSB).

In spite of Satan's efforts to destroy the gospel, Christianity has grown to reach multiple millions over the centuries and as of 2010, of the 6,895,850,000 people on earth, 31.4 percent, or 2.17 billion, were Christians.[21] This means that over two-thirds of the world's population were not Christian. Satan obviously, through his spirit, has hidden or blinded the minds of the vast majority to the truth of the gospel. However, Satan's rule over this earth is drawing short and he desperately wants to destroy not only the existing gospel message but all those whom Christ has commissioned to preach it. There is only one way to do this. That is to pervert the gospel of Christ so that Christ's sacrifice is no longer seen as necessary to receiving eternal salvation. This vital perversion is fostered by the message and doctrine of universalism, also known as inclusionism, Chrislamism, and interfaithism. Almost all religions of the world already believe this lie. The only remaining obstacle on earth to Satan's lie is Christianity.

To eradicate the true gospel message, Satan must pervert its message and replace it with a universalist gospel. This has been and is the missing key needed for Satan to unify all nations and peoples on earth under one political and religious system, producing a New World Order (NWO). This NWO would become a new Tower of Babel, built in defiance of and rebellion toward God. Satan's lie, which negates the necessity of salvation in Christ, is now on the march in the circles of many Christian and non-Christian religions. At last Satan has the ultimate weapon that he is banking on to drive a spiritual dagger into the heart of Christianity and prevent it from bringing many to eternal salvation. This (Christian universalism) is Satan's definitive weapon, his Trojan horse. Satan has now drug it into our churches, movies, music, politics, science, and government, and it is spreading like a prairie wildfire around the world. This spirit of the Antichrist is subtle and most deceptive. Author Mel Sanger stated it beautifully:

> You see many people are talking about looking for the Antichrist and I can agree that I do believe that there will be a coming personal Antichrist. However there is also something called **the spirit of the Antichrist** and whether it's politics, economics, music, Hollywood, religion, science or the envi-

ronmental agenda, the spirit of the Antichrist has infiltrated every aspect of society and has in one of the most lethal ways conditioned us to not even be aware of the changes taking place which are propelling us rapidly into the clutches of a one world government.[22]

In order for Satan to destroy God's light on earth (Christianity), he must drive a spiritual dagger into its heart, which beats the only truth on earth that eternal salvation can come only through Jesus Christ. This will never happen, but it is Satan's only hope for victory. He is hard at work in the political and religious arenas, working to accomplish this mission.

Peace = Political And Religious Unification?

Leaders in the political and religious camps are proclaiming the necessity for political and religious unification. It is recognized by both camps that world unity and peace can come only through a uniting all religions and nations under one religious and political faith. It is recognized also that anything standing in that pathway that opposes this union must be removed if we are to achieve worldwide peace and tranquility. Satan understands this reality that was also stated by Dr. Hans Küng, a professor of ecumenical theology and president of the Global Ethic Foundation: "There will be no peace among the nations without peace among the religions. There will be no peace among the religions without dialogue among the religions."[23] It will be in the name of world peace that interfaith dialogue will be forged by the world's religions. These attempts will eventually usher in the ironclad worldwide rule of the Beast power and its ruler, the Antichrist. Religious inclusiveness is a key phrase that will ultimately bring about the uniting of faiths and nations around the world.

Reverend Irvin Baxter states, "In his book *Perestroika,* Mikhail Gorbachev stated that there are three root causes for war on earth: political conflicts, economic conflicts and religious conflicts. It was Gorbachev's contention that if we could have some form of global governance, a world economy and mutual respect among all the religions of the world, we could realize a society of peace and security."[24] Reverend Baxter asks the question, "Could we outlaw religious conflict? That's what Mr. Gorbachev recommended. He said we must extirpate genocide, apartheid and religious exclusiveness. He put believing your religion is the only correct way in the same category as the crimes of genocide and apartheid."[25] This new interfaith religion would outlaw any faith that would claim any exclusive pathway or right to God; therefore Christians would have to accept that Christ is not the only way to salvation and Islamists would have to accept that Allah would accept non-Islamist's faiths as valid. In short, I agree with how Rev. Baxter summed this new religion. You do not condemn my faith and I will not condemn yours. It seems to me that to totally end religious exclusiveness, various religious faiths would have to recognize and give credence to the various gods of all faiths creating, in effect, a new religion. Reverend Baxter used the term "Interfaithism," which I believe is correct to describe this new worldwide religion.[26]

God And Allah Proclaimed As The Same

In 1893 there was a gathering in Chicago of over eight thousand people representing various religious faiths from around the world. It eventually became known as the first meeting of the Parliament of the World's Religions. It began an international effort to foster inter-religious dialogue worldwide. Its successor today was incorporated in 1988 as the Council for a Parliament of the World's Religions. "Its stated mission is 'to cultivate harmony among the world's religious and spiritual communities and foster their engagement with the world and its guiding institutions in order to achieve a just, peaceful and sustainable world'."[27]

Tolerance among world religions has grown, and this is exemplified by statements from and actions by the Catholic Church. "...there has been a move at reconciliation not only with Judaism, but also Islam. The Second Vatican Council states that salvation includes others who acknowledge the same creator, and explicitly lists Muslims among those...."[28]

285

In August of 1985, Pope John Paul II announced to eighty thousand Muslims in Morocco that he believed Muslims and Christians worshiped the same God. He stated, "We believe in the same God, the one God, the living God, the God who created the world and brought his creatures to their perfection.'[29]

One year later, in spite of resistance from some in the Roman Catholic Church, Pope John Paul II hosted in Assisi, Italy, the 1986 Peace Prayer gathering of various religious faiths. After that, with the support of the Pope, yearly meetings were conducted, "...consisting of round tables on different issues and of a common time of prayer [that] has done much to further understanding and friendship between religious leaders and to further concrete peace initiatives."[30]

It's interesting to note that on May 14, 1999, John Paul II received a delegation (a Shiite imam, a Sunni from the Iraqi Islamic Bank, and an individual from the Iraqi ministry of religion). The Pope kissed the Muslim "holy" book, the Koran (Qur'an) at the Vatican. This was witnessed by Chaldean Catholic Patriarch Raphael, who said: "At the end of the audience *the Pope bowed to the Muslim holy book, the Qur'an, presented to him by the delegation, and he kissed it as a sign of respect* [emphasis added]. The photo of that gesture has been shown repeatedly on Iraqi television and it demonstrates that the Pope is not only aware of the suffering of the Iraqi people, he has also great respect for Islam."[31]

On May 6, 2001, John Paul II was the first Pope in history to step foot into a mosque of Allah. He was in Damascus, Syria, "...calling for brotherhood between Christians and Muslims. The Pontiff went into the Omayyad Mosque accompanied by Grand Mufti Ahmad Kuftaro, the highest Muslim religious authority of Damascus."[32] In addition to comments from the Pontiff, the Muslim sheik delivered an address in the Mosque's patio, "...to Muslim religious leaders, members of the Syrian government, and leaders of the Catholic Church, who came from all over the world to participate in the historic event."[33] He, like the Pope, obviously believed the God of the Christians was one and the same being (Allah) that Islam worships. He said, "We all adore the same God... Peace comes from our God and it returns to him. We are expressions of peace. God, Allah, calls all his creatures to peace, to belief in love."[34]

On September 24, 2015, Pope Francis said to the Muslims concerning the tragedy they suffered in Mecca, "In this moment, I give assurances of my prayers. *I unite myself with you all. A prayer to almighty god, all merciful.*" Allah is known in Islam as "the all-merciful one." This sounds very similar to what Francis said during his first ecumenical meeting as Pope. "I then greet and cordially thank you all, dear friends belonging to other religious traditions; *first of all the Muslims, who worship the one God, living and merciful, and call upon Him in prayer, and all of you.*). It sounds to me like the Pope is praying to a universal god that can be accessed by not only Christians but also Muslims, and other religious too.[35]

This kind of language should not be too surprising when you consider that this kind of sentiment and language was sanctioned in 1964 at the Second Vatican Council, Lumen Gentium 16. It was stated: "But the plan of *salvation also includes those who acknowledge the Creator* [emphasis added], in the first place among whom are the Muslims: these profess to hold the faith of Abraham, and *together with us they adore the one, merciful God* [emphasis added], mankind's judge on the last day."[36] Did this Vatican Council state, in effect, that "salvation" includes Muslims and that Christians and Muslims worship the same god?

Efforts at bridging the divide between Muslims and Christians have not been a one-way street. Before his death, King Abdullah of Saudi Arabia sponsored the World Conference on Dialogue in 2008. It was hosted by King Juan Carlos of Spain, with hundreds of leaders from several nation attending from the various major faiths of the world. It was a gathering of about five hundred delegates that was said to be "...a historic gathering that broke barriers and promoted greater understanding."[37] While there, King Abdullah stated, "I come to you from the place dearest to the hearts of all Muslims. This message declares that Islam is a religion of moderation and tolerance; a message that calls for constructive dialogue among followers of religions; a message that promises to open a new page for humanity in which—God willing—concord will replace conflict."[38] In another meeting later that year, King Abdullah spoke to religious leaders from various faiths (Baptist preachers, Jewish rabbis, Catholic priests, Muslim imams, Sikh Indian leaders, and Greek Orthodox clerics), saying, "We are all brothers and sisters in humanity. Let us join hands to fight the 'deviants' who cause violence and sow hatred in the name of our peaceful religions."[39]

It seems that many Christians and Islamists believe God and Allah are the same being. Are they? This belief is filtering down to many religious faiths worldwide, as you will see in this and the final chapter. This is a crucial question, for it is through this door that the divinity of Christ is being challenged. By accepting this theology you automatically are accepting other pathways to heaven for mankind than through Jesus Christ. I believe that former president George W. Bush expressed what many, if not most, Christians now believe. President Bush was asked in an ABC television interview, "Do you believe we all worship the same God, Christians and Muslims?" His answer was, "I think we do. We have different routes of getting to the Almighty." President Bush also was asked, "Do Christians and non-Christian, do Muslims go to heaven in your mind?" He replied, "Yes, they do. They have different routes of getting there."[40] Did President Bush in effect state that accepting Jesus Christ and His forgiveness of our sins is not necessary to enter heaven?

The religious communities of the world have made giant strides in bridging the divides of world religions since their beginning baby steps in the first meeting of the Parliament of the World's Religions in 1883. For the first time in history in August of 2000, "One thousand of the world's top religious and spiritual leaders came together at the United Nations ... to discuss and devote themselves to world peace."[41] Among the Western and Islamic attendees were "Pope John Paul II, Archbishop of Canterbury George Carey, Sheikh Ahmed Keftaro, the Grand Mufti of Syria, Israel's chief rabbi, Archbishop Desmond Tutu, and the Grand Sheikh of al-Azhar University."[42] They concluded the summit by signing the "Declaration for World Peace," which outlines efforts to be made to achieve lasting international peace."[43] In 2014, Pope Francis allowed Muslim prayers and Qur'an readings at the Vatican. Palestinian President Mahmoud Abbas, Israeli President Shimon Peres, and the Pope prayed together in the Vatican gardens.[44]

In Irvin Baxter's End Time Ministries magazine, in an article by David Robbins, important points were made concerning the current worldwide move toward a one world religion. In 1993 at the one-hun-dredth-year anniversary of the Parliament of the World's Religions in Chicago, "Catholics, Protestants, Hindus, Jews, Muslims, Sikhs, Asto-rians, Wiccans (Witches), indigenous people and many others were in attendance."[45] Religious leaders from around the world met and adopted a global belief statements authored by the eminent Catholic theologian Hans Kung.[46] One important belief statements they agreed to was, "We must sink our narrow differences for the cause of the world community, practicing a culture of solidarity and relatedness."[47]

David's article points out that it looks as though many Christian faiths are willing to give up their "narrow differences," as is demonstrated by the Catholic Church. In the Catholic Catechism in item number 841, it states the following concerning the Church's relationship with the Muslims:

> The plan of salvation also includes those who acknowledge the creator, in the first place amongst whom are the Muslims; these profess to hold the faith of Abraham, and together with us they adore the one, merciful God, mankind's judge on the Last Day."[48]

The sinking of the "narrow differences" of various religious faiths around the world is absolutely necessary and justified because it is rec-ognized by world religious and political leaders that the only way world unity and peace can be achieved. Mr. Robbins article points out a state-ment by Robert Muller, assistant secretary general to three secretaries general of the United Nations, which sums up what I think the Parlia-ment of the World's Religions would like to see happen. Mr. Muller said:

> We have brought the world together as far as we can politi-cally. To bring about true world government, the world must be brought together spiritually.... What we need is a United Nations of Religions.[49]

Could these "narrow differences" someday, in the name of and for the "cause of world community," require that Christians reject the belief that their God is a different God than Allah and that the only way to salvation for every living soul is through Jesus Christ? If Christians accept that God and Allah are the same entity, then the door can begin to be closed to the belief that Jesus Christ is the Son of God and only in Him can salvation be granted. Prophecy shows that accepting these two basic tenets will ultimately be required by the Antichrist.

Christianity +Islam = Chrislam

It is interesting to note that there are interfaith branches of Christianity and Islam sects today all over America that are fostering a new theology called Chrislam. "Rick Warren, Pope Francis and the Lebanese Islamic-Christian National Dialogue Committee have all been attacked by the critics of Chrislam who cite alleged 'irreconcilable differences' between its two component religions. Chrislamic people themselves see no problem with the basic unity of the two religions, because they say that God loves all people and wants us to love all people."[50]

In 2011, in an article under the name "American Churches To Embrace Chrislam on June 26, 2011" by Geoffrey Grider, there was posted a listing of seventy-one individual American Christian churches in thirty-one states that had agreed to an interfaith service to be shared with others of not-Christian faiths. Some of the more recognizable church names that had at least one listing were: Episcopal, Catholic, Presbyterian, Lutheran, Congregational, United Church of Christ, United Methodist, and Baptist.[51] Since this came out five years ago, I can now only imagine how many more churches have embraced the faith of "Chrislism."

Satan's Whore

Scripture says that a religious leader will be critical in forging a final alliance of all nations and faiths. This religious leader is identified as a "another beast" (Rev. 13:11, WEB) and recognized as a great religious leader by all the nations. However, the Scriptures exposes him as a "false prophet" (Rev. 19:20 WEB).

I saw a woman [false church] sit upon a scarlet coloured beast, full of names of blasphemy, having seven heads and ten horns. And the woman was arrayed in purple and scarlet colour, and decked with gold and precious stones and pearls, having a golden cup in her hand full of abominations and filthiness of her fornication: And upon her forehead *was* a name written, MYSTERY, BABYLON THE GREAT, THE MOTHER OF HARLOTS AND ABOMINATIONS OF THE EARTH. ~ Revelation 17:3-5, KJV

The true Church of Christ is referred to in Scripture as a woman (see Ephesians 5:23,32; Revelation 19:7). The woman riding the beast (dictator and ten nations) is called a "prostitute" (Rev. 17:1, WEB) who has committed adulteries with the kings of the earth. This prostitute pictures a fallen church that has abandoned Jesus and has adulterously joined the false religions of the world by embracing their doctrines spawned by the devil.

Devil's Doctrine Of Inclusion

Let's now discuss a bit further how the unlikely union of nations from the East and West could be forged. Satan is the real power masterminding their rise and unification (see Revelation 13:4). Critical in his plan is the need to unify them into one whorish church and state. It will be necessary to use an individual recognized by all the nations as a great religious leader. The Scriptures call him a false prophet and another beast because of his ability to perform great miracles and signs, "…even making fire come down out of the sky to the earth in the sight of people" (Rev. 13:13b WEB). I believe that if the Pope or an Islamic ayatollah today called fire down from heaven in full view of a million people, most of them would be traumatized and greatly impressed, to say the least. When this does happen in the future by the false prophet, it will have a jolting effect on the psyche of those who see it. Because of this miracle, "…it deceived those who dwell on the earth" (Rev. 13:14 BSB). This false prophet will be critical in adulterating all religions under his control. He will accomplish what was once thought was inconceivable; the unifying of all religious faiths under the power of the Antichrist into serving a new god. He will deceive the nations into worshiping the head of the reborn ten-nation Roman Empire (perhaps five nations each from the Middle East and five from Europe).

Consider again the fact that Daniel shows one leg of the revived Roman Empire planted firmly in the Western Empire and one planted in the Eastern Empire. This would clearly indicate that the ten toes representing the Beast power of ten nations would be an alliance of five nations from the Western Empire and five from the Eastern Empire. I believe that the false prophet ultimately riding and helping unite the two empires will most likely profess Christianity, however, it is possible that he might be an Islamist king (like in Saudi Arabia) or other Islamic cleric. Whichever the case may be, this false prophet will preach a god who accepts all faiths.

To prove his status as "God's spiritual leader," this false prophet will perform unbelievable miracles, which he will use to aid the rise of the empire's Antichrist and to deceive the nations into worshiping this Antichrist as God. This false prophet will be critical in binding together the iron and clay nations.

In order to support and consolidate the power of the new world dictator, this false prophet will claim that God sent this Antichrist dictator to head the newly revived Roman Empire to save the world from total destruction and usher in a new world order of peace and harmony. Satan's plan is to use the false prophet, the new revived Roman Empire, and its Antichrist to destroy mankind and God's kingdom.

This religious leader will preach that all faiths of all nations are valid because they all serve the same god. This is the present-day doctrine of inclusion and it will be used to galvanize the various religions worldwide to support and serve the new Beast power. Church and state will be united. A new faith will unite all religions of the world. It will officially reject the acceptance of Jesus Christ as the only way to eternal salvation and entry into God's kingdom. The false prophet will say, "There are many ways to get to heaven. We must stop fighting over our religious differences such as that between Christians and Islamists. It matters not what god a Hindu, Islamist, Jew, Buddhist, or Christian worships; we all worship the same Supreme Being!"

The people on earth will believe the lying pronouncements through Satan's earthly agents, and as the Scripture says, "They worshiped the dragon who had given authority to the beast, and they worshiped the beast, saying, 'Who is like the beast, and who can wage war against it?'" (Rev. 13:4, BSB). Most inhabitants of the nations will worship the dictator ruling this revived Roman Empire. He will seemingly be an invulnerable superhuman being. All will worship this new powerful ruler except the faithful Christians who are not deceived to the true identity of the Beast and its new king god (Rev. 13:8).

The Spirit Of The Antichrist Is Marching

To embrace the new religion of the Antichrist, all individuals of the various nations around the world will have to reject Jesus Christ as the only way to eternal salvation. Rejecting Christ is the only pathway to uniting the various religions around the world. Groundwork for this Antichirst doctrine, as we have seen earlier, is now being laid. The spirit of universalism worldwide seems to be speeding up daily. For example, I was shocked today to hear the following statement from a television news reporter: "The Vatican has declared that Christians should not attempt to convert Jews. In an historic decision a panel of senior Catholic theologians ruled that the Jewish people can obtain salvation without embracing Christianity, therefore advocating Christians to abstain from proselyting the Jews…. The Vatican's commission for religious relations with Jews issued a report reversing Christianity's official stance on the Jewish people, stating that the Jews have a part in salvation because the gifts of the calling of God are irrevocable! It went on to call for the Catholic Church to no longer seek the conversion of Jews and to work toward the elimination of anti-Semitism."[52]

It seems the Vatican has declared a new litmus test in order to enter into heaven. No longer must one recognize that Jesus Christ is the Savior of the world and accept Him as one's Savior to enter heaven. All one must to do is have "the gifts of the calling of God," whatever that means. Sounds to me like a future Vatican panel could easily extend entry into heaven not only to just the Jews but to all non-Christians on the earth who also have "gifts." Who are you going to believe, a decision of a panel of senior Catholic theologians or Jesus, who said, "…I am the way, the truth, and the life. No one comes to the Father, except through me" (John 14:6b, BSB). If the Jewish people can obtain salvation without going through Christ, then why discriminate against the rest of mankind? If the Jews can enter heaven without Christ, then why can't any person on earth also be able to? Whatever the excuse might be, it seems obvious that the Catholic Church no longer believes it is necessary to repent and accept Jesus Christ as one's savior in order to be saved. The spirit of universalism is definitely on the march and spreading rapidly now, not only within Catholicism, but also within its Protestant daughters around the world. In the name of inclusion and peace, religions around the world are now moving at breakneck speed to remove "barriers" between them, Christ being the main obstacle. These attempts will play into the hands of the coming Antichrist, who will co-opt universalism and use it as the key to gather the nations of the world under his power. With it he will forge one religious and political system under his absolute dictatorial tyranny.

21

THE TRIBULATION PERIOD

Scripture does reveal major events that count down to the return of Christ. The following account I give is based in part on Irwin Baxter's teachings on this matter.[1] As we have already seen, World War III will devastate the world, driving almost every nation on earth to unite with the newly revived Holy Roman Empire under its charismatic and seemingly invincible new dictator, the Antichrist. Scripture reveals that there will be at least two and possibly three nations that will not come under the powerful control of the Beast power's world rule. For sure two of the nations who escape the grasp of the Antichrist will be Israel and Jordan (see Daniel 11:41). It is possible that the third nation might be the United States. I will discuss that possibility shortly.

Israel's Peace Treaty

After World War III in which one third of mankind will be destroyed, a devastated world will cry out demanding peace. This will set the stage for a strong man to come forward and take control of the situation and promise to give the world the peace it demands. However, the remaining major hot spot left to deal with will be the dispute between Israel and the Palestinians over a Palestinian State. Negotiations will ensue, but a stalemate will exist because Israel will refuse to give up East Jerusalem to the Palestinians. Though Israel will not be forced under the control of the Beast power, Israel will remain a threat to world peace and will be viewed by the world as the one remaining antagonist because of her obstinate refusal to give the Palestinians their own nation within the confines of the Israeli-controlled territories with East Jerusalem as their capital. The unsettled dispute between Israel and the Palestinians over a Palestinian homeland will by then be a boiling cauldron ready to explode, igniting World War IV. The horrors of World War III will be fresh in everyone's mind and the nations will be willing to do just about anything to avoid another war, even to the extent of giving up national and religious sovereignty.

The Palestinians will be recognized by the new Beast power as having a right to a nation and negotiations under the all-out threat of war on this matter will take place between Israel and the Palestinian allies under the heavy hand of the Beast power. Israel will insist that their right to exist be recognized by the Arab nations and that they be given access to the Temple Mount to rebuild their third Temple to God. On the other hand, the Palestinians will demand that they be given the West Bank (Judea) to establish their own independent nation and that Israel allow East Jerusalem to become their capital. These two disputed stances will stand as roadblocks to a final peace treaty. Israel will obstinately refuse to give up its control over the city of East Jerusalem.[2] The Beast power, mostly in concert with the United Nations, will eventually forge a temporary peace agreement of seven years, after which time all parties will agree to each other's demands except for the matter of who will control East Jerusalem. The resolution of that one remaining issue will be delayed until the end of the seven-year temporary peace agreement. This matter will then be revisited to permanently settle the dispute.[3]

The signing of this peace treaty will mark the beginning of a seven-year countdown to the return of Jesus Christ and the Battle of Armageddon. In the temporary peace agreement between Israel and the Palestinians, Israel's right to exist will be affirmed. In essence, this will verify the covenant God made with Abraham, giving to him and his descendants the land of Israel forever (see Genesis 15:18; Exodus 32:13). The Temple mount will be taken under international control of most likely the United Nations, under which the mount will be shared be-

CHAPTER 21: THE TRIBULATION PERIOD

tween the Israelites and the Palestinians. Israel will be allowed to rebuild its third Temple on the mount after nearly two thousand years. Israel will re-institute daily sacrifices and offerings to God. After this agreement, the Palestinians will establish their new nation comprising the occupied territory of the West Bank (Judea). The Palestinians will allow Israeli citizens to remain in their West Bank settlements if they so desire.[4] The world will rejoice over this agreement. The specter of World War IV will fade and the world will then settle down to enjoy the fruits of unity and peace. This time period of seven years is generally recognized as the tribulation period.

The first three and a half years will experience increasing tensions or, as Christ describes it, "All these *are* the beginning of sorrows" (Matt. 24:8, KJV). However, the first three and a half years will be nothing compared to the final three and a half years, called the "Great Tribulation," which will begin when the Antichrist is suddenly revealed when he breaks the treaty with Israel, stops the sacrifices in the Temple, and proclaims himself the god of his new universal religion. This is the major signpost Christ gave his saints, telling them to flee for their lives because persecution and mass martyrdom of the saints will begin immediately after this proclamation by the Antichrist (see Matthew 24). Daniel describes it this way, "He [the Antichrist] shall make a firm covenant with many for one week [seven years]: and in the midst of the week he shall cause the sacrifice and the offering to cease [in the Temple]... (Dan. 9:27b, WEB). It is when the Antichrist halts the sacrifices in the Temple of God that his true nature will be revealed to God's people as the "lawless one" and "Antichrist." Scripture says:

> He [the Antichrist] will oppose and exalt himself above every so-called god or object of worship. So he will seat himself in the temple of God, proclaiming himself to be God. ...And then the lawless one [who is the Antichrist] will be revealed, whom the Lord Jesus will slay with the breath of His mouth and abolish by the majesty of His arrival. ~ 2 Thessalonians 2:4, 8, BSB

Daniel describes the Antichrist dictator as a "King" and describes his desecration of God's temple: "Forces shall stand on his part, and they shall profane the sanctuary, even the fortress, and shall take away the continual [burnt offering], and they shall set up the abomination that makes desolate" (Dan. 11:31, WEB). It is interesting to note that an angel told Daniel in a vision concerning the Antichrist that, "Neither shall he regard the gods of his fathers, nor the desire of women, nor regard any god; for he shall magnify himself above all" (Dan. 11:37, WEB). The ten nations will already have unified as both one state and one church (iron and clay) to form the power of the Antichrist who will rule them all.

The Beast's union is described in Daniel as part iron and clay. Its unification is partly strong and yet partly weak. This will be due to some extent because of the various cultures and religions of the nations around the world nations that will come under the leadership of the Beast power. This is where the scriptures describe a "false prophet" who will step forward to strengthen the power of the Beast by miracles. "And the second beast [the false prophet] performed great signs to cause even fire from heaven to come down to earth in the presence of the people. Because of the signs it was given to perform on behalf the first beast, it deceived those who dwell on the earth…" (Rev. 13:13-14a, BSB). However, it will not be until the Antichrist stops the sacrifices of the Jews in the temple of God that the Antichrist declares that he is none other than God himself. He may hope this declaration that he is God will strengthen the ten-nation union and his rule over them and the other nations of the world he now controls.

It is at this juncture that Scripture exposes him to true Christians as the Antichrist when he, in the temple of God, declares that he is the personification of what has been sought after by all religious faiths; that he is the reality and perfect union of their heavenly desires. Therefore he will claim that he is the true God they both have desired since the beginning of time. He will proclaim that he is the only one who can maintain peace, economic security, and stability for all nations of the world. He will proclaim that only he can usher in mankind's desired Utopian world. In effect, he will merge the forces of all religions on earth under his control into one new religion with himself as their god. This will strengthen his power and legitimacy as their king. I have believed for the last fifty-four years that the

Antichrist will be a European and the false prophet will be the last Pope. Although I personally believe this is correct, I now have come to believe that one or both could possibly come from the geography of the old Holy Roman's Eastern Empire. Whatever is the case, to unify the nations of the world under the Beast power, the doctrine of inclusion will be the only thing that can make this implausible union plausible. Universalism will become the required faith of all nations of the world. All other faiths will be outlawed as extremist and a threat to the love, peace, and tranquility of the world. It is interesting that the seeds of what eventually will outlaw any faith in the world contrary to universalism are now being planted.[5]

In 2014 Pope Francis visited the Middle East and criticized fundamentalism in Christianity and any extremist religion as a form of violence. The Pope said, "A fundamentalist group, even if it kills no one, even if it strikes no one, is violent. The mental structure of fundamentalism is violence in the name of God"[6] Recently the Pope reiterated these beliefs: "'Fundamentalism is a sickness that is in all religions,' Francis said, as reported by the National Catholic Reporter's Vatican correspondent, Joshua McElwee, and similarly by other journalists on the plane. 'We Catholics have some—and not some, many—who believe in the absolute truth and go ahead dirtying the other with calumny, with disinformation, and doing evil.' 'They do evil,' said the pope. 'I say this because it is my church.' 'We have to combat it,' he said. 'Religious fundamentalism is not religious, because it lacks God. It is idolatry, like the idolatry of money.'"[7] These beliefs will be at the heart and core of the coming one new world religion, which for the sake of peace, love, and happiness will worship the Antichrist and outlaw any faith that is regarded as extremist and therefore a threat to the new faith of universalism.

War In Heaven

At some point, most likely after the signing of the peace treaty and prior to unveiling of the Antichrist, Satan and his army of fallen angels will ascend to heaven to make one final attempt to rip control and rule of the universe from God. Scripture describes the event this way:

> Then a war broke out in heaven: Michael and his angels fought against the dragon, and the dragon and his angels fought back. But the dragon was not strong enough, and no longer was any place found in heaven for him and his angels. And the great dragon was hurled down—the ancient serpent called the devil and Satan, the deceiver of the whole world. He was hurled to the earth, and his angels with him. ~ Revelation 12:7-9, BSB

Satan will be utterly defeated by God's army and cast back to earth to be permanently confined there. In his rage at his defeat in heaven, Satan will turn his wrath on the Jews and Christians to annihilate them. A prophetic dire warning is issued to the nation of Israel and God's saints remaining on earth: "But woe to the earth and the sea; with great fury the devil has come down to you, knowing he has only a short time." (Rev. 12:12b, BSB). Yes, his time is short indeed. This war in heaven will occur just prior to the Antichrist stopping the daily sacrifices and setting up the abomination of desolation in the Jewish temple.[8] Satan will know that he has only three and a half years left before Christ comes to establish His kingdom on earth and bind Satan and his angels in the bottomless pit for the next one thousand years. Satan will be furious and will unleash his fury on two groups of people. First his fury will be directed at Israel in an effort to destroy it. When his efforts are throated, his fury will turn to the Christians. Notice:

> And when the dragon saw that he had been thrown to the earth, he pursued the woman who had given birth to the male child. But the woman was given two wings of a great eagle to fly from the presence of the serpent to her place in the wilderness, where she was nourished for a time, and times, and half a time. Then from the mouth of the serpent spewed water like a river to overtake the woman and sweep her away in the torrent. But the earth helped the woman and opened its mouth to swallow up the river that had poured from the dragon's mouth. And the dragon was enraged at the woman, and went to make to war with the rest of her children, who keep the commandments of God and hold to the testimony of Jesus. ~ Revelation 12:13-17, BSB

To accomplish Satan's aim, he will most likely swoop down to earth to take bodily possession of the Antichrist, who will then break the treaty with Israel, stopping their Temple sacrifices. The Antichrist will stand in the Temple declaring himself to be the head of both church and state of not only the Holy Roman Empire but also of the world. With the help of the False Prophet, the Antichrist will follow this event with a reign of terror and martyrdom of Jews and saints for the next three and a half years in the Great Tribulation. During this time the two witnesses of God will stand strong and powerful in their opposition to the Antichrist. In spite of the Antichrist, God will preserve Israel as a nation and will also spare the nation of Jordan from destruction by the Beast power.[9] The last three and a half years of tribulation and the fury unleashed toward Jews and Christians will be the expression of Satan's wrath on God's people.

Satan's fury will focus first on destroying the nation of Israel. However, Israel will be given "two wings of a great eagle," whereby she will be protected "in her place." Her place is most likely within her boarders of Israel.[10] When Satan sees that he will not be able to destroy Israel, then his wrath will be turned "against the rest of her offspring—those who keep God's commands and hold fast their testimony about Jesus." Their testimony is that the only way to heaven is through Christ, and these Christians will refuse to accept the universal inclusion doctrines being promoted by the Antichrist. It is during these last three and a half years of the Great Tribulation that the Jews living in Palestinian sector of the West Bank will be slaughtered. Many believe that the Great Tribulation will be a result of God's fury at mankind. This is incorrect, for when Satan sees he can't destroy Israel, he will refocus his great wrath on those who keep God's commands and hold fast to Jesus Christ as mankind's only way to salvation. These will be the multiple millions of Christians living in the nations under the control of the Beast power. Many millions of Christians will be persecuted and martyred during this time of Satan's wrath.

Who Is The Woman Of Revelation Twelve?

Let's expand on this question for a moment. I believe this prophecy could be dual in nature. It could apply to the nation of Israel and it could also apply to the Christian Church. When I was a young man and a member of Mr. Herbert Armstrong's Worldwide Church of God (WCG), I was taught that the woman given "two wings of a great eagle" was none other than the WCG, which was the "one and only true Church of God" on earth. We were taught that we'd be physically taken to a place (most likely the red sandstone mountains of Petra in Jordan) where we would be protected from Satan's wrath for the three and a half years of the Great Tribulation. Although I agree with Reverend Baxter that the woman in Revelation twelve is the nation of Israel, I think it is possible that it might also relate to some spiritual Israelites (Christians) who will physically escape the Great Tribulation and be protected somewhere on earth during this time. I believe this is possible because they will heed the warning Christ gave to flee when they see the halting of the sacrifices and the desecration of the Temple by the Antichrist. Jesus warned, "Therefore be watchful all the time, praying that you may be counted worthy to escape all these things that will happen, and to stand before the Son of Man" (Luke 21:36, WEB).

Jesus here was warning Christians to be looking for the events he predicted would happen leading up to the Great Tribulation period. I believe this warning was not only for His disciples concerning the slaughter after the Roman desecration of the Temple in AD 70 but also for us today concerning the soon coming desecration of Israel's third Temple. Do I believe that all Christians alive on earth will have to suffer the Great Tribulation? No, I don't! I do not believe that Jesus' warning was meaningless for saints in the first century, nor is it meaningless for us today. He obviously said we should pray that we might escape from the coming tribulation. Why would he command that we should pray this unless there will be some who do escape the clutches of the Antichrist because they will heed the warning of Jesus? Obviously, some Christians did in AD 70, and it is likely some will also be spared from the coming Great Tribulation. Where will they go? God only knows for sure. Many may be protected in the nation of Israel itself. I believe some Christians may be protected in Jordan. Frankly, God can also protect Christians in areas of United States, South America, Australia, as well as other countries.

I believe Jesus was admonishing Christians today to look for the signposts He said were coming. We don't all have to agree in advance on exactly when, where, and how they will unfold. However, when we see the events Jesus spoke of surface on the horizon, and certainly when we see them happening, we will be better able to recognize them and properly react to them in faith. Doing so may allow some Christians to move to a "place of safety." The fact is that Christ will not make Christians do anything. He gives us signposts to look for that lead into the Great Tribulation, but He does not force us to look for and recognize them. Christ warned Christians, "So be careful, or your hearts will be loaded down with carousing, drunkenness, and cares of this life, and that day will come on you suddenly. For it will come like a snare on all those who dwell on the surface of all the earth" (Luke 21:34-35, WEB). It seems obvious from what Jesus said that some Christians will choose not to heed His warning. Sadly, some who don't pay any attention to Christ's warning will pay the consequence of having to suffer in the Great Tribulation. Christ did not say in vain, "Blessed is the one who reads the words of this prophecy, and blessed are those who hear and obey what is written in it, because the time is near" (Rev. 1:3, BSB). Christians who follow His advice will receive a special blessing. It may even be that they will be spared the Great Tribulation. Will some who heed Christ's warning still go into the Great Tribulation? Yes, they will if God wants them to for a special purpose to glorify His name. As John stated concerning Christians who will experience the Great Tribulation period:

> He who has an ear, let him hear. "If anyone is destined for captivity, into captivity he will go; If anyone is to die by the sword, by the sword he must be killed." Here is a call for the perseverance and faith of the saints. ~ Revelation 13:9-10, BSB

"Perseverance and faith?" I should say so! It will take a lot of it for Christians who will have to endure the Great Tribulation. God will decide who will have to go through it. For many it will not be a matter of whether one is worthy to escape the Great Tribulation. Many of those who go into the tribulation will do so at the will of God to be a special witness for Him. Take, for instance, the two witnesses of God. They will be on a special mission from God, as will you, if you go into the Great Tribulation.

It behooves Christian ministers to preach on these matters in order to inform and warn God's sheep of what is to come. This will aid Christians to watch for and pray that they may escape Satan's wrath during the Great Tribulation. At any rate they will not be surprised when these events come to pass. Therefore, they will be better able to faithfully endure the time period of the Great Tribulation, if that is God's will. For some Christians, being aware of and heeding Christ's warning may result in them being able "to escape from all these coming evils." If the preachers of a pretribulation Rapture are wrong, many of their flock will be ill prepared to follow Christ's imperative to "…watch at all times, and pray that you may have the strength to escape all that is about to happen…(Luke 21:36 BSB).

Who Will Protect Israel?

As I have said, Irvin Baxter believes that the nation of Israel is the one given the "wings of an eagle" and protected "in her place" during the Great Tribulation. As I have also related, I believe this could refer to both Christians and Jews. Reverent Baxter says "her place" is the land of modern-day Israel. It's interesting to note here that the national symbol of the United States of America is the great bald eagle.[11] Is it just possible that this eagle that helps protect Israel is America? Let's consider that possibility. Daniel had a vision showing four animals representing the major nations that would exist just prior to the return of Christ (see Daniel 7). It has been speculated three of these animals are used to depict readily identifiable nations that now exist. Rev. Baxter believes that the bear is Russia. The leopard is Germany. The lion is England.[12] The fourth "beast" is the soon coming ten nations who will rule the world and will seek to destroy Israel and fight Christ in the Battle of Armageddon.

Now let's focus on the lion. Daniel said concerning this lion that it, "...had the wings of an eagle. I watched until its wings were torn off and it was lifted from the ground so that it stood on two feet like a human being, and the mind of a human was given to it" (Dan. 7:4b, WEB). It is interesting to note that the lion is depicted as having wings that were removed from him. Is it possible that this represents the United States of America breaking away from England in the eighteenth century?[13] Reverent Baxter thinks so and draws some interesting points concerning the wings of the eagle which also morphed into a man. He believes that the eagle's wings and the man represents the United States of America which broke away from Great Britton in 1776.[14] I believe Reverent Baxter is correct concerning this prophecy. Note that the American Bald eagle is recognized around the world as a symbol of the United States of America. "The bald eagle is the national bird of the United States of America.... The bald eagle appears on most official seals of the U.S. government, including the presidential seal, the presidential flag...."[15] Also note that scripture says, the wings morphed into two feet like a man with a mind. Not only is the bald eagle used to depict America, but at times a man is also used. We often refer to the United States as Uncle Sam. "Uncle Sam (initials U.S.) is a common national personification of the American government or the United States in general...."[16]

Could the man that Daniel saw in his dream represent America's Uncle Sam? It is at least an interesting speculation. If these prophecies are speaking of the United States, then we do have great reason to hope that America will repent and turn to God in the face of the coming disasters and World War III. Is it possible we will still be powerful enough to not come under the control of the Antichrist and even be able to protect Israel and Jordan from destruction at the hands of the coming resurrected Roman Empire? Scripture prophecies that Israel would be protected during the Great Tribulation. Notice, "Two wings of the great eagle were given to the woman, that she might fly into the wilderness to her place, so that she might be nourished for a time, and times, and half a time [3 1/2 years], from the face of the serpent" (Rev. 12:14 WEB). We can only pray that this will be the case. If this is so, we can take great courage from this prospect. It indicates that the United States will have coming a new

"Great Awakening" by turning back to God.

There have been three or four great religious revivals in the last three hundred years in America. The term "Great Awakening" can refer to several periods of time in which many evangelical Protestant ministers stirred up Christian fervor, resulting in a great increase in church interest and attendance.[17] Let us all pray this will be so for America. America may yet be used by God to support and protect Israel.

The Last Three And A Half Years

We are told in the book of Revelation that the Antichrist was given "…a mouth to speak arrogant and blasphemous words, and authority to act for forty-two months [three and a half years] was given to him" (Rev. 13:5, BSB). Jesus described this period of time, saying:

> When, therefore, you see the abomination of desolation, which was spoken of through Daniel the prophet, standing in the holy place (let the reader understand), then let those who are in Judea flee to the mountains. Let him who is on the housetop not go down to take out things that are in his house. Let him who is in the field not return back to get his clothes. But woe to those who are with child and to nursing mothers in those days! Pray that your flight will not be in the winter, nor on a Sabbath, for then there will be great oppression, such as has not been from the beginning of the world until now, no, nor ever will be. ~ Matthew 24:15-21, WEB

After the Temple sacrifices are stopped and the Beast proclaims his divinity, then the three-and-a-half-year reign of terror that the Bible calls "the Great Tribulation" will begin. This will entail a horrible persecution and mass martyrdom of Jews and Christians. Paul also states that immediately after the revealing of the Antichrist there will be an apostasy from the Christian Church. The Scriptures appropriately name the Antichrist for who he is. The power behind the Beast's throne is none other than the original one that was against Christ, Satan the devil. After the Beast causes the abomination of desolation in the Temple, Scripture exposes him as doing the biding of Satan (Revelation 13:2-8).

After Satan attempts to overthrow God again, Satan will probably then enter and take possession of the Antichrist and declare to all nations, while standing in the Temple, that he is the embodiment of their true god, no matter what faith they hold. Satan will then turn his wrath lose on the Jews and true Christians for having been defeated by the armies of God and confined to earth. This Antichrist will set up his new religion, which worships himself. He will deny that the only way to God is through Jesus Christ. He will declare a death sentence to anyone who believes otherwise. Then, as Jesus described it, "For at that time there will be great tribulation, unmatched from the beginning of the world until now, and never to be seen again" (Matt. 24:21, BSB). Jesus refers to the Antichrist and the false prophet when he states, "For there will arise false christs, and false prophets, and they will show great signs and wonders, so as to lead astray, if possible, even the chosen ones" (Matt. 24:24, WEB).

Is it possible to lead astray the elect of God? Let's examine that question. Paul said:

> The coming of the lawless one will be accompanied by the working of Satan, with every kind of power, sign, and false wonder, and with every wicked deception directed against those who are perishing, because they refused the love of the truth that would have saved them. For this reason, God will send them a powerful delusion so that *they will believe the lie* [emphasis added], in order that judgment will come upon all who have disbelieved the truth and delighted in wickedness. ~ 2 Thessalonians 2:9-12, BSB

When Paul spoke of the attempt by the Antichrist to seduce others by his lie, he said, "But we should always thank God for you, brothers who are loved by the Lord, because God has chosen you from the beginning to be saved by the sanctification of the Spirit and by faith in the truth." (2 Thess. 2:13, BSB). There is only one truth that can save anyone. True Christians believe that Jesus is indeed the only way for anyone to be able to live with God eternally. The Antichrist will tell many lies, but

Paul refers to one particular lie that leads many "professing Christians" to perdition. I can think of no more damaging lie than that which proclaims that there is a way to salvation other than accepting Jesus Christ as your Savior. This is undoubtedly "the lie" that Paul spoke of that the Antichrist would be preaching.

One would think that true Christians called and chosen by God would not be deceived by this lie of the Antichrist and his false prophets. I am inclined to believe that any Saint would never deny that salvation is only through Jesus Christ. However, I am not their judge, God is. I suppose it may be possible due to "political correctness" and the dramatic miracles performed by the false prophet that some saints may become disillusioned and fall away temporarily. Falling away does not necessarily mean they lose their eternal salvation. One can stray from God due to sins or being temporarily deceived doctrinally. Their falling away could be due to the intense persecution and martyrdom of Christians who will not worship the Antichrist as God. Some of these might be some disillusioned Christians whose anticipated Rapture did not occur and therefore were not as prepared for the onslaught of the Antichrist. Most of those who will fall away most likely will be "Christians" in name only and not really born-again children of God. Some saints who are weak or immature in faith may deny Christ with their lips, but retain Him in their hearts. However, whether or not a saint can temporarily be deceived, one thing that's certain is that once an individual is born again, he or she can never be lost by God (see John 10:29).

No one can come to salvation unless God chooses to give them that opportunity (see Acts 2:39, 47; 1 Corinthians 1:26-27). Of those God that offers salvation, He will give salvation only to those who truly believe and accept Jesus Christ. They then are given the Holy Spirit of God, which seals them eternally as His sons and daughters, never to be lost. Paul makes this very plain:

> And in Him you were sealed with the promised Holy Spirit, having heard and believed the word of truth, the gospel of your salvation. The Spirit is the pledge of our inheritance [Kingdom of God] until the redemption of those who are God's possession, to the praise of His glory. ~ Ephesians 1:13-14, BSB

This is why Jesus said of true Christians, "I give them eternal life, and they will never perish. No one can snatch them out of My hand. My Father who has given them to Me is greater than all. No one can snatch them out of My Father's hand" (John 10:28-29, BSB).

That assurance should be most comforting to Christians, for God's hands are pretty strong! Those who are Christians will be made obvious when they publicly refuse to worship the Antichrist, who will be proclaimed the "new god" of all mankind. Only those who profess to worship the Antichrist will escape possible martyrdom. There will be some Christians who live through the Great Tribulation to see Christ return to give them their new eternal body, to resurrect saints, and to avenge the blood of the martyred saints. Paul also described these dire dreary days, warning:

> Let no one deceive you in any way, for it [the coming of Christ] will not come until the rebellion [apostasy of Christians] occurs and the man of lawlessness (the son of destruction) is revealed. He will oppose and exalt himself above every so-called god or object of worship. So he will seat himself in the temple of God, proclaiming himself to be God. ~ 2 Thessalonians 2:3-4, BSB

Martyrs Of The Great Tribulation

Jesus said that a great time of trouble would be unleashed on the earth after the Antichrist stops the Temple sacrifices and sets up the abomination of desolation. Jesus described that time this way: "For in those days there will be tribulation unmatched from the beginning of God's creation until now, and never to be seen again." (Mark 13:19, BSB). When one considers throughout the history of mankind all the horrible times of war, trouble, and distress, it is hard to imagine how the Great Tribulation could be any worse. Yet Jesus clearly said it would be worse than at any time since the creation of the earth. It is at this dark time that the nations of the world will bow the knee to the Antichrist, exposing Christians who refuse to do so. It is during this time that Satan will make his final effort to destroy the only remaining light of God's truth on earth, His bride, the Christian Church.

During these gloomy days on earth, God will fortify His church spiritually and allow it to be a final witness against the wickedness of Satan and his rebellious followers. It will be a horrible time of martyrdom for the possibly multiple millions of Christians who refuse to bow the knee to the Antichrist. The Scriptures do not tell us how many, but they do describe them as "…a great multitude, which no man could number, out of every nation and of all tribes, peoples, and languages…." (Rev. 7:9, WEB). It is possible that a major part or all of these will have suffered martyrdom in the great tribulation. Two other groups of Christians are singled out that are special in God's sight. They are called the 144,000 and two special prophets of God referred to in Scripture as the two great witnesses.

During the Great Tribulation, it seems millions of Christians who will not pay homage to and worship the Antichrist will be killed in various nations under the control of the Roman Empire. The number of the Christian martyrs from around the world during this time will be staggering,[18] for as the scripture states there were so many that no one could count them. They are described as "…standing before the throne and before the Lamb, dressed in white robes, with palm branches in their hands" (Rev. 7:9b, WEB). Their identity is next revealed as "…those who came out of the great tribulation. They washed their robes, and made them white in the Lamb's blood" (Rev. 7:14b, WEB). Many of these, if not all of them, may be martyrs for God and as such will bear witness to the depravity of the Antichrist and all nations who stand with him against Christ.

During the first three and a half years of the seven-year peace agreement between Israel and the Palestinians, the period referred to by Jesus as "the beginning of sorrows," that God will raise up to salvation a great number in the Church. Many of them will be great preachers of righteousness, introducing the last and greatest awakening in history. As a result of their ministry along with that of the two witnesses during the seven-year tribulation period, multiple millions will come to salvation in Christ.[19] Scripture clearly shows that many of the those will be martyred during the last three and half years of the Great Tribulation.

Many millions around the world will hear the true gospel. However, most of mankind will utterly curse them and the God they serve. Scripture records that the two witnesses preach the gospel only to eventually be martyred. Sometime during the Great Tribulation, a series of "seven bowls" of God's wrath will begin to be unleashed, ending in the seventh trumpet and the return of Jesus Christ. At that time Jesus will join the Battle of Armageddon and fight against the nations of the world arrayed against Israel and His return.

Most believe the Rapture will occur prior to the Great Tribulation; others believe it will occur after the Great Tribulation. Some believe the God and Magog war occurs prior to the seven-year peace treaty; others believe it will be at the return of Jesus Christ. God allows us to believe whatever we wish about the signposts He has given us. He just wants us to be aware of those sign posts and to watch for them and recognize them just before or when they happen. Jesus said, "Therefore be watchful all the time" (Luke 21:36a, WEB). It is just possible that being alert to these prophecies and praying for God's direction might actually save us from undue trials during these troubling times the likes of which the world has never seen. Sad to say, Scripture shows that there will be some saints caught unaware because of ignorance to or neglect of these signposts and who will needlessly suffer as a result (see Matt. 24:43-44). For instance, if we are aware of the signpost that says a war is coming where one-third of mankind is killed and then we see it happen at the hands of a two-hundred-million-man army, as is prophesied in the sixth trumpet plague, then we can recognize it as a fulfillment of prophecy, which should give us encouragement to persevere. When we see a peace treaty between Israel and the Palestinians, we then know that the Great Tribulation will begin just three and a half years later. If we are raptured before the Great Tribulation, then our personal problems are solved and we can rejoice together as we meet our Savior. If we are at least aware of the possibility that a belief in a pre-tribulation Rapture could be wrong and that it could occur after the Great Tribulation, then we can look forward in faith to it occurring at the seventh trumpet and the return of our Savior. If we are able to recognize these events when they occur, then our faith will be strengthened and we will be better prepared for each event if God sees fit to allow us to live in them.

During this Great Tribulation period, God will send his two great witnesses, who will preach to the Beast power and the world the true gospel. Many may heed their warnings, but most of the world will not. They will preach in Jerusalem condemning all who are doing wickedly and opposing God. They will be an especially great burden and a thorn in the side of the Antichrist during this three-and-a-half-year period. Scripture says:

> If anyone desires to harm them [the two witnesses], fire pro-ceeds out of their mouth and devours their enemies. If any-one desires to harm them, he must be killed in this way. These have the power to shut up the sky, that it may not rain during the days of their prophecy. They have power over the waters, to turn them into blood, and to strike the earth with every plague, as often as they desire. When they have finished their testimony, the beast that comes up out of the abyss will make war with them, and overcome them, and kill them.
> ~ Revelation 11:5-7, WEB

Their dead bodies will be displayed for three and a half days on a public square in Jerusalem for the world to see. The world and the Anti-christ will rejoice to see them dead. Scripture says they:

> ...all peoples and tribes and tongues and nations will view their bodies and will not permit them to be laid in a tomb. And those who dwell on the earth will gloat over them, and will celebrate and send one another gifts, because these two prophets had tormented them. But after the three and a half days, the breath of life from God entered the two witnesses, and they stood on their feet, and great fear came over those who saw them. And the witnesses heard a loud voice from heaven saying, "Come up here." And they went up to heav-en in a cloud as their enemies watched them. ~ Revelation 11:9b-12, BSB

Can you imagine the horror in the hearts of the Antichrist and the rebellious people on earth when they see this happen?

The Wrath Of Christ

The wickedness of the Antichrist and rebellious mankind will not go unpunished. Most likely sometime during the latter part of the Great tribulation, prior to the return of Jesus, seven bowls of God's wrath will begin to be unleashed on the rebellious nations on earth. "Then I heard a loud voice from the temple saying to the seven angels, 'Go, pour out on the earth the seven bowls of God's wrath'" (Rev. 16:1 BSB). Each angel will pour in succession horrible plagues on rebellious mankind so that they are covered with festering sores; the sea becomes like blood, killing the fish; rivers and springs become blood; and scorching heat from the sun, earthquakes, and huge hailstones torment the earth. At the sound of the seventh trumpet and the pouring out of God's wrath in the sixth and seventh bowl, Christ will appear in the heavens to begin His return to the earth. Before we look at what Jesus says about His return, let's look at the possibility of the Rapture occurring just before Jesus unleashes His wrath upon the armies gathered together against Him at Armageddon. Satan's wrath on Christians will be unleashed during the great tribulation. At some point during the great tribulation God will then unleash His wrath upon the unrepentant people left on earth. As we have just noted, His wrath will be comprised of the seven bowls of Revelation 16 that are sequentially poured out by seven angels.

Christ's Return

The gathering of the world's armies against Israel at Armageddon will be Satan's last-ditch effort to destroy God's plans. Satan's effort will completely backfire with the coming of the Messiah with His saints and angelic armies. The prophet Daniel spoke of a Great Tribulation leading up to the return of Christ in this way:

313

> At that time shall Michael stand up, the great prince who stands for the children of your people; and there shall be a time of trouble [Great Tribulation], such as never was since there was a nation even to that same time: and at that time your people shall be delivered, everyone who shall be found written in the book. Many of those who sleep in the dust of the earth shall awake, some to everlasting life, and some to shame and everlasting contempt. Those who are wise shall shine as the brightness of the expanse; and those who turn many to righteousness as the stars forever and ever. ~ Daniel 12:1-3, WEB

This seems to make it plain that the first resurrection will occur after the Great Tribulation period. Yes, Jesus Christ will end this period of tribulation with the blast from the seventh and last great trumpet (Revelation 11:15). Jesus will then suddenly appear in the sky for all the world to see.

Love Mystery's Revealed At Last!

With the coming of Christ, the time will have come for sixth stage of God's love mystery to be revealed. This is the wonderful love mystery for which God created all things and whose manifestation He sent His own Son to die to make possible. Notice, "But in the days of the voice of the seventh angel, when he is about to sound his trumpet, *the mystery of God will be fulfilled* [emphasis added], just as He proclaimed to His servants, the prophets" (Rev. 10:7, BSB). Here at last will come the time for the manifestation of God's greatest desire. He has kept this marvelous mystery a secret from all of His creations, except for the angels and His chosen saints. The apostle Paul describes this mystery as the manifestation of the Sons of God. Notice: "Listen, I tell you a mystery: We will not all sleep, but we will all be changed— in an instant, in the twinkling of an eye, at the last trumpet [at which time the mystery is accomplished]. For the trumpet will sound, the dead will be raised imperishable, and we will be changed" (1 Cor. 15:51-52, BSB).

Paul gives a specific time marker upon which the mystery or manifestation of God's children (also known as the Rapture) will occur.

Paul says that this Rapture, which produces God's eternal children, will occur immediately after the sounding blast of the "last trumpet." The last trumpet mentioned in the book of Revelation is the seventh one, heralding the return of Jesus and the manifestation of the children of God. "Then the seventh angel sounded his trumpet, and loud voices called out in heaven: 'The kingdom of the world is now the kingdom of our Lord and of His Christ, and He will reign forever and ever.'" (Rev. 11:15, BSB). After the sounding of the seventh trumpet, it is stated that: "The nations were enraged, and Your wrath has come. The time has come to judge the dead, and to reward Your servants, the prophets and saints, and those who fear Your name, both small and great, and to destroy those who destroy the earth" (Rev. 11:18, BSB). Not only has God in great anticipation patiently waited for the manifestation of His wonderful love mystery but all creation has yearned for it. The manifestation or clothing of their new eternal bodies has also been the longing heart's desire of every Christian. Paul put it this way:

> The creation waits in eager expectation for the revelation of the sons of God. For the creation was subjected to futility, not by its own will, but because of the One who subjected it, in hope that the creation itself will be set free from its bondage to decay and brought into the glorious freedom of the children of God. We know that the whole creation has been groaning together in the pains of childbirth until the present time. Not only so, but we ourselves, who have the firstfruits of the Spirit, groan inwardly as we wait eagerly for our adoption as sons, the redemption of our bodies. ~ Romans 8:19-23, BSB

Thank our loving and gracious God and Jesus Christ! We will then be truly free at last with our eternal new bodies incapable of experiencing anything but love, freedom, joy, peace, and happiness forever and ever!

After this wonderful event, the wedding banquet will take place and then the gathered saints will descend with Christ to the earth as He and His angelic army engages and destroys all armies of the world arrayed against Him and Israel. He will save not only Israel but all of mankind from nuclear suicide. Jesus said, "If those days had not been cut short, nobody would be saved. But for the sake of the elect, those days will be shortened" (Matt. 24:22, BSB). But thank God that, at the last minute, when all hope for Israel is lost and worldwide destruction is at hand, Jesus Christ will intervene and crush the armies arrayed against Israel and establish His eternal kingdom on earth.

At last the unity, love, joy, peace, prosperity, and justice that the heart of mankind has vainly sought since Adam and Eve will finally engulf the world. At last the nations of the earth who have been divided over what is truth and freedom and have fought savage, bitter wars will be united in peace under one world ruling government. And guess what? All the divided Christians on earth and in heaven will be united in one doctrine and belief under the tutelage of none other than Jesus Christ. Scripture gives us a peak into the new world that Jesus will establish and rule in righteousness.

> In the last days the mountain of the Lord's house will be established as the highest of the mountains and raised above the hills. All the nations will stream to it. Then many people will come and say, "Let's go to the mountain of the Lord, to the house of the God of Jacob. He will teach us his ways so that we may live by them." The teachings will go out from Zion. The Lord's word will go out from Jerusalem. Then he will judge disputes between nations and settle arguments between many people. They will hammer their swords into plowblades and their spears into pruning shears. Nations will never fight against each other, and they will never train for war again. ~ Isaiah 2:2-4, GW

> They will sit under their grapevines and their fig trees, and no one will make them afraid. ~ Micah 4:4a, GW

> Wolves will live with lambs. Leopards will lie down with goats. Calves, young lions, and year-old lambs will be together, and little children will lead them. Cows and bears will eat together. Their young will lie down together. Lions will eat straw like oxen. Infants will play near cobras' holes. Toddlers will put their hands into vipers' nests. They will not hurt or destroy

anyone anywhere on my holy mountain. The world will be filled with the knowledge of the Lord like water covering the sea. ~ Isaiah 11:6-9, GW

The Seventh Stage Of God's Love Mystery

As wonderful as this may sound, this is not the end of the story. As a matter of fact, all of history up until this point has been nothing more than a stepping stone to reach this seventh platform of God's plans. The creation of this new reality is the reason God allowed all of history to begin with. All of history, at this point, will have occurred to set the stage for the entry into an eternity of unbelievable, beauty, love, and happiness. This coming future is the focal point and God's reason for everything. History compared to this new coming reality is as the old adage declares, "You haven't seen anything yet!" A real adventurous life for all who accepted Jesus as their savior will be just beginning. An existence in a Utopian universe will be born which will be far greater than all the dreams and desires of mankind. That which mankind has sought, lived, fought, and died for throughout history will finally emerge. By then all of mankind will have made their choice to accept or reject Jesus Christ as their Savior. All who embraced eternal salvation through Christ will have received their new eternal bodies as God's children. They all will be citizens of God's eternal Kingdom and universe.

Satan and his kingdom of devils along with all of mankind who refused to accept Jesus Christ will be delivered to hell to receive their just eternal damnation. Peter describes the next event to occur which prepares the way for the eternal seventh stage of God's love mystery. Peter reveals, "…the heavens will pass away with a great noise, and the elements will be dissolved with fervent heat, and the earth and the works that are in it will be burned up…. [That day] will cause the burning heavens to be dissolved, and the elements will melt with fervent heat" (2 Pet. 3:10b, 12b, WEB). Peter then describes what happens next which is the seventh platform from which God will launch His eternal creations into an unbelievable awe inspiring joyful journey. Peter simply states the basics, "But, according to his promise, we look for new heavens and a new earth, in which righteousness dwells." (Ibid, 13). What a mouth full Peter stated in these few words. The apostle John adds to Peter's commentary:

> Then I saw "a new heaven and a new earth." For the first heaven and the first earth had passed away, and there was no more sea. I, John, saw the Holy City, the New Jerusalem, coming down out of heaven from God, prepared as a bride adorned for her husband. And I heard a loud voice from heaven, saying, "Look! The tabernacle of God is with men, and He will dwell with them. They shall be His people, and God Himself will be with them and be their God. God shall wipe away all tears from their eyes. There shall be no more death.' Neither shall there be any more sorrow nor crying nor pain, for the former things have passed away." ~ Revelation 21:1-4, MEV

A new universe and earth will be fashioned by God. This creation by God of the New Earth and universe prepares the way for Heaven's move to the New Earth to be its headquarters for all eternity. The past, present, and future has been planned around the manifestation of God's love mystery, Jesus Christ and His superhuman brothers and sisters. All that has been, is, and to come will be eternally centered around God's love mystery in Heaven.

So what will life really be like in Heaven on this New Earth? I was recently surprised to hear a minister conducting a funeral say, "The Bible doesn't say much about Heaven." Is that true? That is very strange when Paul commands us to "…seek the things that are above [Heaven], where Christ is, seated on the right hand of God. Set your mind on the things that are above, not on the things that are on the earth" (Col. 3:1b- 2 WEB). Randy Alcorn in his awesomely inspiring book "Heaven," from God's Holy Word, paints a vivid picture of what Heaven will be like.[20] How is it that we can greatly desire things that we can't see or imagine? If the Bible doesn't paint a vivid picture of heaven for us, how is it that we should be expected to fervently desire it? As Randy Alcorn properly says, "We can only desire what we can imagine. If you think you can't imagine Heaven—or if you imagine it as something drab and unappealing—you can't get excited about it."[21] How was it that all the saints of old where able to endure all their unbelievable sufferings and even martyrdom for the Kingdom of God? Scripture states that was because, "they were longing for a better country—a heavenly one."[22] They set their desires on an eternal Kingdom whose builder and maker is God (Heb. 11:10). Scripture says that even Jesus: "… for the joy [Heaven] set before Him endured the cross [emphasis added], scorning its shame, and sat down at the right hand of the throne of God" Heb. 12:2b BSB). Randy goes on to explain: "The problem is not that the Bible doesn't tell us much about Heaven. It's that we don't pay attention to what it tells us" (Ibid).[23]

Actually you'd think that since the Bible tells us that Heaven is to become our home that it would have a lot to say about it. Questions arise when we think about it. What will Heaven on the earth look like? Will we enjoy our present family and friends in wonderful dinners and social occasions? Will there be music and dance? Will we work? Will there be mountains, rivers, plants, trees, and animals? Will there be clouds, rain showers, sunshine, flowers and beautiful singing birds? Is it possible your favorite pet might live there? Well, why not? Will there be beautiful and wonderful exciting places to visit and explore? Will there be cities, farms, nations and kings? And what about the new universe? Will God's new superhuman race be allowed "to go where no man has ever gone before" to explore the universe with all of its billions of stars and plants? Well my friend, Randy Alcorn's book answers these questions and much more. If you read it, it will definitely fire up your imagination concerning Heaven, and I believe it will permanently change your life for the better, so much so that you will never be willing to give Heaven up for anything in this present world.

END NOTES

Chapter 1
1. "Winston Churchill," *Brainy Quote,* accessed April 5, 2016, http://www.brainyquote.com/search_results.html?q=Churchill+russia.

Chapter 3
1. "Covenants in the Bible," *Grace Communion International,* accessed April 5, 2016, https://www.gci.org/law/covenants.

2. "Has the New Covenant Been Made?," *Grace Communion International,* accessed September 16, 2013, http://www.gci.org/law/newcovq.

3. Ibid, accessed September 23, 2013.

Chapter 4
1. "Ten Commandments," *Wikipedia,* accessed March 19, 2016, https://en.wikipedia.org/wiki/Ten_Commandments.

2. "Covenant (biblical)," *Wikipedia,* accessed September 10, 2013, http://en.wikipedia.org/wiki/Covenant_(biblical)#Mosaic covenant.

3. "Parchment," *Wikipedia,* accessed September 10, 2013, https://en.wikipedia.org/wiki/Parchment#Jewish_parchment.

4. "Torah," *Wikipedia,* accessed March 21, 2016, https://en.wikipedia.org/wiki/Torah.

Chapter 5
1. "When did God create the angels?" Got Questions?, accessed January 28, 2013, http://www.gotquestions.org/Printer/when-angels-created-PF.html.

2. "What are archangels?" Got Questions?, accessed January 28, 2013, http://www.gotquestions.org/Printer/archangels-PF.html.

3. Ibid.

4. Ibid

5. Ibid

Chapter 6
1. "Universe," *Wikipedia,* accessed September 10, 2013, https://en.wikipedia.org/wiki/Universe.

2. "1961.hayah," *Bible Hub,* accessed September 16, 2013, http://bible-suite.com/hebrew/1961.htm.

3. "Barnes' Notes on the Bible," *Bible Hub,* accessed September 16, 2013, http://biblehub.com/commentaries/genesis/1-2.htm.

4. "Clark's Commentary on the Bible," *Bible Hub,* accessed September 16, 2013, http://biblehub.com/commentaries/clarke/genesis/1.htm.

5. "Dinosaur," *Wikipedia,* accessed September 10, 2013, http://en.wikipedia.org/wiki/Dinosaur.

6. "When Dinosaurs Roamed America," *Wikipedia,* accessed September 10, 2013, https://en.wikipedia.org/wiki/When_Dinosaurs_Roamed_America.

7. 60 Minutes, "A Dangers Game of Cosmic Roulette." *CBS,* 12:25, October 6, 2013, accessed October 6, 2013, http://www.cbsnews.com/videos/a-dangerous-game-of-cosmic-roulette/.

8. "When Dinosaurs Roamed America," *Wikipedia,* accessed September 10, 2013, https://en.wikipedia.org/wiki/When_Dinosaurs_Roamed_America.

9. "Human Evolution," *Wikipedia,* accessed September 10, 2013, http://en.wikipedia.org/wiki/Human_evolution.

Chapter 9
1. "Romans 16:25," *Bible Hub,* accessed April 12, 2014, http://biblehub.com/romans/16-25.htm.

2. Ibid.

Chapter 10
1. "Man's Search for Meaning," *Butler-Bowdon.com,* accessed July 8, 2015, http://www.butler-bowdon.com/manssearch#.VZ7QowR8qhE.yahoomail.

2. Dima, "The Person With No Conscience," *Mind Forums,* April 2, 2009, accessed July 12, 2015, http://mindforums.com/antisocial-personality-disorder.

Chapter 11
1. Joseph Tkach, *Transformed By Truth* (Sisters, OR: Multnomah,

1997), 99.

2. Ibid.

3. Ibid, 94.

4. Ibid, 95.

5. Ibid, 92.

6. Ibid, 92–93.

7. Ibid, 94.

8. Ibid.

9. Ibid, 101.

10. Ibid, 102–103.

11. Ibid.

12. Mary Fairchild, "Christian denominations: The History and Evolution of Christian Denominations and Faith Groups," *About.com,* updated August 5, 2015, accessed September 17, 2013, http://christianity.about.com/od/denominations/a/denominations.htm.

13. Joseph Tkach, *Transformed By Truth* (Sisters, OR.: Multnomah, 1997), 65.

14. Ibid.

15. Ibid, 113.

16. Ibid, 115.

17. Ibid, 65.

18. Ibid, 116.

19. Ibid, 66.

20. Ibid, 66–67.

21. J. Michael Feazell, *The Liberation of the Worldwide Church of God,* (Grand Rapids: Zondervan, 2001), 11.

22. Ibid, 12.

23. Ibid, 184.

24. Ibid, 185.

25. Ibid.

26. Ibid.

27. Joseph Tkach, Transformed By Truth (Sisters, OR.: Multnomah, 1997), 209-211 (Worldwide Church of God Organizational Splits)

Chapter 12

1. Kendra Cherry, "What Is Locus of Control? Are You In Control of Your Destiny?" About.com, updated March 3, 2016, accessed March 14, 2016, http://psychology.about.com/od/personalitydevelopment/fl/What-Is-Locus-of-Control.htm.

2. "4166. poimé," Bible Hub, accessed May 21, 2014, http://biblehub.com/greek/4166.htm.

3. "Compare and contrast three different models of church governance (Episcopal, Presbyterian and Congregational) based upon

the Scriptural evidence for each," chkproject.files.wordpress.com, accessed May 18, 2016, http://r.search.yahoo.com/_ylt=A0SO8wm-FyP-JWqAwAJTpXNyoA;_ylu=X3oDMTEycW4yNTgyBGNvbG-8DZ-3ExBHBvcwMzBHZ0aWQDQjE3MjRfMQRzZWMDc3I-/RV=2/RE=1458780421/RO=10/RU=https%3a%2f%2fchkproject.files.word-press.com%2f2012%2f05%2fproject-church-government.doc/RK=0/RS=IJC7AQrnU3FmeQvqREi.TXTQvw0-.

4. "Become An Ordained Christian Minister online," Ministerregistra-tion.org, accessed May 5, 2014, http://www.ministerregistration.org/.

5. "Become an Ordained Minister Get Your Ordination Here," Christian Harvest Church, accessed May 21, 2014, http://www.christian-har-vestChurch.com/.

6. J. Lee Grady, "6 Ways to Prevent an Embarrassing Ministry Scandal," Charisma News, February 27, 2014, accessed May 21, 2014, http://www.charismanews.com/opinion/42939-6-ways-to-prevent-an-em-barrass-ing-ministry-scandal/.

7. Ibid.

8. "Power Corrupts Quotes," Brainy Quote, accessed March 14, 2016, http://www.brainyquote.com/quotes/keywords/power_corrupts.

9. J. Lee Grady, "6 Ways to Prevent an Embarrassing Ministry Scandal," Charisma News, February 27, 2014, accessed May 21, 2014, http://www.charismanews.com/opinion/42939-6-ways-to-prevent-an-em-

barrass-ing-ministry-scandal/.

10. Ibid.

11. J. Lee Grady, "6 Really Bad Charismatic Doctrines We Should Retire," Charisma News, May 8, 2014, accessed March 22, 2016 http://www.charismanews.com/opinion/43768-6-really-bad-charismat-ic-doc-trines-we-should-retire?showall=&start=1.

12. Ibid.

13. "Waco Siege," Wikipedia, accessed May 21, 2014, https://en.wikipe-dia.org/wiki/Waco_siege.

14. "Jonestown," Wikipedia, accessed May 21, 2014, http://en.wikipe-dia. org/wiki/Jonestown.

15. J. Lee Grady, "6 Really Bad Charismatic Doctrines We Should Retire," Charisma News, May 8, 2014, accessed March 22, 2016 http://www.charismanews.com/opinion/43768-6-really-bad-charismatic-doc-trines-we-should-retire?showall=&start=1

Chapter 13

1. "Compare and contrast three different models of church governance (Episcopal, Presbyterian and Congregational) based upon the Scrip-tural evidence for each," chkproject.files.wordpress. com/2012/05/proj-ect-church-government.doc, accessed, July 4, 2016,

http://r.search.yahoo.com/_ylt=AwrBT8.du3tXv8UAKEFXN-yoA;_ylu=X3oDMTEyb29zOWx1BGNvbG8DYmYxBHBvcwMx-BHZ0aWQDQjE4NzlfMQRzZWMDc3I-/RV=2/RE=1467755550/RO=10/RU=https%3a%2f%2fchkproject.files.wordpress. com%2f2012%2f05%2fproject-church-government.doc/RK=0/RS=1d-UURcO_6Jy.4otd4_1oBi5JIbQ-

2. "Ecclesiastical Polity," Wikipedia, accessed May 20, 2014, http://en.wikipedia.org/wiki/Ecclesiastical_polity

3. "Compare and contrast three different models of church governance (Episcopal, Presbyterian and Congregational) based upon the Scrip-tural evidence for each," chkproject.files.wordpress. com/2012/05/proj-ect-church-government.doc, accessed, July 4, 2016,

http://r.search.yahoo.com/_ylt=AwrBT8.du3tXv8UAKEFXN-yoA;_ylu=X3oDMTEyb29zOWx1BGNvbG8DYmYxBHBvcwMx-

BHZ0aWQDQjE4NzlfMQRzZWMDc3I-/RV=2/RE=1467755550/
RO=10/RU=https%3a%2f%2fchkproject.files.wordpress.
com%2f2012%2f05%2fproject-church-government.doc/RK=0/RS=1d-
UURcO_6Jy.4otd4_1oBi5JIbQ-

4. "Patriarch of Alexandria," Wikipedia, accessed May 18, 2014, http://
en.wikipedia.org/wiki/Patriarch_of_Alexandria .

5. "Episcopal Baptists," Wikipedia, accessed July 5, 2016,

https://en.wikipedia.org/wiki/Episcopal_Baptists

6. "Presbyterian," Merriam-Webster, accessed May 18, 2014, http://
www.merriam-webster.com/dictionary/presbyterian.

7. "Compare and contrast three different models of church governance
(Episcopal, Presbyterian and Congregational) based upon the Scriptural evidence for each," chkproject.files.wordpress. com/2012/05/proj-
ect-church-government.doc, accessed, July 4, 2016,

http://r.search.yahoo.com/_ylt=AwrBT8.du3tXv8UAKEFXN-
yoA;_ylu=X3oDMTEyb29zOWx1BGNvbG8DYmYxBHBvcwMx-
BHZ0aWQDQjE4NzlfMQRzZWMDc3I-/RV=2/RE=1467755550/
RO=10/RU=https%3a%2f%2fchkproject.files.wordpress.
com%2f2012%2f05%2fproject-church-government.doc/RK=0/RS=1d-
UURcO_6Jy.4otd4_1oBi5JIbQ-

8. Ibid.

9. Ibid.

10. Ibid.

11. "Government of the Seventh Day Adventist Church," Wikipedia,
accessed accessed July 5, 2016, https://en.wikipedia.org/wiki/Polity_of_
the_Seventh-day_Adventist_Church

12. "Congregationalism," Britannica, accessed May 18, 2014, http://
www.britannica.com/EBchecked/topic/132545/Congregationalism.

13. "Compare and contrast three different models of church governance (Episcopal, Presbyterian and Congregational) based upon the
Scriptural evidence for each," chkproject.files.wordpress. com/2012/05/
project-church-government.doc, accessed, July 4, 2016,

http://r.search.yahoo.com/_ylt=AwrBT8.du3tXv8UAKEFXN-
yoA;_ylu=X3oDMTEyb29zOWx1BGNvbG8DYmYxBHBvcwMx-
BHZ0aWQDQjE4NzlfMQRzZWMDc3I-/RV=2/RE=1467755550/

RO=10/RU=https%3a%2f%2fchkproject.files.wordpress. com%2f2012%2f05%2fproject-church-government.doc/RK=0/RS=1d-UURcO_6Jy.4otd4_1oBi5JIbQ-

14. "Congregationalist polity," Wikipedia, accessed, July 4, 2016, https:// en.wikipedia.org/wiki/Congregationalist_polity

15. "Compare and contrast three different models of church governance (Episcopal, Presbyterian and Congregational) based upon the Scriptural evidence for each," chkproject.files.wordpress. com/2012/05/ project-church-government.doc, accessed, July 4, 2016,

http://r.search.yahoo.com/_ylt=AwrBT8.du3tXv8UAKEFXN-yoA;_ylu=X3oDMTEyb29zOWx1BGNvbG8DYmYxBHBvcwMx-BHZ0aWQDQjE4NzlfMQRzZWMDc3I-/RV=2/RE=1467755550/RO=10/RU=https%3a%2f%2fchkproject.files.wordpress. com%2f2012%2f05%2fproject-church-government.doc/RK=0/RS=1d-UURcO_6Jy.4otd4_1oBi5JIbQ-

16. "Church Government," Theopedia, accessed May 4, 2014, http:// www.theopedia. http://www.theopedia.com/church-government.

17. "Compare and contrast three different models of church governance (Episcopal, Presbyterian and Congregational) based upon the Scriptural evidence for each," chkproject.files.wordpress. com/2012/05/ project-church-government.doc, accessed, July 4, 2016,

http://r.search.yahoo.com/_ylt=AwrBT8.du3tXv8UAKEFXN-yoA;_ylu=X3oDMTEyb29zOWx1BGNvbG8DYmYxBHBvcwMx-BHZ0aWQDQjE4NzlfMQRzZWMDc3I-/RV=2/RE=1467755550/RO=10/RU=https%3a%2f%2fchkproject.files.wordpress. com%2f2012%2f05%2fproject-church-government.doc/RK=0/RS=1d-UURcO_6Jy.4otd4_1oBi5JIbQ-

18. Ibid.

19. Ibid.

20. Ibid.

21. Junno Arocho Esteves, "Pope Appoints Group of Cardinals to Advise on Church Governance," Zenit, April 15, 2013, accessed May 18, 2014, https://zenit.org/articles/pope-appoints-group-of-cardinals-to-advise-on-Church-governance/

22. Christopher Beam, "You're Defrocked!," Slate, March 17, 2010, ac-

cessed May 20, 2014, http://www.slate.com/articles/news_and_politics/ explainer/2010/03/youre_defrocked.html

Chapter 15

1. Michael Snyder, "New Trend: 'Radically Inclusive' Churches That Embrace All Religions and All Lifestyles," *InfoWars,* March 25, 2015, accessed March 23, 2016, http://www.infowars.com/new-trend-radical-ly-inclusive-churches-that-embrace-all-religions-and-all-lifestyles/.

2. Ibid.

3. Ibid.

4. Ibid.

5. Ibid.

6. "2 Corinthians 5:20," *Bible Hub,* accessed March 19, 2016, http://bi-blehub.com/commentaries/2_corinthians/5-20.htm.

7. "Jesus in Islam," *Wikipedia,* accessed April 29, 2016, https://en.wiki-pedia.org/wiki/Jesus_in_Islam.

Chapter 16

1. "The Doctrine of Inclusion: Why It Appeals, How It Misleads," *Escape to Reality,* accessed March 19, 2016, http://escapetoreality.org/ resources/study-notes/.

2. Ibid.

3. Ibid.

4. "Universalism," *Wikipedia,* accessed May 4, 2015, http://en.wikipe-dia.org/wiki/Universalism.

5. "Christian Universalism," *Wikipedia,* accessed March 24, 2016, http://en.wikipedia.org/wiki/Christian_Universalism.

6. "Fallen Angel," *Wikipedia,* accessed May 21, 2015, https://en.wikipe-dia.org/wiki/Fallen_angel.

7. Paul Ellis, "50 Scriptures Inclusionism Can't Explain," *Escape To Reality,* accessed March 24, 2016, http://escapetoreality.org/2014/12/12/ scriptures-inclusionism-cannot-explain/.

8. Ibid, "Study Notes," *Escape To Reality,* December 12, 2014, accessed March 24, 2016, http://escapetoreality.org/resources/study-notes/.

9. "Universal Reconciliation," *Wikipedia,* accessed December 21, 2015, https://en.wikipedia.org/wiki/Universal_reconciliation.

10. Paul Ellis, "Job's Grace Encounter," *Escape To Reality,* November 4, 2015, accessed March 24, 2016, http://escapetoreality.org/2010/08/02/does-god-give-and-take-away/.

Chapter 18
1. "When was Noah's Flood?" *Creation Tips,* accessed March 19, 2016, http://www.creationtips.com/flooddate.html.

2. "Nimrod," *Wikipedia,* accessed March 19, 2016, https://en.wikipedia.org/wiki/Nimrod.

3. Joel C. Rosenberg, "Three Existential Threats Facing America," *Joel C. Rosenberg's Blog,* accessed March 25, 2016, https://flashtrafficblog.wordpress.com/2015/03/12/three-existential-threats-facing-america-my-address-to-the-national-religious-broadcasters-convention/.

4. Ibid.

5. John Bolton, interview by Bill Hemmer, *FNC, 2,* accessed March 17, 2015. I documented everything at the time I viewed this interview except for the name of the Fox News segment that Mr. Hemmer and Mr. Bolton appeared in. I have searched but have not been able to find that information. However, I am very certain that it was during his regularly scheduled week day segment call, "America's Newsroom."

6. Matt Spetalnick, "Obama tells Netanyahu U.S. to 'reassess' policy on Israel, Mideast diplomacy," *Reuters,* March 19, 2015, accessed March 20, 2015, http://news.yahoo.com/netanyahu-backs-away-rejection-palestinian-state-white-house-203520106.html.

7. Hazel Ward, "Netanyahu faces pressure over Palestine state after win," *AFP,* March 19, 2015, accessed March 19, 2015, http://news.yahoo.com/results-confirm-big-win-netanyahus-likud-111316437.html.

8. "Middle East Caught in 'Apocalyptic Fervor,'" *WND,* March 11, 2015, accessed March 25, 2016, http://www.wnd.com/2015/03/middle-east-caught-in-apocalyptic-fervor/.

Chapter 19
1. Rapture," *Wikipedia,* accessed May 13, 2016 https://en.wikipedia.org/wiki/Rapture#Timing

2. Ibid.

3. Ibid.

4. Ibid.

5. Ibid.

6. Ibid.

7. Ibid.

8. Ibid.

9. Ibid.

10. Ibid.

11. Ibid.

12. Ibid.

13. Ibid.

14. "Endtimes Conference Proves Post-Trib Rapture," post-tribor-pre-trib.blogspot.com, accessed March 19, 2016, http://post-tribor-pre-trib.blogspot.com/2007/06/endtimes-conference-proves-post-trib.html

15. "Pseudo-Ephraem does not teach the Rapture!" Bible.ca, accessed April 30, 2016, http://www.bible.ca/rapture-pseudo-ephraem-latin-syraic-texts.htm

16. "Ephraem the Syrian: Early Christians Believed Pre-Tribulation Rapture," Are We :Living In The Last Days, accessed May 2, 2016, http://www.arewelivinginthelastdays.com/com/ephraem.htm.

17. "Pseudo-Ephraem does not teach the Rapture!" Bible.ca, accessed April 30, 2016, http://www.bible.ca/rapture-pseudo-ephraem-latin-syraic-texts.htm

18. Ibid.

19. Ibid.

20. Ibid.

21. Ibid.

22. "Endtimes Conference Proves Post-Trib Rapture," post-tribor-pre-trib.blogspot.com, accessed March 19, 2016, http://post-tribor-pre-trib.blogspot.com/2007/06/endtimes-conference-proves-post-trib.html

23. Ibid.

24. End of the Age, Dave Robbins, "Post-Tribulation Rapture," You-Tube, 59:00, accessed July 11, 2016, https://www.youtube.com/watch?v=3IHBrLUYj5g

25. Strong's Concordance, "646. apostasia," Bible Hub, accessed May 5, 2016, http://biblehub.com/greek/646.htm.

26. Strong's Concordance, "868. Aphistémi," Bible Hub, accessed May 5, 2016, http://biblehub.com/greek/868.htm.

27. Pulpit Commentary, "2 Thessalonians 2:7," Bible Hub, accessed February 21, 2015, http://biblehub.com/commentaries/pulpit/2_thessalonians/2.htm

28. Gerald B. Stanton,"Kept from the Hour, Chapter Five, Who Is 'TheRestrainer'?" Rapture Ready, accessed October 20, 2015, https://www.raptureready.com/resource/stanton/k5.htm.

29. Todd Strandberg, "The Pre-tribulation Rapture," Rapture Ready, accessed October 20, 2015, http://www.raptureready.com/rr-pretribulation-rapture.html

30. Tomorrow's World, "The Mysterious Day of the Lord," You-tube, 28:31, accessed May 8, 2016, https://www.youtube.com/watch?v=14HWsInZJUU.

31. End Times Ministries, "What the Book of Revelation Reveals About the End Times," Endtime.com, accessed May 10, 2016 , http://www.endtime.com/blog/book-revelation-reveals-end-times/

32. Eddie Sax, "Remember the Plagues," End Time Ministries, accessed May 10, 2016, http://www.endtime.com/endtime-magazine-articles/remember-plagues/.

33. Ibid

34. Ibid..

35. EndTime Youth, "Is the Book of Revelation in Chronological Order?" Endtime.com, accessed July 11, 1916, http://www.endtime.com/q-and-a/book-revelation-chronological-order/

36. Dave Robbins, "Events of the Final Seven Years," EndTime Ministries, accessed July 9, 2016, http://www.endtime.com/endtime-magazine-articles/events-final-seven-years/

37. Ibid.

38. Ibid.

39. Pulpit Commentary," 2 Thessalonians 2:10, Bible Hub, accessed July 10, 2016, http://biblehub.com/commentaries/pulpit/2_thessalonians/1.htm

40. Irvin Baxter, "A Harvest Caught Up and Harvest of Wrath," End-Time Ministries, accessed July 10, 2016, http://www.endtime.com/end-time-magazine-articles/two-simultaneous-harvests/

41. Roger Armstrong, "The Second Coming of Christ… 'Rapture,' Calvary Chapel Men's Conference, accessed July 10, 2016, http://post-tri-borpre-trib.blogspot.com/2007/06/endtimes-conference-proves-post-trib.html

42. Ibid.

43. Ibid.

44. Ibid

45. End of the Age, Dave Robbins, "Post-Tribulation Rapture," YouTube, 59:00, accessed July 11, 2016, https://www.youtube.com/watch?v=3IHBrLUYj5g

46. Ibid.

Chapter 20

1. "About Irvin Baxter," *End Time Ministries,* accessed November 11, 2015, http://www.endtime.com/irvin-baxter/.

2. Politics and Religion, "Are The Antichrist And The False Prophet Alive Today," *YouTube,* 58:58, accessed March 26, 2016, https://www.youtube.com/watch?v=JCungDpmYTI.

3. End of the Age with Irvin Baxter. "World War 3," *YouTube,* 50:58, accessed March 26, 2016, https://www.youtube.com/watch?v=U6jv_Qz6FWo.

4. Understanding the Endtime, "The 7 Trumpets." *YouTube,* 50:39, accessed March 26, 2016, https://www.youtube.com/watch?v=00ERb-Z5nWGI.

5. Noah Browning and John Irish, "Saudi Arabia announces 34-state Islamic military alliance against terrorism," *Reuters,* December 15, 2015, accessed March 19, 2106, http://news.yahoo.com/saudi-arabia-announces-34-state-islamic-military-alliance-002409921.html;_

ylt=A0SO80TL2nFWfhwAJ85XNyoA;_ylu=X3oDMTEyNjFxaW03B-
GNvbG8DZ3ExBHBvcwMzBHZ0aWQDQjEzMjVfMQRzZWMDc3I-.

6. Tom Olago, "The Growing Russia/China Alliance," *Prophecy News Watch,* October 6, 2015.

7. Pamela Engel, "Ben Carson is defending an odd claim about China and Syria he made during the last GOP debate," *Business Insider,* November 11, 2015, accessed November 11, 2015, https://ca.finance.yahoo.com/news/ben-carson-defending-odd-claim-204141996.html.

8. Nicola Slawson, "Saudi execution of Shia cleric sparks outrage in Middle East," *Guardian,* January 2, 2016, accessed March 19, 2016, http://www.theguardian.com/world/2016/jan/02/saudi-execution-of-shia-cleric-sparks-outrage-in-middle-east.

9. Ibid.

10. Catherine E. Shoichet and Mariano Castillo, "Saudi Arabia-Iran row spreads to other nations," *CNN,* updated January 4, 2016, accessed January 5, 2016, http://www.cnn.com/2016/01/04/middleeast/saudi-arabia-iran-severing-ties-whats-next/.

11. "About KT," *KT McFarland,* accessed March 19, 2016, http://ktmcfarland.com/?page_id=2.

12. KT McFarland, interview by Stewart Varney, FBN, *Direct TV* 359 8 AM January 5, 2016.

13. "US and World Population Clock," *United States Census Bureau,* accessed September 1, 2015, http://www.census.gov/popclock/.

14. "Middle East War," *Are We Living in the Last Days?,* 10:35, accessed January 5, 2016, http://www.arewelivinginthelastdays.com/road/mewar.html.

15. "Islamic Apocalypse," *Islamic Beast Rising,* accessed August 19, 2015, http://www.islamicbeastrising.com/.

16. End of the Age with Irvin Baxter. "World War 3," *YouTube,* 50:58, accessed March 26, 2016, https://www.youtube.com/watch?v=U6jv_Qz6FWo.

17. "Elites Preparing Last Phase of New World Order?," *WND,* accessed March 26, 2016, http://www.wnd.com/2015/08/elites-preparing-last-phase-of-new-world-order/.

18. "Islamic Apocalypse," *Islamic Beast Rising,* accessed August 19, 2015, http://www.islamicbeastrising.com/.

19. Ibid.

20. "Western Roman Empire," *Wikipedia,* accessed September 10, 2015, https://en.wikipedia.org/wiki/Western_Roman_Empire.

21. Ishaan Tharoor, "Chart: There will be almost as many Muslims as Christians in the world by 2050," *Washington Post,* April 2, 2015, accessed November 3, 2015, https://www.washingtonpost.com/news/worldviews/wp/2015/04/02/chart-there-will-be-almost-as-many-muslims-as-christians-in-the-world-by-2050/.

22. "The Antichrist Identity V," *Antichristidentity.com,* accessed August 6, 2015, http://www.antichristidentity.com/.

23. "Interfaith Dialogue," *Wikipedia,* accessed November 10, 2015, https://en.wikipedia.org/wiki/Interfaith_dialogue.

24. Irvin Baster, "The Crime of Religious Exclusiveness," *Endtime Magazine,* May / June, 2008, accessed March 27, 2016, http://www.endtime.com/blog/the-crime-of-religious-exclusiveness/.

25. Ibid.

26. Ibid.

27. "Parliament of the World's Religions," *Wikipedia,* accessed November 5, 2015, https://en.wikipedia.org/wiki/Parliament_of_the_World%27s_Religions.

28. "Christianity and other religions," *Wikipedia,* accessed November 5, 2015, https://en.wikipedia.org/wiki/Christianity_and_other_religions#Modern_.28post-Enlightenment.29_Christian_views.

29. Jeffery Weiss, "Do Christians, Muslims and Jews worship the same God?" *Belief Blog,* September, 2, 2013, accessed March 29, 2016, http://religion.blogs.cnn.com/2013/09/01/do-christians-muslims-and-jews-worship-the-same-god/.

30. "Christianity and other religions," *Wikipedia,* accessed November 5, 2015, https://en.wikipedia.org/wiki/Christianity_and_other_religions#Modern_.28post-Enlightenment.29_Christian_views.

31. "Church Revolution in Pictures," *Traditioninaction.org,* accessed November 10, 2015, http://www.traditioninaction.org/RevolutionPhotos/A055rcKoran.htm.

32. Zenit staff, "In Visit to Mosque, John Paul II Asks for a New Era of Dialogue," *Zenit,* May 6, 2001, accessed November 10, 2010, http://

www.zenit.org/en/articles/in-visit-to-mosque-john-paul-ii-asks-for-a-new-era-of-dialogue.

33. Ibid.

34. Ibid.

35. Steve Watson, "In New York, Pope Francis embraced Chrislam and laid a foundation for a one world religion," Infowars, September 28, 2015, accessed December 21, 2015, http://www.infowars.com/in-new-york-pope-francis-embraced-chrislam-and-laid-a-foundation-for-a-one-world-religion/.

36. Juan Cole, "Do Christians and Muslims worship the same God?" Juancole.com, December 18, 2015, accessed December 21, 2015, http://www.juancole.com/2015/12/do-christians-and-muslims-worship-the-same-god.html.

37. "New Age gods—Awakening," Thenewagegods.com, accessed December 11, 2015, http://www.thenewagegods.com.

38. Ibid.

39. Ibid

40. ABC News, "George W. Bush: All Religions Go to Heaven," *Good Morning America,* 1:51, October 26, 2004, accessed November 6, 2015, https://www.youtube.com/watch?v=JHaTamomFlc.

41. "Millennium World Peace Summit," *Berkley Center,* accessed November 9, 2015, http://berkleycenter.georgetown.edu/events/millennium-world-peace-summit.

42. Ibid.

43. Ibid.

44. Jennifer LeClaire, "Why So Many People Think Pope Francis Is the Antichrist," *Charisma News,* July 29, 2015, accessed March 29, 2016. http://www.charismanews.com/opinion/watchman-on-the-wall/50752-why-so-many-people-think-pope-francis-is-the-antichrist.

45. David Robbins, "One-World Religion Part 1," *End Time Ministries,* accessed March 19, 2016, http://www.endtime.com/endtime-magazine-articles/one-world-religion-part-1/.

46. Ibid.

47. Ibid.

48. Ibid.

49. Ibid.

50. "Chrislam," *Wikipedia,* accessed March 19, 2016, https://en.wikipedia.org/wiki/Chrislam.

51. Geoffrey Grider, "American Churches to Embrace Chrislam on June 26, 2011," *Nowtheendbegins.com,* June 23, 2011, accessed October 7, 2015, http://www.nowtheendbegins.com/blog/?p=5441.

52. Israel Now News, "Episode 211," *YouTube,* 28:31, accessed March 29, 2016 https://www.youtube.com/watch?v=7e3PDQgwogc.

Chapter 21

1. Irvin Baxter, "World War III — Entrance Ramp for the Antichrist," *YouTube,* 51:33, accessed March 30, 2016, https://www.youtube.com/watch?v=GtRejWfQEo8.

2. Ibid, "The Future of Israel," *End Time Ministries,* 59, accessed March 31, 2016, http://www.endtime.com/podcast/the-future-of-israel/.

3. Ibid.

4. Ibid.

5. End of the Age with Irvin Baxter, "World War 3" *YouTube,* 50:58, accessed March 30, 2016, https://www.youtube.com/watch?v=U6jv_Qz6FWo.

6. AFP and Arutz Sheva staff, "Pope Condemns Religious Fundamentalism, Middle East Violence," *Arutz Sheva,* June 13, 2014, accessed March 19, 2016, http://www.israelnationalnews.com/News/News.aspx/181689#.VpUvDJsm6cy.

7. Michael, "Pope Francis Declares that Christian Fundamentalism 'Is a Sickness,'" *The Most Important News,* December 1, 2015, accessed December 1, 2015, http://themostimportantnews.com/archives/pope-francis-declares-that-christian-fundamentalism-is-a-sickness.

8. Irwin Baxter, "The Great Tribulation," *End Time Ministries,* 59:01, accessed March 31, 2016, http://www.endtime.com/podcast/the-coming-great-tribulation/.

9. Ibid.

10. Ibid.

11. Irvin Baxter, "The Future of Israel," *End Time Ministries,* 59, accessed March 31, 2016, http://www.endtime.com/podcast/the-future-of-israel/.

12. Irwin Baxter, "World War III- Entrance Ramp For The Antichrist," *YouTube,* 51:33, accessed March 30, 2016, https://www.youtube.com/watch?v=GtRejWfQEo8.

13. Irvin Baxter, "The Future of Israel," *End Time Ministries,* 59, accessed March 31, 2016, http://www.endtime.com/podcast/the-future-of-israel/.

14. Irvin Baxter, "United States In The Bible," *YouTube,* 1:01:40, accessed April 1, 2016, https://www.youtube.com/watch?v=XVOJ3X-137Hk.

15. "Bald eagle," *Wikipedia,* accessed April 1, 2016, https://en.wikipedia.org/wiki/Bald_eagle#National_bird_of_the_United_States.

"Uncle Sam," *Wikipedia,* accessed April 1, 2016, https://en.wikipedia.org/wiki/Uncle_Sam.

16. "Uncle Sam," Wikipedia, accessed April 1, 2016, https://en.wikipedia. org/wiki/Uncle_Sam.

17. "Great Awakening," Wikipedia, accessed September 13, 2015, https://en.wikipedia.org/wiki/Great_Awakening.

18. "144,000 And The Great Multitude," Arewelivinginthelastdays.com, accessed December 28, 2015, http://www.arewelivinginthelastdays.com/article/144/144.htm

19. "144,000 Jewish Evangelists." YouTube, 4:37, accessed December 28, 2015, https://www.youtube.com/watch?v=2JW5om3bczY.

20. Randy Alcorn, Heaven (Carol Stream, ILL: Tyndale House, 2004)

21. Ibid, 79-80.

22. Ibid, 80.

23. Ibid, 79.

Made in the USA
Middletown, DE
18 October 2016